Advocacy and
Social Work Practice

Advocacy and Social Work Practice

Tom Wilks

Open University Press

Open University Press
McGraw-Hill Education
McGraw-Hill House
Shoppenhangers Road
Maidenhead
Berkshire
England
SL6 2QL

email: enquiries@openup.co.uk
world wide web: www.openup.co.uk

and Two Penn Plaza, New York, NY 10121-2289, USA

First published 2012

A catalogue record of this book is available from the British Library

ISBN-13: 9780335243037 (pb)
ISBN-10: 0335243037 (pb)
e-ISBN: 9780335243044

Library of Congress Cataloging-in-Publication Data
CIP data has been applied for

Typeset by Aptara Inc., India
Printed in the UK by Bell and Bain Ltd, Glasgow.

Fictitious names of companies, products, people, characters and/or data that may be used herein (in case studies or in examples) are not intended to represent any real individual, company, product or event.

MIX
Paper from
responsible sources
FSC® C007785

The McGraw·Hill Companies

Contents

Tables and Figures

Tables

Figures

Acknowledgements

I would like to thank all my social work colleagues at London South Bank University for their support during the writing of this book. I won't name people individually for fear of inadvertently missing someone out. Particular thanks must go to John Prosser from Brunel University, whose ideas have had an influence on certain sections of the book. Finally I want to thank my family, Clarissa, Felix and Hector, for all their help.

Introduction

As a social worker the idea of advocacy can be a beguiling one; as an advocate you are working in a way in which the most ambitious and noblest aspirations of the profession can be met. 'Advocacy is crucial to social work and social change, inasmuch as it creates the foundation for social justice and seeks to protect human rights' (Goldberg Wood and Tully 2006 p141). However, much of the time the reality of practice is that advocacy is marked by pragmatism and a realism about what can be achieved. Doel and Best (2008 p44) describe a piece of advocacy work undertaken by a student helping a service user to get re-housed, and of the student fighting hard to achieve her end and having to ruffle a few feathers on the way. Although the victory achieved was a small one in the wider scheme of things, for the service user concerned it was clearly of immense importance. The importance of advocacy to social work is that such small but important victories keep us in touch with the spirit of social justice, which has been such a pervasive influence on our profession.

Advocacy is a growing area of practice in and around social care (Henderson and Pochin 2001). It is also seen as a key part of the changing face of social care within the personalisation agenda (Williams et al. 2009, Windle et al. 2010, DoH 2006). It is marked by great diversity in relation to the nature of advocacy services and who they are provided for. This book adopts a broad view of what advocacy and social work are (as anyone confronted with its diversity I think has to). The book explores some of the boundaries of advocacy and sees social work as an activity which takes place in a range of different social care contexts and internationally. Social work is not understood or defined by a statutory function, but rather by the skills and values that practitioners bring to their work. In the increasingly diverse social care marketplace this type of understanding may be better suited to the future of practice.

The experience of social work students in practice placements in relation to advocacy has shaped the purposes of the book. I have often found that students in statutory settings struggled to understand how what they were doing in placement might be called advocacy. Yet often they were fighting for resources for service users both within and outside their agencies, sometimes using sophisticated presentation and negotiation skills. For those students placed in advocacy-specific settings, the theoretical frameworks available to analyse practice were limited at times. I hope that the book may provide something for both sets of students.

I started this brief introduction with rather a grand idea of why advocacy is important to social work. I want to finish with three equally important but more prosaic ones. Advocacy remains a very important part of social work practice. Social workers devote considerable time and energy to fighting for resources for service users in a wide range of ways and ensuring that their voices are heard, and need skills in order to do this successfully. Social work and social care services are delivered in an environment where advocacy is a constant feature and undertaken in a wide variety of ways. Social workers therefore need to know something about the history of advocacy, its purposes and the different ways in which it carried out. Finally social workers, particularly those in statutory settings (and elsewhere), need to know something about how to work alongside advocacy. How can social workers encourage the development of a culture of advocacy (Henderson and Pochin 2001) and work in a way which is consistent with some of its values? How can they be supportive of new statutory advocacy roles? These three elements – how to do advocacy, how to understand it and how to work with it – recur throughout the book.

The overall structure of the book

The first part of the book, Chapters 1 to 4, provides a general introduction to advocacy. Beginning with the historical background to advocacy and its place within social work as a professional activity, it then explores different definitions and understandings of advocacy, and a range of practice models presenting a multi-dimensional model as an analytic framework. As part of this exploration the value base of advocacy is addressed within the context of social work's professional ethics. The current practice context is addressed, as are the new statutory IMHA and IMCA roles.

The second part of the book, Chapters 5 to 7, is more practice focused and concerned with advocacy in general terms. It looks at process models of advocacy and how advocacy fits with social work methods and theories of intervention. It then goes on to address the skills an advocate needs in order to present a case and negotiate an outcome.

Finally the last chapter looks at a range of specific issues which will impact on the future of advocacy.

1 Advocacy's Place Within Social Work Practice

In the first chapter of this book, how to do advocacy, how to understand and how to work with it are all addressed (albeit to differing degrees). The main concern in this chapter is defining advocacy or at least trying to understand some of its core characteristics and trying to start to see the types of role it can have in social work. The historical place of advocacy in social work (and the enormous impact of the service user movement on the history of advocacy) provides further background to questions about advocacy within a professional context. One important feature of this text is a concern with skills, and the chapter ends by looking at advocacy issues in practice and an overview of some of the skills needed to undertake advocacy.

Definitions of advocacy

I want to start with what Atkinson (1999 p15) describes as 'a deceptively simple question', what is advocacy? As you might guess from Atkinson's description she did not find it a straightforward question to answer and nor I suspect will we. In fact one of the main features of this book is that it attempts to describe the range and scope of advocacy services, and the picture that emerges from this process is one of the variety and diversity of activities that fall under the heading of advocacy. Advocacy is also a changing and contested field of activity with some disagreement about what should or shouldn't fall within it. So a single definition may be beyond us. To fully understand what advocacy is requires an appreciation of the context within which it takes place, its aims and purposes, the values which inform it and its historical roots. However, what we can do at this point is to begin to identify some of its core features.

Fortunately not all those writing about advocacy have been as reluctant as me to define it and so a good starting point in exploring advocacy is to look at some of the definitions of advocacy which have been put forward and identify their common features. Although this will not provide a definition it will give us a sense of what the key elements of advocacy might be. I am going to start by considering David Brandon's definition of advocacy. There are two reasons for this; firstly, Brandon's influence over the field of advocacy has been considerable and secondly the definition he supplies us with identifies some its most salient features:

> Advocacy involves a person(s), either a vulnerable individual or group or their agreed representative, effectively pressing their case with influential others, about situations which either affect them directly or, and more usually, trying to prevent proposed changes which will leave them worse off. Both the intent and outcome of such advocacy should be to increase the individual's sense of power; help them to feel more confident, to become more assertive and gain increased choices. (Brandon 1995b p1, cited in Brandon and Brandon 2001)

There are a number of key elements of advocacy identified here. The idea of advocates pressing a case is there and the idea that it can be conducted on a group or individual level. Also important is the idea of advocacy as an empowering practice and one which may bring psychological benefits to those involved, giving greater self-confidence and building assertiveness. Let's look at another definition.

> Social work advocacy is the exclusive and mutual representation of clients or a cause in a forum attempting to systematically influence decision making in an unjust or unresponsive system. (Schneider and Lester 2001 p65)

Implicit in Brandon's definition of advocacy, within the notion of pressing a case, is the idea of trying to persuade decision makers to take a particular course of action. Schneider and Lester make this idea more explicit; for them advocacy is about systematic influence. They also put a name on advocacy at a group level pursuing a collective issue, cause advocacy; more than just working to address group concerns, but actively pursuing social causes. Finally Schneider and Lester introduce the concept of mutual and exclusive representation, of the advocate having the service user's needs as his or her primary concern (exclusivity) within a relationship where the direction of the advocacy is agreed upon together as part of a shared enterprise (mutuality).

Henderson and Pochin's (2001) definition of advocacy also addresses the nature of the relationship between advocate and service user:

> Advocacy can be described as the process of identifying with and representing a person's views and concerns, in order to ensure enhanced rights and entitlements, undertaken by someone who has little or no conflict of interest. (Henderson and Pochin 2001 p1)

This part of Henderson and Pochin's definition introduces the idea of advocacy as representation, as making sure the service user's voice is heard. This is a slightly different thing from persuasion (although Henderson and Pochin do acknowledge the place this also has to play in advocacy). Action for Advocacy take this idea further in their definition identifying advocacy as 'taking action to help people say what they want' (Action for Advocacy 2002). Here the goal of advocacy is not merely to represent the views of another, but also to enable that person to speak themselves. Henderson and Pochin's definition also clarifies further what the idea of exclusiveness in the relationship between advocate and service user might mean. An advocate needs to be aware of potential conflicts of interest in their advocacy role and to be as independent as possible.

Finally I want to look at a couple of definitions of citizen advocacy. We will look in more detail at citizen advocacy in the next chapter, but it has a very specific orientation, which ought to be included in any consideration of the definition of advocacy. Atkinson (1999 p6) defines Citizen Advocacy in the following way: 'citizen advocacy is typically seen as a one-to-one relationship between a volunteer spokesperson and their disadvantaged partner'. Citizen advocacy developed as part of normalisation with or for people with learning difficulties and 'occurs when an ordinary citizen develops a relationship with an ordinary person who risks social exclusion or other unfair treatment' (Bateman 2000 p24). In citizen advocacy the relationship between advocate and service user is of vital importance. This approach representing the service user's views goes alongside support and empowerment more generally. What can we learn from citizen advocacy about defining and understanding advocacy more generally? An essential precept of this approach is that the relationship between advocate and the person being represented is an vital aspect of advocacy and, echoing Brandon's definition, we cannot ignore the important role that advocacy can play in enhancing confidence and self-esteem.

So what does all this tell us about the nature of advocacy? Firstly, I think we can see that advocates can represent the views of individuals, groups and wider communities of interest and that advocacy can also involve campaigning for collective rights. Secondly, advocates can be involved in the process of persuading others to change and also giving voice to the perspectives of service users and ensuring their views are heard. In doing this they can speak for service users and help to enable them to speak. It is also important that advocates are aware of any conflicts of interest which may exist in relation to this role. Finally there is an important emotional and psychological component in advocacy.

Before we leave the definition of advocacy, it is worth thinking about two other related themes which are present in many accounts of advocacy's essential features, over and above the dimensions we have just considered. The first of these is the relationship between advocacy and empowerment. Thompson (2002 p302), looking at social work with adults, views advocacy as 'an important form of empowerment in which relatively powerless individuals or groups are supported in their attempts to influence or challenge more powerful elements in society'. In Thompson's view advocacy has a significant part to play in empowering practice in social care and has the capacity to increase service users' sense of autonomy and make real changes in the world; to empower people psychologically and structurally. However, advocacy may have the scope to do more than this. It may have a 'radical potential' (Boylan and Dalrymple 2009 p2) to play a part in the pursuit of social work's transformational goals (Payne 2006) 'enabling disadvantaged and oppressed people to gain personal and social empowerment through changes in society' (Payne 2006 p14).

A central tenet of anti-oppressive practice has been the belief that social work has the capacity both to empower the individual and, through the adoption of practice approaches sensitive to the impacts of difference, to begin to alter power relationships between individuals, within communities and in society more broadly. Advocacy's clear links with empowerment, therefore, may offer an approach to practice consistent with these important aims of anti-oppressive practice.

One thing which thinking about the definitions of advocacy tells us is that there is not unanimity about what advocacy is or how it should be carried out (and nor perhaps should there be). The search for a single unifying definition may therefore prove illusory. In Chapter 4 we will look at the value base of advocacy and it may be here where we find the most common ground between different approaches. There is a clear distinction in practice however between those who identify themselves as being advocates and those who undertake advocacy as part of a wider professional brief.

Advocacy as part of a professional role

Discussion point

Consider the following roles. Most of these describe activities which on the face of it would not be called advocacy. Think about the characteristics of advocacy we outlined when we were thinking about how to define it. To what extent do you think the following roles fit with these dimensions? Could any of them be identified as advocacy? If not do they have elements of advocacy within them? Where you think you can see an element of advocacy you need to think about why this is the case.

A mediator who works for a not-for-profit family mediation service and who works with couples going through the process of separation and divorce. The service provides a safe, secure environment within which couples can discuss their differences together, sometimes in circumstances where domestic violence has been an issue. The role of the mediator does not involve taking sides, but is about enabling both parties to put forward their views and facilitating negotiation between them.

A worker in what is known in one local authority as brokerage. She worked for many years as a home care organiser, responsible for managing a group of local authority home helps. The new brokerage role involves liaising with a range of private companies who are approved to provide home care for residents of the local authority, monitoring the quality of those services, or when a service user has a personal budget which they wish to spend themselves, supporting that person to find suitable providers of whatever care services the person requires and monitoring the quality of those services.

A social worker employed by the local authority who works in a day centre for people with mental health problems and who is setting up a service user consultation group to contribute towards planning what services should be provided.

A shop steward working on behalf of the union UNISON, who represents the views of union members working in a busy children and families division of a social services department. She has been approached by union members expressing concerns about workloads within the authority, and that the pressure of work gives insufficient time and space for social workers to properly assess risk, and perform their duties to the standards demanded by their professional body. She plans to raise these concerns at the regular joint meeting between the union and senior managers within the local authority.

A group of young service users who have experience of the looked after children's system and are part of an advocacy group, who are offering a peer mentoring scheme for

(*continued*)

social work students within a particular local authority. They are each paired with a social work student and meet every week to look at how they can develop approaches to practice which are empowering for young people and respect their rights.

The members of a Mental Health Act monitoring group, made up of representatives of the police, ambulance services, social services, health and service users, experts by experience, who meet each month to look at how the Mental Health Act is being applied in their locality and to try and ensure that practice across the board conforms to the legal requirements and respects the rights of service users. Where problems with practice are identified then the group acts to rectify these.

An inspector from the Care Quality Commission (CQC), who is about to undertake an inspection of a residential care home for older people. A number of relatives of elders living in the home have approached the CQC to express concerns about the standards of care residents have been receiving.

A cognitive behavioural therapist who has set up an assertiveness group for women, in a hospital for people with mental health problems. The group aims to make members more assertive in negotiating with psychiatrists about their treatment.

I would argue that there are clearly identifiable advocacy roles in the examples above. Those involved in the inspection, regulation and quality assurance of services are often acting as advocates on behalf of people at their most vulnerable. Aspects of negotiation may involve enabling people to voice their concerns or more forcefully pressing for service users' needs to be met. Involvement can empower service users and lead to lobbying for changes in the way services are structured and delivered. Work with a psychological focus can empower people to be more effective in advocating for themselves.

Advocacy is not just something social workers do as part of their professional role. The Nursing and Midwifery Council requires nurses and midwives to 'act as an advocate for those in your care, helping them to access relevant health and social care information and support' (Nursing and Midwfery Council 2008 p2). Doctors also often take on advocacy (Waterston 2009).

A brief history of advocacy

We have looked at how to define advocacy. Another way of understanding it is through a consideration of its history. I want to look briefly at two, at times, interwoven strands of this history, advocacy within social work and social care, and advocacy without. This distinction is not at all a clear one. Some approaches to advocacy are hard to categorise in this way, Citizen Advocacy for example. However, it serves as a loose framework for an historical overview.

The origins of social work lie in attempts to address the causes of and alleviate the consequences of poverty. One way in which this was achieved was through the efforts of the Charity Organisation Society and the distribution of charitable support to the deserving poor (Payne 2005b). However, as Manthorpe and Bradley (2002 p279) point out, many 'early amateur social workers...appreciated that social change would be necessary to challenge cycles of deprivation and systems of inequality'. The Settlement Movement, which grew up at the end of the nineteenth century, offered a new way of understanding poverty and attempting to address it. The basic idea of the settlement movement was that students from Oxford and Cambridge colleges would come to settlements to spend time amongst the poor in large cities (most notably in London's East End) and engage in what modern parlance might describe as community development activities. These included setting up youth clubs and activities, organising and sponsoring holidays, and active advocacy on behalf of the poor. From these rather inauspiciously patrician beginnings some important aspects of advocacy emerged. A notable example, where individual advocacy and campaigning (cause advocacy) were combined, is the poor man's lawyer scheme, which started at the Mansfield Settlement in 1891 with the provision of pro-bono legal advice and then spread to other settlements. From within the settlement movement a campaign was launched for state support for the provision of legal services, which eventually led to the current legal aid system (Spencer 2009).

It is the more radical tradition in social work in the UK which has been most keen to embrace advocacy as a practice tool. Community development, which can trace some of its origins back to the Settlement tradition (Mayo 1994) has a long tradition of encouraging self-help, advocacy, and community activism and campaigning. Radical social work allied itself with campaigning and advocacy groups such as the Claimants Union (Bateman 2000) and embraced both campaigns and self-help, 'alternative forms where people can organise collectively to help themselves over particular social problems' (Wilson 1980 p36). Recent interest in a more radically orientated practice has tried to refocus social work's attention on poverty (Ferguson and Woodward 2009). Mantle and Backwith (2010) make a strong case for the adoption of a more community orientated social work with advocacy as a central feature.

Jordan (1987 p135) argues that 'two powerful paradigms of the social worker have dominated the profession's self-image. The first is that of counsellor – skilful, attentive, accurately empathetic and accepting of the client's vulnerability. The second is that of advocate, who champions the oppressed, and turns the tables on those who exploit or exclude the client.' Jordan sees these two approaches as being at the ends of a sort of continuum of practice. Our exploration of history shows us that for certain practitioners at certain points in the history of social work the advocacy end of this continuum has been a very important part of practice.

Advocacy and the service user movement

Moving on to look at the impact of advocacy outside of social work, the role of service user movements has been crucial. The self-advocacy movement, which we will look at in more detail later on in the book, enabled groups of people with learning disabilities to collectively begin to advocate and lobby for greater control over their care. The Independent Living Movement sought and achieved increasing control by disabled people over their care, first through Centres for Independent Living and then through the successful campaign for the institution of direct payments via the Community Care (Direct Payments) Act 1996. Mental health services were also an important focal point for advocacy and campaigning. These movements, with their dual interest in case and cause advocacy, were driven by some common factors. The move away from institutional care was important as was a critical re-evaluation by service users of what care more generally meant and what assumptions underlaid it.

For people with disabilities this critical re-evaluation came through the development and adoption of the social model of disability. The central thesis of the social model, that it is not impairments themselves which create the disadvantages and restrictions that disabled people experience, but the responses of society to those impairments, has come to have increasing influence on social care in the field of disability (Oliver 2009). In relation to mental health services the anti-psychiatry movement presented an important theoretical backdrop to the burgeoning service user movement in the 1980s. The work of Szasz (1961) and Rosenhan (1973) was influential as was Romme and Escher's work (Romme and Escher 2000 for example), which destigmatised voice hearing. A central concern of the service-user-led organisations that emerged – UKAN (UK advocacy network) and Survivors Speak Out – was supporting advocacy by service users at the grass roots level whilst at the same time lobbying for changes in policy (the inclusion of a statutory right to advocacy in the 2007 amendments to the 1983 Mental Health Act for example).

Another way of looking at the history of advocacy and social work

I am going to look at another version of the history of social work now and the place of advocacy within it. What I want to do is look at the life of 'a pioneer of social work' (Oxford University Press 1992 (DNB) p3330) within the UK, Eileen Younghusband, and to reflect on Jordan's idea of social work's dual mandate in the context of one individual's experience of social work.

Eileen Younghusband was born at the beginning of the twentieth century in Kashmir, where her father, a well-known explorer, was a colonial diplomat and administrator. The wider world beyond Great Britain and global issues were always of concern to her and this international early childhood may have influenced this interest. Socially reformist Anglicanism was also an important influence on Younghusband when young, and the pacifist priest Dick Sheppard's sermons, which emphasised the social responsibilities of Christians, were important in shaping her life and thinking. Younghusband's early social work experiences were among the settlements in the East End of London, where she was involved in youth work and later as a JP with a particular interest in young people and crime, an area of judicial and social policy in which she campaigned for changes (Payne 2005).

Younghusband spent many years teaching social work at the London School of Economics and had a profound impact on the development of social work education and

(continued)

training. Her report on the education and training of social workers (Younghusband 1947) was instrumental in the profession's development and the models of education and training which we see today. Younghusband's vision of social work practice was a broadly based one. Her chairing of the committee which produced the 1968 report on the education of community workers is just one indicator of this (Younghusband 1968). She also had a strong interest in the welfare of refugees. 'Sharing a home with Helen Roberts, a part-Jewish worker with refugees from Hitler's Germany' (Payne 2005 p60) led her into this area of work. She was instrumental in the foundation of the first Citizens Advice Bureau during the war, dealing with debt, poverty, homelessness and evacuation. In her later life much of her work was concerned with the international context of social work and she made 'a significant contribution to the spread of ideas about organisation of services, training and practice beyond the UK' (Lyons 2003 p3)

Her view of social work was that it encompassed both work with the individual and social activism on a wider level within society as a whole. This quote sums up that philosophy: 'To a considerable extent the old case work question, 'who is the client?' is undergoing a change as social work replies that the client is not only the individual or even the family but also the school, the prison, the hospital, the work place, the neighbourhood, or indeed some power group in the functional or geographic community' (Younghusband 1971 p. 131)

What can we learn about the place of advocacy in social work historically by looking at Eileen Younghusband's life? Firstly the importance of working to counteract poverty and the recognition of the role it played in the life of service users is a theme running through her work. Her involvement in the settlements of the East End and her work in establishing the Citizens' Advice Bureau are good examples of this aspect of her professional life. The Citizens' Advice Bureau was the origin of much poverty orientated case-based advocacy. Her work on juvenile crime shows a combination of an appreciation of the individual causes of crime, but also a dissatisfaction with the way it was managed by the system which she campaigned to change. Campaigning and cause-based advocacy were consistent features of her work. In her international activities and interest in community work she demonstrated a broad conception of what social work might be and do and its potential to have a more radical edge, both in communities in the UK and in development abroad. In her Eileen Younghusband memorial lecture to the International Federation of Schools of Social Work, Briskman (2008) draws on the example of the advocacy of social workers in response to the detention of asylum seekers in Australia, to argue that social work has the capacity to carry out a role in the political realm, responding to human rights abuses through political activism, a position consistent with Younghusband's 'deep sense of social justice and commitment to social reform' (p13). There is obviously danger in thinking, to paraphrase Thomas Carlyle (Carlyle 1888 p2), that 'the history of the world is but the biography of great women', but the life of Eileen Younghusband does exemplify how advocacy historically has been associated with and been a core part of social work.

Discussion point

As social workers we all have our own particular perspectives on which approaches to practice should be at the heart of social work, informed in part by what we think social work is about, what role it plays in society more broadly. Think about Eileen Younghusband. From what we know about her from the brief biographical details I've included here, it is possible to get a sense of how she understood social work and why she therefore saw advocacy as important. Think at this point about your own motivations for being a social worker and what you see the profession as being for. Advocacy is important in social work. How would advocacy fit into your personal model of practice?

Advocacy and current approaches to understanding practice

We can see that the history of social work is one in which advocacy features strongly. At this stage I want to move our discussion forward to the present and explore recent understandings of social work and how advocacy might fit with these. Dominelli (2002a) and Payne (2006) provide us with two very similar accounts of the purposes of social work and its function in society. Both present three different competing accounts of social workers' wider social role. I am going to look at each of these in turn and think about how advocacy might relate to this framework of theories about what social work is about. I am going to start with what Dominelli calls the maintenance approach to social work, an idea very similar to Payne's individualist reformist perspective. In this account social work is seen as a mechanism for maintaining order in society, for fixing tears in its fabric and helping individuals through problems to a point where they can function successfully. The social workers' interventions here are marked by pragmatism and a non-therapeutic focus. The primary concern is with the individual and social change which enhances individual strengths and stability.

How would advocacy fit into this framework? Advocacy here would have a pragmatic and personal focus. Martin Davies provides us with the following example. 'The social worker acts on behalf of a harassed mother in a face-to-face confrontation with a housing manager or landlord wanting to evict her and her family for non-payment of rent' (Davies 1994 p90). However, the role might extend to lobbying for resources for a local community perhaps, or specific resources to meet particular types of service user need.

Therapeutic approaches are 'best exemplified by counselling approaches' (Dominelli 2002a p3) and their primary concern is with psychological functioning. The social worker role is seen as the promotion of 'growth and self-fulfilment' (Payne 2006 p12). The relationship between the social worker and the service user is a mechanism through which the service users can explore their lives and through this exploration manage the problems they are encountering more effectively. Within this model advocacy might primarily be concerned with psychological empowerment and spiritual growth. Southgate (1990 in Brandon 1995a) identifies the importance of nurturing and supporting as part of the advocacy role. 'Above all advocates must support the inner advocacy and creativity of the individual' (Brandon 1995a p10). This approach emphasises the undoubted importance of interpersonal skills as a way of facilitating advocacy and empowerment. 'Empowerment and advocacy in social work are enabled through counselling skills' (Seden 2005 p89).

Finally we come to what Dominelli calls the emancipatory perspective on social work, that others (Pease and Fook 1999, Payne 2006) have termed transformational. Within this social work paradigm the purpose of social work extends beyond the individual's psychological make-up and their immediate environment to a broader consideration of the structural factors impacting upon their lives. Promoting social justice and combating oppression are very much to the fore in this approach. It is in this account of social work that the synergies with advocacy are most obvious. The type of advocacy envisaged within this model is one that engages with social campaigns and in which power is firmly in the hands of service users. So user-led approaches to advocacy are particularly important in this context. Advocacy offers the opportunity for service users to come together collectively to pursue a particular cause, something very much in keeping with the ethos of the transformative approach. Finally this type of collective approach to advocacy has the potential to raise political consciousness and produce political change. It is for this reason that 'advocacy and empowerment strategies have proved attractive in recent years as a development and implementation of critical social work' (Payne 2005 p313).

The international definition of social work with its emphasis on human rights and social justice seems most closely connected to the transformational account of social work:

> The social work profession promotes social change, problem solving in human relationships and the empowerment and liberation of people to enhance well-being. Utilising theories of human behaviour and social systems, social work intervenes at the points where people interact with their environments. Principles of human rights and social justice are fundamental to social work. (IFSW 2000)

Certainly advocacy offers an important mechanism 'to allow social workers to address issues of rights and social justice and to support efforts to help people obtain services and resources in the community' (IFSW 2000).

Discussion point

Before we move on to look at advocacy skills and some case examples of advocacy practice it might be helpful at this point to revisit the question we asked earlier, how does advocacy fit into your personal model of practice? Does the Dominelli/Payne distinction between the maintenance, therapeutic and transformational approaches to practice help you think through this issue?

Advocacy skills in practice

At this point I want to look at the stories of a couple of users of social services to think about how advocacy might play a part in the support which social workers might offer. Both cases see social workers operating in situations where they have a duty to protect the welfare of vulnerable people, and in both skills in advocacy are important.

Practice example: Sonia

Sonia's story

Sonia is a 21-year-old mixed race woman who has two children aged 4 and 6 years old, both girls. Sonia had an upbringing which was difficult at times. She spent quite a lot of her young life in foster care after her mother was imprisoned for a drug dealing offence. After the birth of her first daughter she left her foster parents and lived in a flat found by her social worker. With a lot of help and support she managed to cope and now lives with her children in a small house owned by a housing association. Over the years Sonia has had some difficulties with her drinking and with the use of cocaine, which has had an impact on her role as a parent. Sonia has sought help with these issues from the Community Drug and Alcohol Team, and although she occasionally drinks too much has been drug free for a couple of years. Sonia's older daughter attends a local primary school and her younger daughter goes to the nursery there, which runs in the mornings only. Up until this point the girls have been doing well at school. However, the school has recently made contact with the social services department to express their concerns about both girls' sporadic attendance and high level of sickness. In relation to her youngest daughter this is putting her place in the nursery in jeopardy as there are other children on the waiting list for the place, and Sonia has breached the agreement all parents using the nursery sign up to when their children start there, that they will make sure their child attends regularly.

When Sonia is seen by the duty social worker, Grace, the girls are at home with her. Sonia seems very anxious for the social worker to leave and tries to rearrange the appointment for the following morning. The social worker does not want to do this, and eventually Sonia starts to talk more with Grace about what has been happening to her recently.

About six months ago Sonia's boyfriend Alex moved into the house. Neither Alex nor Sonia was working when he moved in. Sonia was keen that if they were going to live together they needed to make sure their benefits situation was all clear. So they made a new joint claim for Job Seekers' Allowance and Sonia thought that she had stopped her old Income Support claim. All her benefits are paid directly into her Post Office bank account. About a month or so ago Alex tried to get a crisis loan for the family. However, when the benefits agency looked into this they found that they had been paying them two lots of benefits and a fraud investigation was started. At this point all the family's benefits were suspended. Alex also left at this point. The relationship between him and Sonia had been a difficult one, and in many ways she was glad he had left. He had been using drugs and

(continued)

been violent towards her and the children. Since he has been gone he has sent Sonia a number of threatening texts and emails. She did make contact with the police about this, but Sonia says they haven't done anything.

Sonia feels stupid that she left her bank statements unopened and hadn't properly looked at letters she had received. Since her benefits have been suspended she has been working cash-in-hand at a pub quite close by. They insist she works an 11am to 5pm shift (which is why she wanted Grace to come back tomorrow) so sometimes she has had to take the girls out of school and nursery to allow this to happen, because she can't pick them up if she's working. Sometimes she leaves them at home on their own. But she is nervous about doing this because she worries that Alex may come back. So sometimes they stay with her in the pub when she's working in a room behind the bar. This hasn't always worked perfectly and the youngest child went running round the pub on one occasion. The pub is quite rough and used by drug dealers. Sonia has been offered drugs but so far not accepted any. Without benefits Sonia is building up rent arrears. Alex left an old car he was 'working on' outside the house and there have been complaints about this. The housing association have written to her about this, but Sonia hasn't opened the letter.

Sonia's story is not untypical of referrals to social work. She faces a range of practical problems which she is struggling to deal with. For Grace, advocacy will be an important element in her intervention here. She may want to have some initial contacts with the benefits agency to explore what has happened and see if there is an immediate solution, but also support Sonia in seeking more expert benefits advice, advocacy and legal support. With Sonia's daughter's nursery place under threat Grace may need to contact the school to advocate on Sonia's behalf for the place to be kept open. Equally it might be important for Grace to be pressing for an adequate police response to the threats made by Alex and linking Sonia to agencies which can support her in this area and if necessary advocate on her behalf. It might also be important to address the precarious nature of Sonia's relationship with the housing association, again presenting a case to them and supporting Sonia to make sure they understand her perspective. Skills in negotiation and in presenting a case will be important in ensuring the protection and well-being of Sonia's children.

Practice example: Marija

Marija's story

Marija is a 66-year-old woman who was born in Croatia but who has lived in the UK for the past 30 years after marrying an English man, Alfred. She worked in a florist store until three years ago. Marija has a long history of mental health problems and has been diagnosed by her psychiatrist as having bi-polar disorder. She has been in the psychiatric unit of the local hospital on a number of occasions since she has been in the UK. She was admitted under a compulsory order and 'sectioned' under the Mental Health Act the first time she

(continued)

went into hospital, but since then has been persuaded to come in when her mental health has deteriorated. She has a good relationship with her psychiatrist, Dr Jones, but he thinks she can sometimes be unreliable in the way she takes her medication, stopping for a few days and then restarting. Crises seem to happen when she stops altogether. Marija has one sister, two years younger than her, but they have not spoken for a number of years. Marija ended the relationship when her sister married a Serbian, shortly before the Yugoslav war, and moved to Serbia. They have not spoken since this time.

Alfred has been becoming increasingly worried about Marija over the past few weeks. She has been speaking less and less English and has taken to shouting in Croatian, a language that Marija knows he can only speak a little. She has had difficulty sleeping and smashed a plate near him. (In the past she has hit him with several other things.) He has approached his GP, just to talk through his concerns. Her behaviour has been a little bit different on this occasion and she seems to be taking her medication fairly regularly and is less talkative and more upset. The GP asks Alfred to ask Marija to come into the surgery to see him, but she refuses to do this. He decides to go out with a trainee GP and a community psychiatric nurse (CPN) to see her after surgery finishes. Both Marija and Alfred are a little bit surprised by the visit. Marija, who opens the door, doesn't want to let this group of professionals in and after speaking in English at first goes back to using Croatian. Alfred tries to persuade her that she should let them in. Quite a lengthy dialogue ensues between the GP, Alfred and Marija in the hallway, with Marija pacing the hall and occasionally interjecting, and Alfred explaining in a lowered voice that he is worried about her and suggesting perhaps Dr Jones should come out to see her and see if a change in medication would be helpful.

Carol is the duty Approved Mental Health Professional who has been contacted by Dr Smith, a consultant psycho-geriatrician, the following morning. Dr Smith explains that Marija's GP, who saw her yesterday, has spoken to him and asked him to assess her under the Mental Health Act for compulsory admission to hospital and asks if Carol can be there for an assessment that afternoon. Carol begins to gather information about the situation. She speaks to Alfred, to the community psychiatric nurse at the GPs surgery, and to an occupational therapist, who knows Marija well, in the Community Mental Health Team (where Dr Jones works) that has supported Marija in the past. Everyone is a bit confused that Marija is not being seen by Dr Jones, who knows her well. Eventually Carol is able to speak to Dr Jones, who explains that he is planning to transfer her to the older age psychiatry team (where Dr Smith is the consultant) and that as a consequence he can't see her or admit her to the hospital beds in Drake Ward, which are for under 65s only (and he explains they're full anyway). When Carol goes to see Marija with Dr Smith, Marija is able to talk with them with the help of an interpreter, although she breaks off at times to pace up and down the hall. She acknowledges that things aren't going well and that hospital might be a good idea, although she thinks at the moment things have not reached that point, but she only wants to go to Drake Ward which she knows and has been going to for years and years. At one point she says to Dr Smith, 'See, see I'll come, take me to Drake Ward' and tugs at his arm indicating towards the door. However, Dr Smith remains adamant that she needs to be in hospital and that the only option is to be admitted to

(continued)

this unit. Alfred is very reluctant for this to happen. He knows that Marija will only go to Dr Smith's ward if she is under a section of the Mental Health Act, but knows that the situation will get more difficult at home if things continue the way they are. Carol is reluctant for Marija to go into hospital at all, as she feels that it might still be possible to support her at home. She knows that Marija might go willingly if the right bed in the right ward were available so, for both of these reasons, does not think she can support a compulsory admission to hospital.

For Carol now the only option seems to be further negotiation with the doctors involved in Marija's care. Carol speaks to the GP and Drs Smith and Jones. She draws their attention to their common interest in seeing that Marija's mental health improves and of the fact that patient choice features strongly in the current culture of health care, and tries to behave in an assertive way. Dr Jones is adamant that Marija must now be treated within the older age psychiatry service and anyway, even if he were to keep her as a patient, he has no beds available in Drake Ward. The end point of the negotiations is to try a more creative solution. Dr Jones concedes that the rules about transferring patients at a particular age do have some flexibility in them. Everyone acknowledges that there is no bed available on Drake Ward but, after exploring all the options, it emerges that Dr Jones can refer patients to a crisis intervention team which works with people in their own homes in an intensive way. Marija and Alfred agree to try this approach. The outcome is a positive one; with intensive support from a CPN and social worker within the team Marija starts taking medication again. However, she is also able to reveal her reasons for thinking things have been difficult for her recently. She has learnt that her younger sister died over a year ago from breast cancer. Her brother-in-law has only recently contacted her by letter to tell her. She had not felt able to tell Alfred as she still feels guilty about their estrangement.

At first sight looking at Marija's story we might ask where the advocacy is here. This is after all an account of quite a coercive area of social work practice. This not like Sonia's situation, where the social worker was involved with benefits, housing and securing a nursery place. Advocacy in social work is often seen as being about this sort of thing. However, a closer look at what happened to Marija reveals that advocacy was an important part of Carol's work, even when working within a framework of coercion. A key part of the work Carol did with Marija was enabling her voice to be heard, when she was in a relatively powerless and vulnerable situation and was finding it difficult to express herself. Carol's use of an interpreter to try to open up the communication options available for Marija is a good example of this. However, this aspect of Carol's work also involved a representational element, giving voice to Marija's views about her treatment and making sure that the doctors, in positions of considerable power, took account of her perspective. The use of negotiation is very characteristic of advocacy and assertive negotiation skills are crucial in doing this successfully. Carol demonstrates – in seeking the underlying shared interest in the negotiation, in looking at external criteria which are relevant to the process and in trying to generate a range of creative options in the search for an agreed outcome – the skills she has in this area. Finally being a guide for a service user through the complex landscape of health and social care can also be an important part of advocacy, making sure that the information is available to that person to make an informed choice. Social workers are often presenting a perspective within multidisciplinary working which is a corrective to a very medically orientated model of practice, advocating for the social perspective on mental health care. Carol is doing this here in offering Marija support which gives her the space to start to talk about what she sees as being at the heart of her current problems.

Advocacy skills: an introduction

We can see from these case studies that advocacy requires a certain set of skills and I wanted to get a general overview of this area by looking at where advocacy fits into the GSCC key role framework (Topss 2002). The Social Work Reform Board's proposals for a new capabilities framework (Social Work Reform Board 2010) may have an impact on the types of skills identified as central to practice. However, there is no indication that the proposals will make a radical change to the social work skills base. The starting point of this process should be key role 3, and particularly unit 10 of the framework. This key role to 'Support individuals to represent their needs, views and circumstances' relates directly to advocacy. Both unit 10, where advocacy is addressed, and unit 11, in which the participation in decision making forums is discussed, are particularly relevant to advocacy. I want to begin by looking at Unit 10, which covers advocacy 'on behalf of, individuals, families, carers, groups and communities'.

This unit is made up of three elements:

10.1 Assess whether you should act as the advocate for the individual, family, carer, group or community.

Here social workers need to be aware where there might be a conflict of interest between their professional role and undertaking advocacy (we will see a little later in this chapter how this might work) and when they might need to seek out specialist advocacy skills. In these circumstances 10.2 will become important.

10.2 Assist individuals, families, carers, groups and communities to access independent advocacy.

Working effectively alongside independent advocacy is an important part of advocacy friendly practice.

10.3 Advocate for, and with, individuals, families, carers, groups and communities.

This final unit addresses direct advocacy roles across a whole range of different areas.

However, the relevance of advocacy to social work skills extends beyond unit 10 of the National Occupational Standards. As we can see from our case study advocacy requires a range of skills:

Information gathering The analysis of information and its evaluation is important in advocacy (units 2.2. and 1.3). We can see this in the work with Sonia where the social worker is presented with a complex interrelated set of problems.

Negotiation skills and assertiveness The case of Marija shows the importance of complex inter-professional negotiation as a key element in advocacy (units 6.1 and 6.5). Assertiveness is also important in this context (unit 19.2).

Skills in presenting a case Again, for social workers undertaking advocacy this is important. Grace is presenting a case for keeping open Sonia's nursery place for example and Carol is arguing why a particular approach to treatment is the right one for Marija. Units 11.1, 11.2 and 11.4 are all relevant here.

Skills in working with groups Advocacy can be an individual or group based activity and often the two areas are linked together. So it can be important for advocates to develop skills in participatory approaches to working with groups.

The brief review above of social work skills gives us a sense of where advocacy fits within current understandings of the social work skills base. It is important to remember, however, that advocacy skills have applicability in other contexts. Skill in presenting a case can be important in a wide range of contexts. Negotiation skills and assertiveness have a relevance that extends across social work.

Before we leave this area I wanted to add a little postscript to the work on the two cases we described earlier. Both cases represent instances of intervention in a crisis. (It is interesting that theories of crisis intervention stress the importance of practical assistance alongside psychological support in which advocacy can have an important role (Roberts 2005).) Although advocacy can be important in the short term, it can also be part of providing support in the longer term. To illustrate this, a 'what happened next' exercise is helpful.

Sonia

Sonia managed to sort out a number of her problems, and an assistant social worker has been involved in supporting her over the past couple of months. She is linked to a solicitor who has helped her with the fraud enquiry and the possible prosecution. Social services representations to the school mean that the nursery place has been kept open and the girls are attending school. The assistant social worker has helped Sonia with debts accrued when she was without benefits and to deal with the housing association. As a final suggestion before he closes her case the assistant social worker asks whether she would be interested in being part of a mentoring scheme for other young people from the looked after system who are moving into independent living. The scheme involves giving assistance, advice and support based on personal experience.

Marija

Some weeks later and Marija's situation is much more settled. She is still concerned about being referred on, away from a team and consultant psychiatrist who have been involved in her care for a long time, at what seems to her like the arbitrary age of 65. Carol has formally raised this issue with the health trust following the Mental Health Act assessment and been told informally that the trust might make an exception in Marija's case. Carol feels that, although she is not an employee of the trust, she is managed by them and that the most effective way of supporting Marija might be to exert pressure from outside the trust as well. She has suggested that Marija also makes contact with the local MIND advice service about this. When Marija does this she discovers that a number of other service users have complained about being transferred from adults' to older people's services and a campaign to change the way this works is now under way.

Both of these examples show the potential of advocacy to be more than just a single-issue-based task-orientated approach. It can generate more extensive networks of support. Our postscript shows how this can be achieved through service users themselves becoming involved in mentoring and advocacy and through cause advocacy and campaigning.

I want to finish this chapter by looking at the place of advocacy within practice models. We have looked, when thinking about Dominelli and Payne's account of social work's purpose in society, at how a particular orientation to practice can shape the view a practitioner has of advocacy. However, in this instance I wanted to look at an overall model of practice and how advocacy fits within it. Goldberg Wood and Tully (Goldberg Wood and Tully 2006) present a structural model of social work practice which identifies advocacy as one of eight key roles undertaken by social workers: the conferee, the broker, the mediator, the advocate, the therapist, the case manager, the group worker and the community organiser. The pivotal roles in this account are those of conferee, broker, mediator and advocate. It is valuable to look at this approach for number of reasons: it is an unusual thing; a generic model of practice; derived from social workers' practice experience; with its origins in North America it provides us with an idea of the place of advocacy in an international social work context; it is also of interest because it comes from a particular value base. Underlying it is the view 'that opportunities and resources are unevenly distributed and that members of deprived populations are structurally victimised' (Goldberg Wood and Tully 2006 p21). It is a strengths-based model which sees problems as stemming fundamentally from the environment rather than the service user, and emphasises the importance of power in understanding their impacts. A key theme of the model is the link between the individual and the wider world, between actions that social workers undertake at the micro level and those they can engage in with groups to promote social change. Goldberg Wood and Tully (2006 p139) argue 'that without advocacy the profession [social work] would be like a deodorised skunk – never really able to make a stink about individual victims or classes of victims who are unable to obtain access to basic human needs or human rights'. In the two cases studies we have looked at advocacy is a conduit to collective engagement and action. Goldberg Wood and Tully's approach sees making these links between the local and the broader community as essential and as having the potential for leading social work into campaigning and social change.

Key learning points

- Advocacy covers a very broad range of activities which are difficult to encapsulate in a single definition
- We can, however, identify some key dimensions of advocacy and its potential as a force for change in social care
- Advocacy has an important role in social work historically, but service user movements have also been instrumental in the development of what we now understand as advocacy
- Our overall view of social work, how far it can be a force for social change for example, can influence how we think about the role of advocacy within it
- Advocacy in social work can be undertaken in a variety of different contexts and requires a wide range of skills

Further reading

Atkinson, D. (1999) *Advocacy: A review*, Brighton, Pavillion/Joseph Rowntree.

Dominelli, L. (2009) Anti-oppressive practice: the challenges of the twenty-first century in Adams, R., Dominelli, L. and Payne, M. (eds) *Social Work, Themes, Issues and Critical Debates* (3rd ed), Basingstoke, Palgrave Macmillan.

Goldberg Wood, G. and Tully, C. (2006) *The Structural Approach to Direct Practice in Social Work*, New York, Columbia University Press.

Schneider, R. and Lester, L. (2001) *Social Work Advocacy: A New Framework for Action*, Belmont CA, Brooks Cole.

2   Dimensions of Advocacy

This chapter looks in more detail at what advocacy means in practice, both for independent advocacy services and for social workers. Traditionally what we call advocacy has been understood as being made up of a range of distinct but related forms. Beginning with a discussion of legal advocacy this chapter explores these different ways of doing advocacy using a multi-dimensional model to critically analyse the areas they have in common and their differences. The model presents four dimensions of advocacy, each a continuum (from speaking for to enabling to speak, for example), that provide a framework within which different forms of advocacy can be located, analysed and understood. The final part of the chapter begins to consider the roles of social workers undertaking advocacy, addressing the commonalities and differences between social work and independent advocates and the types of advocacy roles social workers can undertake.

Advocacy is quite a broad concept; a heading under which many interrelated activities take place. As we saw in the last chapter it is not always straightforward to define. However, falling within the broad definitions we explored there, we can identify a number of reasonably specific quite well understood headline approaches to advocacy. Legal advocacy, formal advocacy, citizen advocacy, peer advocacy, self-advocacy and group advocacy are key areas we will look at in this chapter. In addition there are statutory advocacy roles which help decision making in statutory contexts, which we will also touch upon here before a more detailed examination in Chapter 3. Advocacy can be however a bit of a slippery fish and individual advocacy projects often have their own particular ways of delivering services, which will conform in differing degrees to the headline approaches listed above.

Writers exploring this area have tended to identify key characteristics of the advocacy role and to construct a typology of advocacy services based around these characteristics. So Brandon and Brandon (2001) and Payne (2005) identify advocacy's key representational functions and contrast advocacy at an individual level with collective approaches. Brandon and Brandon (2001) (drawing upon the work of Hodgson (1995)) also call attention to the distinction between active and passive roles in advocacy. We can also order different types of advocacy by identifying who undertakes it (Brandon 1995a). Bateman (2000) in contrast identifies three core approaches – self-, citizen and legal advocacy – of which other forms of advocacy are variants. Our strategy for navigating through this area adopts some of these ideas, but fits them into a multi-dimensional model of advocacy where four key defining parameters of advocacy as an activity are defined: purpose, perspective, focus and scope.

A good starting point for our discussions of the nature and range of activities which fall under the title of advocacy is to look at legal advocacy, what we might call the legal archetype. This legal archetype often involves representation in courts or formal tribunals of some kind by an advocate with specific skills and expertise. Typically this person might be a lawyer, but the legal model has close affinities with other types of expert advocacy (an area we will explore later on in this chapter), and the two are often seen as a single approach (Mind 2010).

Legal advocacy

Why is it important to consider legal advocacy? Well one reason why this approach has had such an influence is its pervasive presence within our lives. Historically, recourse to the law has been crucially important in instigating and supporting social change, and pursuing goals of social justice. Brandon (1995a) outlines the important role that legal advocacy has played in attaining rights for people with mental health problems and physical disabilities. Bateman (2000) quite rightly argues that 'fundamental rights around homelessness, community care and discrimination have been usefully clarified and improved by lawyers acting as advocates' (p28). This is also a model of advocacy with which people are generally very familiar: representation in a formal context, whether it be in help buying a home, pursuing a claim in a court or tribunal, or appearing in a criminal court, is a relatively common experience. From *Perry Mason* via John Grisham novels to *Judge Judy*, accounts of the legal process within the media influence our expectations of the advocacy process. Many key concepts which stem from this approach have been prominent in shaping other types of advocacy. How we understand the concept of independence in advocacy, the nature of the advocate's representational role, and the way we present the process of advocacy have all been influenced by the legal archetype.

What are the key characteristics of the legal approach? It is possible to identify a number of core features:

A contractual or financial basis to the relationship   The relationship between lawyer and client is usually contractually or financially based (Bateman 2000, Brandon and Brandon 2001). One impact that this has is on the scope of the advocacy undertaken within the legal archetype. It is normally focused on a particular problem taking place within a specific timeframe.

Expertise   Our expectation of our legal representatives is that they should possess a particular range of knowledge of both the specific legislation with which they are dealing and also the process of the legal system through which they are seeking redress. The legal system has its own often abstruse language, which can make access and understanding difficult for the lay person. One role that legal representatives undertake in this area therefore is as translator.

Access to systems of redress   The courts are not easily open to all. As Bateman points out barristers 'have a legally protected virtual monopoly on appearances in the higher courts' (Bateman 2000 p27). When we engage a lawyer we are also buying a means of access to the legal system.

The adversarial context   Most legal advocacy takes place within an adversarial framework, where the role of the advocate is two-fold: firstly, it is to take instructions and to ensure that the client's voice is heard; secondly, it is to put a case to persuade and win an argument. This partisan perspective, arguing a case rather than just presenting another's views, is very characteristic of the legal approach.

Power   Power is a central issue in both social work and advocacy. The relationship between service user and professional within the legal archetype is one of expert and non-expert. The legal frame of reference for the advocacy process is inherently prone to establish a power differential between lawyer and client, to make advocacy become 'remote from the client' (Bateman 2000 p28), despite positive moves that can be made to breach this gap. Legal advocacy is not primarily about providing service users with skills and knowledge that they themselves can use in the future.

Social work, advocacy and human rights

As part of our discussion of legal advocacy within social work there is some value at this point in considering the role of human rights within social work. This is a theme to which we will return in the final chapter when we consider social work advocacy within a wider global context. The introduction to the UN Centre for Human Rights manual *Human Rights and Social Work* (1994, p3) stresses their fundamental value:

> The International Federation of Social Workers (IFSW) and the International Association of Schools of Social Work (IASSW) consider it imperative that those involved in the field of Social Work Education and practice have a clear and unreserved commitment to the promotion and protection of human rights.

Ife (2008) argues that 'one of the privileges of being a social worker is that it brings one constantly into contact with people whose commitment, determination and self-sacrifice provide a daily lesson in human rights and their importance' (p165).

There are essentially two ways in which this 'unreserved commitment' can be expressed through practice. The first is through the specific application of human rights codes and the law in relation to particular cases and areas of practice. In the UK the incorporation of the European Convention on Human Rights into the 1998 Human Rights Act has the potential to 'promote a real culture of rights which is empowering for service users' (Bramer 2009 p114). The Act has had an influence on the drafting of new guidance, *No Secrets*, covering the safeguarding of vulnerable adults, for example (Department of Health 2000, Bramer 2009). It has also had an impact on case law (Williams 2001) and the way in which social workers and advocates work with individual cases. Action for Advocacy's Human Rights Toolkit (Action for Advocacy 2009) includes a case example of a service user on a psychiatric ward, where patients' access to water has been restricted to meal times, because 'another person on the ward has a problem involving water retention' (p15). This situation, they argue, represents a potential breach of Article 8 of the Act, the right to private and family life, home and correspondence, which proves a very helpful reference point and source of support for those advocating for the end of the practice.

However, both Ife (2008) and Reichert (2003) argue that social work advocacy should adopt a broader interpretation of human rights which goes beyond the specifics of individual cases towards a human-rights-sensitive advocacy practice. Reichert suggests four elements to an approach to social work grounded in human rights:

- A strengths perspective to combat the fact that 'structural injustices have isolated many individuals and groups from necessary resources and fair treatment' (p230)
- A focus on empowerment linking personal experiences with broader structural factors
- Systematically challenging oppression 'which clearly relates to the exercise of human rights' (p229)
- A critique of power relations in society addressed through the adoption of feminist and 'ethnically sensitive' practice and cultural competence

Ife (2008) similarly argues that individual case advocacy has limits and has the potential to be disempowering; 'for the powerless and the disadvantaged it may well be argued that the last thing they need is to have yet another person, however well-intentioned, speaking on their behalf' (p42). Ife goes on to argue that 'if advocacy is not to be conservatory it needs to be practiced within an empowerment framework which seeks to show how the advocacy approach, far from reinforcing the dependence of the client on the social worker, is actually geared towards skilling the client' (p42). Ife moots a broader conception of human rights and advocacy which goes beyond the individual rights to incorporate wider economic, social and cultural rights, and collective rights. The struggle for environmental rights, for example, would fit with this broader conception of advocacy. Only critical empowerment based practice at the community as well as individual level can address this wider human rights agenda.

Our brief exploration of human rights reveals some of the strengths and weaknesses of the legal approach. The use of the law has the capacity to create real changes in systems of social care. However, it may not always be the most effective way of empowering service users. I want to look at this point at the four-dimensional model of advocacy that was introduced earlier and to consider its application to the legal archetype. The model covers four areas: the purpose of advocacy, and its perspective, focus and scope.

Purpose   When we consider the purposes of legal advocacy it is primarily about an expert speaking for a service user, rather than enabling the service user to speak for themselves by equipping them with the skills and knowledge they need in order to do this.

Perspective Within our legal archetype the perspective on advocacy which is adopted is one of persuasion, of arguing a case within an adversarial system, rather than trying to convey exactly what the service user wants to be heard or creating a set of circumstances where this can happen.

Focus The legal approach has quite a narrow focus on the specific issues that a particular case presents in law. This is in many ways a strength. Bateman (2000) argues that asking advocates to be 'friend, counsellor, legal advisor and general supporter' (p25) places too great a burden upon them. However, the process of advocacy does have other aspects to it. A service user's fight for decent housing, for example, does not take place in an emotional vacuum. Legal advocacy may only peripherally touch upon these expressive elements of the advocacy task.

Scope Legal advocacy is very much focused on the needs of the individual rather than the collective needs of a group and a shared interest or cause. Even in circumstances where a collective issue is at stake the legal system operates via single cases. Ife points out in his discussion of human rights (Ife 2008) that legal action takes place in a broader social context, where wider social goals may be being pursued. With its narrow scope there is the potential for these social and political aspects of advocacy to be downplayed in the legal approach.

It is important to reiterate at this juncture a point we touched upon, that the general styles of advocacy we have identified, of which legal advocacy is an example, do not represent unvaried monolithic ways of doing things. Legal advocacy, for example, encompasses a whole range of approaches which we can loosely fit under an overarching umbrella. This is one of the great strengths of the multi-dimensional model of advocacy. It essentially highlights a set of parameters which we can use to describe and analyse particular types of advocacy, an approach which reflects the diverse ways in which advocacy services are delivered in reality. It is relatively straightforward to think of legal advocacy services which don't fit neatly with the framework we have just outlined. Legal advocacy, for example, was an important element in the carers' movement, which also involved a group of carers working collectively to lobby for a cause. There are good examples of legal advocacy the purposes of which are much more aligned to empowerment and enabling service users to speak for themselves. The Claimants Union, which fought for the rights of welfare benefits recipients in the 1960s and 1970s, was a self-help group which combined campaigning with legal work in the area of welfare benefits, often undertaken by claimants themselves (Bateman 2000).

A multi-dimensional model of advocacy

Before we go on to explore the full range of approaches to advocacy I want to look in a little more detail and more generally at the multi-dimensional model we have used

Table 2.1 Dimensions of advocacy

Dimension	From	To
Purpose	Speaking for	Enabling to speak
	For example From . . . . Expert advocacy . . . . to . . . . Peer advocacy	
Perspective	Persuasion	Giving voice
	For example From . . . . Legal advocacy . . . . to . . . . IMHA role	
Focus	Instrumental elements	Expressive elements
	For example From . . . . Benefits advice . . . . to . . . . Citizen advocacy	
Scope	Individual needs	Collective concerns
	For example From . . . . Self-advocacy . . . . to . . . . Group advocacy	

in relation to legal advocacy. Table 2.1 outlines how this model works and provides examples of the types of advocacy which most closely conform to each of the dimensions (bearing in mind the caveat that individual advocacy projects will have their own specific ways of carrying out their work). The model does not attempt to adopt a fixed view of where a particular approach to advocacy can be located. What it does is to provide a framework we can use to critically analyse a range of ways of doing advocacy and identify similarities and differences between them. It will also serve as a framework we can use to structure our discussions of advocacy as part of the social work role.

I will explore each dimension in turn.

Purpose

The purpose dimension looks at the goals of advocacy and the extent to which the approach under consideration is concerned with speaking for a service user or enabling them to speak for themselves. In approaches to advocacy where expert advice is given (the legal archetype being a very good example), it is often the role of the expert to act as an intermediary between the service user and those in positions of power, the other party involved in the advocacy process. So typically 'speaking for' would involve representing another person in a formal decision-making forum, a tribunal for example, or writing letters on that person's behalf. There is a great value in this approach to advocacy. It is potentially a powerful way of addressing the problems service users face and is undoubtedly effective. At the other end of this dimension is advocacy whose primary goal is to enable service users to speak for themselves. Here the emphasis is on equipping service users with the skills they need in order to achieve this end, and on the wider goal of developing mechanisms for effective participation which can help this to happen. This is a similar distinction to the one used by Hodgson (1995) between active and passive advocacy; passive advocacy involves an advocate speaking for another person, active advocacy that person speaking for themselves. When we were looking at advocacy and human rights we considered a case of a service user whose access to water was restricted to meal times. There are two different approaches to this problem which serve as a good illustration of how this dimension of the advocacy process works in practice. One strategy which could be used to address this issue would be for the service user to take it to the MIND hospital advice service and then for a professional advocate to raise it formally with the management of the hospital, perhaps detailing their concerns in writing. Alternatively the patient themselves might, with support from a peer advocacy project (where service users support each other in getting their views heard), draft a brief outline of her concerns which can be raised by the service user at the weekly ward forum, linked to a patients' council, which has been established to enable service users to bring matters of concern to the attention of the hospital management. Both of these routes offer viable ways of resolving this issue and there will be many local issues which will make either strategy more or less likely to succeed. However, they do illustrate how the same issue can be addressed in different ways, each of which sits in a slightly different place in our dimensional model.

Perspective

One important question facing advocates is the extent to which their role is to present a case or to give voice to the perspective of the service user. (This is quite a common dilemma in advocacy as we shall see in Chapter 4.) One perspective in advocacy is that the role is primarily about persuasion. When we try to persuade we may emphasise particular elements of a situation whilst down-playing others in order to achieve a particular outcome. Advocacy which adopts the perspective of persuasion is often orientated to a particular goal. We can see how this might work in social work practice. For example a social worker seeking financial support from his or her local authority for a place in a supported housing project may present a service user's case in a way which emphasises the service user's vulnerability as this will be a key criterion which will determine eligibility for the service concerned. On the other hand, in presenting the case to a multidisciplinary team the social worker may place greater stress on the user's strengths and capabilities, aware that a risk focus can be dominant in the medical model of care and that it can be difficult for the service user's voice to be heard in multidisciplinary meetings.

Legal advocacy is an area where concern with outcome and the presentation of a case to persuade can (quite appropriately) be dominant. A contrast with this is provided by the role of the Independent Mental Capacity Advocate (IMCA) (Brown et al. 2009). This is a role enshrined within the 2005 Mental Capacity Act, which relates to particular sorts of important decisions (around medical treatment and changes in accommodation) faced by those who lack capacity and do not have family or friends whose views decision makers can ascertain to help inform the decision-making process. The IMCA role is summed up in the Mental Capacity Act Code of Practice as being to 'work with and support people and represent their views to those who are working out their best interest' (The Stationery Office 2007 p178).

Focus

The next dimension I want to consider is focus. Brandon (2001), drawing on the work of Wolfensberger (1977), makes a distinction between instrumental tasks in advocacy and expressive tasks. Instrumental tasks are practical and specific roles which look at discrete areas of a person's life. So a typical instrumental task in advocacy might be the provision of practical advice and possibly representation around a particular issue or problem; addressing inadequate housing, and issues with benefits or legal problems would be good examples. Expressive tasks are primarily focused around the provision of emotional support, particularly during times of stress and crisis, and the maintenance of 'sympathetic communication and interaction' (Brandon 2001 p31). So an advocacy approach such as citizen advocacy, where relationship building and the provision of practical help go hand in hand, falls into the expressive end of this dimension. The extent to which advocacy is about emotional support has been a matter of some debate. Bateman presents quite a convincing argument for a narrow focus, seeing advocacy as most effective in relation to problems which have clear boundaries. However, unless advocates can create rapport with a service user and form a constructive relationship, advocacy is not likely to be entirely successful. It is difficult therefore to see advocacy purely as an instrumental activity, particularly in social work where attention with psychological well-being goes hand and hand with a concern for ensuring access to resources.

Scope

Our final dimension is scope, which provides a measure of the extent to which advocacy addresses the needs of the individual or of the collective. One common distinction made when describing advocacy services is between case advocacy, working with an individual on issues germane to their specific circumstances, and cause advocacy, working with a group pursuing wider collective concerns (Schneider and Lester 2001, Payne 2005). This is an area we will pursue in more detail in subsequent chapters. Even within an advocacy service with a common ethos approaches with a different scope can sit side by side. So, for example, within service-user-led advocacy, self-advocacy and group advocacy can operate together: self-advocacy concentrating on supporting individuals in developing their skills and the emotional resilience to express their own views; group advocacy bringing collective concerns to the attention of decision makers. One important benefit of the pursuit of collective concerns is that it sets advocacy within a broader social context. Exploring and pursuing shared concerns can help raise awareness of issues of social injustice, discrimination and oppression.

Different approaches to advocacy

I now want to look in more detail, and in the context of our multi-dimensional model, at some of the different types of advocacy we identified earlier in the chapter: formal advocacy, citizen advocacy, peer advocacy, self-advocacy and group advocacy. We have already addressed legal advocacy (and touched upon some other approaches). I want to start with the approach which is closest to legal advocacy, which I have termed formal advocacy.

Formal advocacy

Formal advocacy describes an approach which has much in common with its legal counterpart. Within formal advocacy schemes those undertaking advocacy, whether paid professional advocates or trained volunteers, have a particular expertise in a specific area of law or policy. This is what we might term expert advocacy with a focus on providing informed advice and individual case work where the advocate often presents a case to a decision maker. Often advocates will have access to legal advice to support their work. This advice centre tradition is an important and extensive one within advocacy in the UK. It covers a range of projects with different degrees of specialisation in the work they undertake. The Citizens' Advice Bureau, housing advice agencies, welfare rights advice centres and money advice agencies all adopt this general approach. Formal advocacy tends to have an instrumental focus in its case work approach. However, many organisations involved in individual case work also make more general approaches to policy makers about issues of collective concern to the users of their services. The work of Shelter exemplifies this approach, combining the provision of advice to individuals facing homelessness with representations to government and policy makers about matters of collective concern, often with other advice agencies. An example is the *Taking the Strain* report produced by the Money Advice Trust (Reynolds and Smith 2009)

Citizen advocacy

As we saw in Chapter 1, citizen advocacy is an important strand in the history and development of advocacy services. It has its roots in normalisation (Emerson 1992, Tyne 1992, Pochin 2002) and is an approach which contrasts with the formal advocacy which we have just looked at in that its focus is on advocacy in a broad sense, within the context of a sustained relationship between service user and advocate, providing 'a major vehicle by which people are to be enabled to belong to communities' (Walmsley 2002 p27). The aim of citizen advocacy is to provide a support for vulnerable people that encourages participation in the community and provides emotionally supportive reciprocal relationships which can help service users negotiate choices they have to make and problems they may face. Unlike formal advocates, citizen advocates do not have specific expertise. They focus primarily on the expressive elements of advocacy, on first and foremost building a supportive relationship with a service user over a long period of time. This can be helpful both in supporting the service user to speak for themselves, and in understanding and voicing their perspective, what Atkinson (1999) terms 'spokespersonship'.

Advocacy and empowerment-orientated mental health care in the community – Rose and Black's approach

---

Rose and Black (1985) consider the role of advocacy and empowerment in supporting a group of people with mental health problems in the community as part of what they describe as a deinstitutionalisation programme. Their work is interesting because within it a broad understanding of advocacy forms the backbone to an empowering approach to practice (Payne 1991). Rose and Black believe 'that advocacy activities designed to confront the structures and ideologies of oppression are central to any direct services programme' (p18). For Rose and Black 'advocacy activities' include both the support and pursuit of service users' legal rights, and the provision of case management and day care services. The overall orientation of the support programmes they discuss is one of empowerment – 'a constant guide to our relationships with clients' (p18) – whilst advocacy permeates all aspects of the specific support offered. Rose and Black's approach is explicitly informed by the work of Freire (Freire 1972) and envisages the advocacy/empowerment process as a transformative one, supporting service users in increasing their sense of personal autonomy and awareness of oppression, whilst developing and sustaining networks of support, helping people become 'subjects rather than objects in their lives' (Payne 1991 p226). Rose and Black argue (p60) that 'the purpose of the advocacy/empowerment action orientation is to produce change or movement of the deinstitutionalized former patient from a position of passive powerlessness and self-destructive alienation to one of increased self-conscious autonomy through a series of action phases'. These phases of the work between service user and worker perhaps most importantly include:

- *Verstehen* – understanding the service user's perspective on their world and establishing a relationship of trust
- *Thematization* – the establishment of generalised themes within the service user's life particularly around oppression, alienation and powerlessness
- *Problematization* – a critical exploration of how service users can change their world and begin to gain validation as a person

The model moves through these phases of work to a point where the worker's primary role is to support the choices and actions of service users: two key elements of autonomy (and so often absent from the experience of those who have been institutionalised). Rose and Black's work allies a focus on specific targeted elements of advocacy, particular issues with landlords and rent payments for example, with a broader focus on the expressive aspects of advocacy, supporting empowerment and autonomy. The approach makes much use of group work and sees 'constituency building for change' (p141) around collective issues faced by service users as central to the ethos of the empowerment/advocacy orientation.

Self-advocacy, peer advocacy and group advocacy

The final point in our exploration of different forms of advocacy is a consideration of three approaches which are user led: self-advocacy, peer advocacy and group advocacy. As we will see, these three approaches are interlinked; peer advocacy is often seen as a mechanism which enables service users to speak for themselves and group advocacy enables individuals to express similar views collectively. There is the potential for these three approaches to act in concert each supporting the other, with those who have developed skills in self-advocacy passing these on to others through peer-advocacy schemes. It is probably most helpful to begin with **self-advocacy**, which it has been argued 'should be the goal of all other forms of advocacy' (Atkinson 1999 p6). Self-advocacy has often been defined in quite broad terms encompassing the act of an individual speaking out for themselves, self-advocacy as a group activity, and as a more general process of campaigning for change (Brandon and Brandon 2001). I want to focus here on people speaking for themselves, representing their views to those in positions of power. However, I think we can clearly learn from the broad view of self-advocacy, in that to speak for yourself requires a particular set of skills, a framework for support and a commitment from professionals to enabling this process to work. The Social Care Institute for Excellence (Lawton 2007) identifies three ways in which successful self-advocacy can be supported. The first of these is through self-advocacy groups. Groups can help service users develop skills in understanding their own needs, strengths and preferences; communication and assertiveness skills; and a knowledge of potential sources of support. However, group support and the development of skills need to be complemented by the existence of pathways of access to decision makers. For health and social care professionals this means establishing systems that enable service users to express their views and influence the care they receive. Finally user-led organisations can lend their support to the self-advocacy process and provide a potential route to decision makers through which changes can be achieved. Self-advocacy brings many potential benefits, empowering service users and building self-esteem. Rai-Atkins et al. (2002) use the concept of self-definition as a framework for describing some of the benefits of self-advocacy for service users from the African, Caribbean and South Asian communities: 'the journey towards self-definition provides a powerful opportunity for black service users to challenge externally defined stereotypes which often result in psychological attacks on their personhood and dignity' (p5).

How does self-advocacy fit within the multi-dimensional model? If we start by considering its scope, it is essentially an individually focused approach although when allied with group advocacy it has the potential to address collective issues and concerns. Interestingly it can have both an instrumental and expressive focus; as we have argued to advocate for oneself is a potentially empowering thing to do. Furthermore, when speaking for yourself you may seek to have your voice heard and to persuade others of your case.

Crisis cards – a form of self-advocacy

Crisis cards are an interesting example of self-advocacy in the mental health field. Crisis cards were developed by the service-user-led organisation Survivors Speak Out and the International Self-Advocacy Alliance at the end of the 1980s. The small cards which could be carried in a wallet, purse or pocket allowed a service user to nominate a friend or relative to be a key point of contact should they find themselves in a mental health crisis at some future point. The cards also identified the types of treatment and help a service user would like to receive if they were too ill to express their views. This was conceived as a form of self-advocacy by Survivors Speak Out (Sutherby et al. 1999, Mind Information Unit 2010). A number of research projects have been carried out to assess the effectiveness of the cards (Sutherby et al. 1999, Henderson et al. 2004, Henderson et al. 2008) and have found that the cards have an impact, both improving the success of treatment in the event of a crisis, and increasing service users' self-confidence and confidence in those responsible for their treatment.

Peer advocacy and group advocacy both have the potential to support and build upon self-advocacy. In **peer advocacy** the main thrust of the approach is towards supporting service users to advocate for themselves. Peer advocacy schemes work in a range of different ways. One approach is the establishment of a supportive group of peers who can work together around particular issues and problems faced by group members. The boundaries between peer and group advocacy are a little blurred here, particularly when peer groups feedback their views collectively. A more distinct approach to peer advocacy is what Harnett (2004) calls 'peer demonstration/mentoring' (p37). This involves service users with more experience of speaking for themselves supporting those who are less confident, 'saying "look I can do this and so can you" and showing them how it could be done' (Harnett 2004 p37). The purpose of advocacy here is very much about enabling service users to speak and using group support to address individual needs. Group support in peer advocacy is often focused on the expressive elements of advocacy, on building confidence and emotional resilience, which can be very important. Maglajlic et al. (2000) identified the role of this type of peer support in helping service users take up direct payments. Direct mentoring roles within peer advocacy where individual service users are linked with a more experienced peer, 'an insider, someone who is in the know through personal experience' (Atkinson 1999 p7), rather in the manner of citizen advocacy (Boylan and Dalrymple 2009 p104), can take this expressive focus a stage further. The St Mungo's Peer Advocacy Link project is a good example of this approach. It focuses on the move from supported housing to independent living; those with experience of this transition help those without. It helps both the recipients of advocacy and the advocates themselves, many of whom use their voluntary advocacy experience when applying for work. These types of peer advocacy projects are able to offer a wider range of support with a more holistic expressive focus going beyond a specific problem.

Finally we come to **group advocacy**. This is an approach which offers the opportunity for groups of service users to come together to address shared issues, so its scope is broadly looking at wider collective concerns. Boylan and Dalrymple (2009) identify four models of group advocacy:

- The autonomous model, where advocacy groups are user led and work outside formal organisations
- The divisional model, where service users' group advocacy is one section of a larger social care organisation
- The coalition model, where organisations representing service users' views band together to present group concerns
- The service system model, where groups are located within the service delivery system

Patients' councils are a good example of the service system approach to group advocacy and provide us with a general overview of how this approach works. Essentially they work to collectively represent the views of patients of a particular hospital in order to improve the service they receive, acting as a conduit through which patients' perspectives can be collated and then placed before managers and decision makers. Group advocacy is often about speaking for a particular community of interest (in this case the hospital patients) and the perspective is therefore one of giving voice with a primarily instrumental focus. However, there are clearly potential weaknesses in the service system model. Group advocacy can be dependent upon a receptive approach to service users' perspectives from decision makers and the extent to which a commitment to advocacy is part of the culture of the organisation. However, group advocacy's link to campaigning and cause advocacy makes it a potentially powerful way of addressing social injustice.

Practice example

Different approaches to advocacy – Rose Terrace

Rose Terrace is a small supported living project for a group of service uses with learning disabilities. It is part of a small voluntary sector agency, set up a number of years ago by a group of parents for their children, but it now takes referrals from a range of health and social care agencies. Over the years the project has grown. Attached to the supported living accommodation there is now a drop-in centre and a community café, which is a social enterprise. It employs people with learning disabilities who prepare and serve a range of meals during the day. It is quite popular with people who live and work locally. The back room and garden of the café are used for a variety of group activities. An art group meets there and it serves as the base for a gardening project and a scheme helping young people to learn to use public transport independently. The projects under the Rose

(continued)

Terrace umbrella are run by a management committee, which comprises the manager of the café and of the supported living project, some parents of users of the service past and present, a supportive local GP, a service manager from the local authority social services department, and the vicar of a nearby church.

For some time the project has been considering the establishment of some kind of advocacy service and over a number of months has looked at a range of options.

- One suggestion has been a peer advocacy scheme. Users of the supported living project would be paired with ex-residents who have now moved on and would be supported in a range of areas particularly around dealing with bureaucracy and having a voice in plans for their care and support.
- A citizen advocacy approach has also been mooted. Under this scheme members of the public would be recruited and linked to the project. Their role would be two-fold: befriending with the aim of creating a relationship with a user of Rose Terrace; trying to help the users become involved in community based activities. One user of the Rose Terrace supported living project has a longstanding link to a citizen advocate (which predates his joining the project). They regularly meet for a cup of tea and a chat and periodically go fishing together.
- Another option is to establish an advocacy group. This would bring together those living in the supported housing and the users of the café so they could present ideas to the management committee to develop and improve the service. Rose Terrace itself has for a number of years been supported by a grant from the local authority supplemented by other sources of income such as Housing Benefit and support from the local adult education college. However, some of this funding is now under threat, a fact which users of the project have become aware of so there is a need to lobby more widely to ensure the service's continued existence.
- Over the past year or so a number of those attending the café and the groups have had their needs reassessed by the local authority in order to ensure that the services they receive are tailored to their needs. Some of those who have completed self-directed support assessments have been upset by the local authority appearing rather dismissive of their ideas for support. The idea of using a personal budget to buy a season ticket for a local football club suggested by one service user was met with considerable resistance. One advocacy option available to the project would be to bring a link worker to the project each week from a local advice centre, with experience of the community care legislation, to carry out individual advocacy work focused on these reassessments, and to advocate to the local authority on behalf of individual service users.

Obviously the four approaches to advocacy outlined here are not mutually exclusive. It would be possible for the project to pursue all four choices. However, Rose Terrace does have limited staff resources and adopting all four of these approaches to advocacy may not therefore be possible.

Discussion point

The first part of this exercise involves thinking about these four options. In doing this it is important to consider the four dimensions of advocacy we looked at earlier.

- Perspectives
- Purposes
- Focus
- Scope

What do you think Rose Terrace would gain from each of the four options?

Now imagine you had the casting vote on the management committee as they decide which option to go for and could therefore sway the decision. Which option would you choose and why would you choose it? What would be the downside of this choice?

The situation we have outlined here is a hypothetical one. The provision of advocacy services in the real world is shaped by local historical factors, pragmatism and serendipity. It is also worth restating that advocacy services do not necessarily fit neatly into categories such as peer advocacy or citizen advocacy, for example, but a range of elements of different advocacy approaches may be encompassed within the same service. However, what a consideration of this choice does help us to do is to think about the breadth of activities which fall under the rubric of advocacy, and to reflect upon the impacts of different approaches and their fit with a particular context.

Advocacy and the social work role

Thus far in this chapter we have looked at an overall model of advocacy and at how particular advocacy roles fit within that model. I now want to think about advocacy as part of a professional brief and as a key element in social work practice. In doing this I want to explore what social work can bring to the advocacy role and also at what limitations professional constraints can place on this particular aspect of the work.

A good way of kicking off this discussion is to look at a case study. Trina's case which is described below is adapted from a case example used in the Equality and Human Rights Commission report on the provision of care within a human rights framework, *From safety net to springboard* (Equality and Human Rights Commission 2009 p16) and in Hurstfield et al. 2007, but retains almost all the key features of the case presented there.

Practice example – Trina

Trina is a 35-year-old white woman with a learning disability who lives in her own flat and has shared custody of her 10-year-old son, Daniel. Trina's father, who had always lived close by, died about 6 months ago. Following his death Trina felt very low and started

(continued)

drinking heavily. She also got into a lot of debt. As a consequence she fell behind with her rent payments. Daniel's school attendance had become rather sporadic: he often arrived late at school and sometimes not at all. His school clothes were quite unkempt and it was clear to teachers he was not eating properly. Trina had worked for nearly 10 years for a local supermarket. However, following her father's death she was frequently absent and when she did go into work she had sometimes clearly been drinking. Trina struggled to understand letters she had received from her landlord and people she owed money to. The school were so concerned that they referred her to social services and she was seen by a social worker in the children's centre attached to the school.

At this point Trina was referred to an advocacy project for people with learning difficulties. At first her advocate, Carolyn, focused on building rapport with Trina. She looked at different ways in which she might address her problems starting by looking at the correspondence Trina was receiving. They went through the letters together. Everything was explained in plain English and Carolyn went with Trina to court hearings and meetings with her solicitor. Carolyn was able to persuade Trina to see her GP and through this route she was referred to a community based alcohol detox programme. Linked to a debt counselling project, Trina was able to put together payment plans to deal with her debts and creditors. With Trina's permission Carolyn contacted the supermarket where she worked. They were completely unaware of the emotional difficulties that she had been facing and she was able to continue working. Daniel's school attendance improved and he became much happier and more settled.

This is an interesting overview of an advocacy based intervention, which addresses a wide range of issues and incorporates a number of different approaches to advocacy. Looking at Trina's story we can see Carolyn's advocacy here incorporates a number of different intervention strategies, quite a standard practice for an independent advocate. I want to look at each of these in turn.

- One key part of Carolyn's work is building a relationship with Trina. Carolyn recognises that Trina is going through a crisis, that she is potentially quite distrustful of people, and that she lacks any real system of support, with a key relationship upon which she depended no longer there. So Carolyn sees the creation of trust and rapport as essential before she can undertake more formal advocacy roles. She recognises that early on in her work her advocacy will need to be focused on Trina's expressive needs before instrumental elements can be addressed. Throughout the advocacy process Carolyn is aware of the emotional impact that dealing with her problems can have on Trina and combines instrumental advocacy with emotional support.
- Another key role that Carolyn undertakes here is representation, something we identified in Chapter 1 as a core component of advocacy. So Carolyn is representing Trina's views to her employer, for example, speaking for Trina in this particular instance.
- Carolyn's work, however, is not simply about speaking up for Trina. She also works with her: for example, helping her to understand the correspondence

she has received. The purpose of this is to enable Trina to 'speak': to deal with this aspect of the problems she faces herself.

- Linking Trina into networks of care and support (what we might loosely term brokerage) is also an important part of Carolyn's work. It is essential that Trina maintain a relationship with her GP and her solicitor if she is to successfully get her life back on track. Carolyn's work offers a bridge into these services and she has oversight over all the systems supporting Trina.

- Empowerment is a key feature of Carolyn's work. She is clear with Trina about the nature of her intervention and she explains her role, and no doubt the end goals for the advocacy are agreed between them. Their aim is to re-establish Trina in the workplace and to move her to a stage when she can begin to manage her life independently again.

- Despite Carolyn having a primary concern with Trina's debts and housing situation, she recognises that in order to address these problems she will need to consider Trina's situation in broader terms. So without Trina addressing her alcohol problems, for example, she will not manage to remain debt free or sustain her employment.

One of the most striking things about this example of an intervention by an independent advocate is the extent to which it resembles a social work intervention. Atkinson in her review of advocacy services (Atkinson 1999), suggests that in practice advocates were doing more than 'supporting people to have a say in their lives', but seemed to be 'offering a range of practical and emotional support to the disadvantaged and vulnerable people who come their way' (p34). Looking at this case we can immediately start to identify a range of common features between the approach of independent advocacy and of social work. So where is the common ground and what are the differences?

Social work and independent advocacy – similarities and differences

The importance of the relationship between worker and service users is one key shared aspect (Ruch et al. 2010). The holistic nature of the intervention is also important. Networking and managing interfaces between different services are again core social work activities and lie at the heart of care management (Payne 1995, Trevillion 1999). Empowerment is a central element of anti-discriminatory practice; social workers accept the importance of building upon and enhancing service users' strengths (Adams 2008). Finally, the representational tasks undertaken by Carolyn, speaking to Trina's employer for example, are far from inconsistent with a social work role.

As we can see there is plenty of common ground here. Where might the differences lie? One important difference is that social work is generally informed by a range of theories. So the work of a social worker intervening in Trina's situation might be influenced by crisis intervention (Roberts 2005) or by models of bereavement (Currer 2007, Weinstein 2008). In thinking about Trina's use of alcohol the social worker might well consider the cycle of change model or the use of ideas from motivational interviewing (Miller and Rollnick 2002). Network and systems theories might influence a social worker's understanding of how to strengthen and extend Trina's networks of support (Trevillion 1999). Interestingly a social worker's professional standing and power might help in accessing resources and in negotiation with other professionals. It would not be unreasonable to expect a social worker to have a knowledge of housing law and debt management, as Carolyn no doubt has. So presented in this light it would seem that social work has the potential to provide the sort of advocacy outlined in the case study, in perhaps a more theoretically informed and reflective (given that theory can only aid reflection) way.

However, there are key differences between independent advocacy and social work. The 'prefix' independent is perhaps the most important source of the differences between the two. Before we go on to examine this area I want to look at some of the other differences between social workers undertaking advocacy as part of their professional role and independent advocates, particularly where, as in Trina's case, the roles are so similar.

Breadth of professional responsibility

One key difference between a social worker's role and Trina and Carolyn's role relates to the breadth and nature of the social worker's professional responsibility. The relationship between Trina and Carolyn is one in which Trina essentially has control. Trina can disengage at any point and more importantly she has much more say about the nature of the work undertaken. For a social worker a much wider range of professional responsibilities exists. The most obvious of these are responsibilities in relation to the safety and well-being of both Trina and Daniel. Obviously there might well be instances where Carolyn's concerns for Daniel's well-being, say, might mean that she had to raise a concern about his welfare. However, for a social worker intervening in a way which was largely focused on advocacy, well-being is a more overarching concern and more clearly part of the professional brief. The professional expectation that we might have of an independent advocate is that were a particular threshold in relation to risk to be reached they might seek help from another service. The expectation of a social worker is that risk and well-being are always part of the picture of any work undertaken and not just at the point at which a threshold for intervention is reached. This difference in approach is not just something which springs from the organisational context within which most social workers practise, working within a statutory service. It is a central part of social work practice, reflected in the GSCC Codes of Practice and Key Roles, and in the proposed Capabilities Framework, where 'ensuring safety whilst balancing rights and risks' (Social Work Reform Board 2010 p7) is identified as a key element of social work intervention. If a social worker was operating within a voluntary sector organisation, but undertaking advocacy as part of a social work role, then this breadth of perspective would still shape their work.

Professional judgement and assessment

This difference of approach is also apparent when we consider the 'assessment' phase of the intervention. For an independent advocate, 'assessment' does not exist in quite the same form as it does for a social worker. Assessment for the advocate involves an identification of key problem areas and perhaps a judgement by the advocate of how these can be addressed. It is the service user who identifies the problems. (Chapter 5 contains a further discussion of this aspect of the process of advocacy.) Social workers do adopt this approach but it is only one element of a wider process of 'gathering information, sifting it carefully and coming to an "objective" and "accurate" conclusion' (Milner and O'Byrne 2002 p6). This is not a straightforward process (Milner and O'Byrne 2009, Parker and Bradley 2010) as the inverted commas around 'objective' and 'accurate' in our quote from Milner and O'Byrne indicate. However, it does involve a professional judgement (Sheldon and Macdonald 2009). Social workers' assessments tend to be broad in scope and combine a service-user-led element with an exploration by the social worker of a number of key domains, which extend the process beyond the immediate presenting issue with which the service user arrives. The process is one which is informed by theory. So a social worker seeing Trina, for example, might well incorporate a judgement about the impacts of bereavement on Trina (which they would share with her) in their initial assessment, informed by theory, but which might well go beyond the scope of the sort of problem investigation which marks the initial phase of the advocacy process.

Knowledge and expertise

The fact that social workers come to an encounter with a service user equipped with a certain set of knowledge and expertise can be important not only because it informs the assessment process, but also because it is a key source of social workers' professional power. Smith argues that this appearance of 'impartiality, objectivity and technical expertise' has the potential to create a situation where 'problems for individuals become defined as problems of individuals' (Smith 2008 p111). Obviously this can be tempered by social workers adopting a collaborative approach to assessment, but the professional role still has the potential to create distance between social worker and service user.

The impacts of the organisational context on advocacy

Thus far I have looked at differences in approach between social worker and independent advocate which are primarily the product of their differing professional roles. However, as we suggested earlier, the differing organisational contexts of advocacy and social work can also impact upon the approach adopted. This is where the idea of 'independence' is important. Social work is often carried out in statutory health or social care agencies; independent advocacy generally takes place within the voluntary sector in agencies where there is a greater degree of service user control and independence. This is obviously a generalisation, and specific advocacy schemes may be more or less 'independent'. However, it is worth exploring the impacts of this general distinction on the advocacy role.

Gates in *Advocacy: A Nurse's Guide* (1994) looks at the differences between independent advocacy and advocacy within a professional role (Table 2.2). I want to build

Table 2.2 Social worker and independent advocate – organisational context

Social worker	Independent advocate
Multiple loyalties	Primary loyalty to service user/client
• Colleagues • Organisation • Profession	
Acting within professional constraints	Acting with 'profound commitment' (Gates 1994 p27)
Acting as an employee with an employer in mind	Independent with the interests of the service user to the fore

on some of the key distinctions he identifies to look at the organisational context of social work and its impact on the advocacy role.

As we can see from Table 2.2 there are clearly tensions within the advocacy role for social workers within statutory settings.

This is a theme we will explore in future chapters. As we have already seen, many of the skills social workers bring to their work are consistent with effective advocacy. The knowledge base of social work also provides a useful backdrop to this area of practice. Social workers do need to adopt a critically reflective approach in this area, however, and be aware of the potential limitations of advocacy within a professional role, whilst remembering the crucial importance of advocacy in the pursuit of goals around social justice.

Advocacy as part of social work practice

I want to move on now to consider how social workers can make advocacy a key element of their practice. I am going to look at two aspects of this. Firstly, the distinction between direct and indirect advocacy roles (Brandon and Brandon 2001) in social work provides a helpful way of mapping the types of work that social workers undertake which fall into the category of advocacy. Secondly, Freddolino et al. (2004) identify four distinctive ways in which advocacy forms a key part of the work social workers provide for their clients.

Direct and indirect advocacy roles

One clear distinction in advocacy is between supporting service users directly and supporting advocacy indirectly. Brandon and Brandon (2001) argue that within these two categories it is also possible for social workers to have an impact at a micro level and at a macro level. Table 2.3 summarises Brandon and Brandon's perspective.

Table 2.3 Direct and indirect advocacy

Representing service users directly	
Micro level	*Macro level*
Examples – making a case around benefits or housing	Examples – drawing attention to deficiencies in a whole service or lobbying for improved benefit provision
Supporting advocacy indirectly	
Micro level	*Macro level*
Examples – supporting a self-advocacy group to raise concerns about the provision of care or encouraging self-assessment	Examples – helping a neighbourhood group to collectively put forward their views on problems with the repair of council property

(Adapted from Brandon and Brandon 2001 p64)

Essentially Brandon and Brandon's view is that social workers can work at a range of different levels to effect change through advocacy. In representing service users directly, work on individual cases is extremely important, but it is also vital to consider macro-level issues for groups of service users. Indirect support for advocacy may encompass the micro-level advocacy of helping a self-advocacy group to develop and flourish, or the macro-level approach of working at the level of the whole community.

Freddolino et al. (2004) identify four ways in which social workers provide advocacy: advancing claims and appeals, protecting vulnerable people, creating support that enhances functioning, and fostering identity and control. Although these are seen as distinctive areas there are clearly links between the four.

Advancing claims and appeals is the aspect of social work practice which can most straightforwardly be aligned with advocacy as it is traditionally conceived. For example, social workers play active roles in supporting service users in benefit claims and applications for housing, representing their views to other professionals and accessing resources. As part of this approach 'social work advocates may engage in the most adversarial forms of advocacy' sometimes adopting 'quasi legal roles' (Freddolino et al. 2004 p124). **Protecting vulnerable people** is an interesting and often underplayed way in which social workers advocate for others. 'Advocacy in this context means that the social worker not only may speak on behalf of the individual but would also muster the resources needed to protect the individual and advance his or her safety and well-being' (Freddolino et al. 2004 p121). There are obvious ways in which this can happen. For example, a social worker working with a victim of domestic violence may well be actively involved in seeking access to resources to support the victims as well as the provision of a range of practical help. However, advocacy in a broader sense is an important aspect of the protecting and safeguarding role. It is worth considering the following cases and thinking about how advocacy might play a part in them.

Practice examples

George

George is a 73-year-old man who lives on his own in a local authority flat. He has a long history of mental health problems and has been admitted to psychiatric hospital on a number of occasions. His flat can appear fairly chaotic. He is a voracious reader of newspapers and the flat is full of papers going back over a number of years piled in a particular order. He often feels anxious and restless and spends his days wandering around the estate where he lives and where he is quite a well-known figure. George is seen every week by his community psychiatric nurse and his social worker. On a recent visit they discovered him very agitated and upset. His newspapers had been moved and the floor of his flat was covered with empty cans, and remains of cigarettes and joints. The door was partially off its hinges and the word 'nutter' had been sprayed on one of his windows. George reveals that local youths have been visiting his flat in the evening for a considerable period of time, and using it as a venue for drinking and listening to music and he hasn't felt able to tell any one about it. When George has asked them to leave they have refused.

Denise

Denise is a 13-year-old girl. She lives at home with her mother, younger sister and step-father. Recently teachers at her school have noticed that she has lost weight and sometimes seems quite withdrawn, sometimes quite angry. She has frequently been absent and pays little attention in class – a change from her previous behaviour. After a number of altercations with teachers she has been spending an increasing amount of time in the learning support unit, for 'disruptive' pupils.

Kalisha, the social worker based within the school, has spent quite a lot of time chatting to her trying to establish if anything is wrong at home. She eventually reveals that her stepfather has been coming into her room at night, getting into bed with her and touching her inappropriately. In a police interview, however, Denise says nothing, and her mother the following day contacts the police to say that Denise wants to withdraw the allegations, which she had made up to get back at her stepfather.

Discussion point

Think about these two brief case outlines. Both of these service users are finding it difficult to speak out and communicate their concerns – a common experience of so many people in need of help and protection (Davies and Duckett 2008). As we know, advocacy is about enabling people to find a voice. What might be preventing George and Denise from protecting themselves? How could advocacy be part of an approach to social work which helped their voice be heard?

Both of these examples show how advocacy can be an important element in the safeguarding process. For George an important task will be mobilising resources, speaking for him, and representing his views to the police and the housing department, for example, presenting a case for a range of different types of support and help. Equally it may be important to support George to tell his own story in circumstances where he may be upset and afraid. In Denise's case Kalisha may need to maintain some oversight of her situation, keeping an eye on her relationships with staff and peers, perhaps dropping into the learning support unit when she knows Denise will be there. Here her purpose is partly creating the conditions that could enable Denise to speak – building a relationship and encouraging her to believe in herself and in the fact that her voice will be listened to (Howell 2003).

Often, in social work, advocacy goes hand in hand with other aspects of practice. Freddolino et al.'s other two categories of advocacy orientated practice, **fostering identity and control**, and **creating support that enhances functioning**, focus upon the empowering aspects of practice. For more direct advocacy to be successful it needs to be undertaken within a framework at the centre of which is enhancing service users' capabilities, and in which their control is maximised. This will involve working with risk. It also means that social workers' advocacy has to be attentive to both instrumental and expressive issues. So in fostering identity and control a practitioner may need to build relationships with service users which help develop the confidence they need to speak for themselves and to engage with collective approaches to making their voice heard. Supporting collective campaigns and fighting to address discrimination and oppression is an important part of this work at a macro level. Social workers will also need to be aware that they may need to refer service users to other advocacy services where the formal nature of the social work relationship may hinder this taking place. In creating support that enhances functioning, social workers have a responsibility to work towards the development of services which are consistent with this goal. At the micro level this can mean seeking creative shared responses to service user need. At the macro level 'in this tradition the social work advocate demands service improvements or asks for a service system to increase the quality of care through the investment of more resources into the support of a particular individual or group of individuals' (Freddolino et al. 2004 p122).

How does this range of social work interventions in which advocacy plays an important role fit with the multi-dimensional model we presented earlier? Returning to our model we can see that social workers can incorporate advocacy into their work in a variety of different ways. The purpose of advocacy can on occasion be to speak for another, presenting a case to a decision making forum or to those in positions of power who control resources, for example. However, a key goal of social work is to find a route to a set of circumstances where that person is enabled to speak for themselves. In arguing for resources persuasion may be an appropriate perspective, although giving voice will be a key part in many types of advocacy, from supporting self-assessment to working with independent advocacy groups. Social workers can also make links between individual and group causes: at a macro level protesting about cuts in services or changes in benefit rules, for example; at a micro level canvassing the views of service user groups in the development of new service initiatives.

Key learning points

- Advocacy covers a wide range of activities and comes in a variety of different forms. Legal advocacy has provided an important blueprint for other approaches and has been influential in shaping the delivery of advocacy services, particularly formal advocacy. Citizen advocacy provides a more holistic approach, where the relationship between advocate and service user is key. The linked areas of self-, peer and group advocacy are strongly orientated towards service user control and collectively lobbying for change. Human rights and theories of empowerment have also had an influence in shaping advocacy within social work.
- A multi-dimensional model of advocacy covering purpose, perspective, focus and scope provides a framework which can be used to differentiate between and analyse the different types of activity which fall under the broad heading of advocacy.
- Independent advocates and social workers share areas of common ground in their approaches to practice. However, the professional and organisational context of social work shapes the nature and scope of advocacy as part of the social work role.
- Advocacy plays an important role in social work across a wide range of areas of practice, and the multi-dimensional model can help us to understand the nature of this role.

Further reading

Atkinson, D. (1999) *Advocacy: A review*, Brighton, Pavillion/Joseph Rowntree

Brandon, D. and Brandon, T. (2001) *Advocacy in Social Work*, Birmingham, Venture Press

Freddolino, P., Moxley, D. and Hyduk, C. (2004) 'A differential model of advocacy in social work practice', *Families in Society* 85 (1) pp 119–128

Ife, J. (2008) *Human Rights and Social Work: towards rights-based practice*, Cambridge/New York, Cambridge University Press

MIND (2010) *The MIND Guide to Advocacy*, London, MIND

Rose, S. and Black, B. (1985) *Advocacy and Empowerment: Mental health care in the community*, London/New York, Routledge

3   Current Practice Issues

The recent history of advocacy has been marked by an expansion in the range of advocacy services available and the extension of advocacy into areas where hitherto it had had only limited influence (Henderson and Pochin 2001). Some of these new developments are dealt with elsewhere in the book. In this chapter we are going to concentrate on three key aspects of the recent development of advocacy which share a common underlying theme, enabling the views of those least able to give voice to be heard. The chapter begins with an overview of 'non-instructed advocacy', advocacy with people who find it difficult to express a view on what is happening in their lives and who find decision making difficult. A discussion of this relatively recent development leads into an exploration of statutory advocacy roles, recently introduced as part of mental health and mental capacity legislation. We finish by looking at the self-advocacy movement and its relationship with social work.

Advocacy when people find making decisions difficult

For all professionals working with those who find getting their message across to other people difficult, the problem of communication and how best to identify the service user's choice and preference will be very much to the fore. So much of what I am about to say has a relevance which extends beyond advocacy and is applicable to practice more generally.

Best interest advocacy and *non-instructed advocacy* are often seen as being very much the same thing and the terms are used interchangeably (MIND 2010). However, they essentially describe two slightly different things and neither adequately gets to the crux of what advocacy is about with those who find decision making difficult. This type of advocacy is also sometimes described more specifically referring to the particular group of service users who face communication difficulties; the term *dementia advocacy* is an example of this (Cantley et al. 2003, Dementia Advocacy Network 2011a). The picture in relation to advocacy for this group of service users is further complicated by the existence of statutory advocacy roles outlined in the Mental Capacity Act 2005 and the Mental Health Act 2007 (which we will explore later in this chapter), which sit alongside non-statutory independent advocacy.

I think at this point it would be useful to look a little more at this terminology and at the limitations of the *best interest* and *non-instructed* approaches as ways of describing advocacy where service users find making and expressing a choice difficult.

The limits of a *best interest* approach

It seems something of a truism that advocacy should serve the best interests of the service user. However, there are clearly circumstances where an advocate's role in enabling a service user's voice to be heard, and the perception of professionals (or even the advocate themselves) of how a service user's needs might most effectively be addressed, might be in conflict. A service user might wish to do things which have risks attendant to them, for example. In general terms advocacy is not about deciding on what might be best for a service user, but about enabling their voice to be heard. However, when undertaking advocacy with service users who are not able to make clear a preference, because of a problem in understanding or retaining information, or in expressing themselves, the purpose of speaking on behalf of another becomes challenging to fulfil. We will explore how this can most effectively be achieved a little later on, but for now I want to draw attention to the limitations of describing this process as best interest advocacy.

It is important to remember that if advocacy is to retain its distinctive role then representing the views of another has to be its main concern. Best interest may be the driving principle behind the help that many other professionals offer service users. However, 'for an advocate to also take such an approach only adds to the range of views that may be presented and as such may do little more than muddy the waters' (Boylan and Dalrymple 2009 p110).

Practice example – Tony

Tony is an 84-year-old white man. He is quite physically fit for his age but has become increasingly forgetful over the past three years and after a number of incidents when he would not let carers into his flat, and where he made himself dangerously ill through eating mouldy food, has ended up living in a residential care home. By a stroke of good fortune the residential care home is only a few hundred yards from his old flat. Tony has for almost 30 years been visiting a local pub very close to the flat and the residential home in which he now lives. He generally goes there three or four times a week, and stays for a couple of hours or so, drinking two or three pints of Guinness. The staff and regulars in the pub know him well. He has a regular seat in the corner and they are used to his sometimes slightly difficult to follow conversations. The walk from the residential home to pub is only about 200 yards. John, the social worker who helped Tony in his move to the residential home, has come to attend the first review before the case is handed over to a reviewing officer. In the review he discovers that Tony has not been out to the pub for the past couple of months. He moved into the home about three months ago. He now sits in the communal lounge with a can of low alcohol lager each night watching the TV. The home explain that they feel that if Tony goes out to the pub he may well wander off somewhere and put himself at risk. They point out that on one occasion when he went out he didn't get back until nearly midnight and that he is much more settled now and likes the current arrangements.

(continued)

For John here there is clearly a role in advocating on Tony's behalf and enabling Tony to express his views. The staff at the home have a very clear view of what is in Tony's best interest and want to minimise any risk to him. What the case shows is how important the voice of an advocate can be in articulating a service user perspective and the limits of best interest as the criteria for determining any course of action.

Non-instructed advocacy

Given some of the difficulties with best interest as a way of describing advocacy where people find communicating and making decisions difficult, non-instructed advocacy offers an alternative way of capturing this approach. However, it also has its limitations. Again I would argue that it does not quite convey what advocacy is about with those who lack the capacity to give voice. Although instructing the advocate as traditionally perceived is impossible, the whole thrust of the non-instructed approach is towards asserting what the views of the service user or client were likely to have been, using a range of techniques in order to do this. So although instruction in its traditional sense is absent, the spirit of this approach is driven by this idea. The term *non-instructed advocacy* also fails to convey the fact that service users' capacity to express themselves may vary. Marshal and Tibbs (2006) talk about 'fluctuating competence' in their discussion of communication in dementia and the 'need to persevere or wait until a better time to maximise the effectiveness of communication' (p97). They argue that, with a carefully developed strategy and flexible approach, communication can take place. This partial communication is also partial instruction.

So we are left with a situation when describing advocacy where the service user finds it hard to direct an advocate, where neither best interest nor non-instructed advocacy fits the bill entirely adequately. My own preference in deciding between these two is to use the term non-instructed advocacy. Although not perfect it avoids some of the pitfalls of best interest, the more problematic of the two terms. So in this chapter we will abandon the term best interest and use non-instructed advocacy when addressing this area (and dementia advocacy when specifically talking about dementia).

The purpose of the preceding discussion has not just been to clarify terminology. It also serves as a useful introduction to the complexity of non-instructed advocacy and gives us a taste of some of the difficult issues faced by advocates working in this area. I want to move this discussion forward now and begin to look at this area.

Non-instructed advocacy and decision making

At this juncture I want to begin our exploration of non-instructed advocacy by considering some of the core issues which impact upon this area of practice, before looking in more detail at a range of practice models. One central problem for advocates working in a non-instructed way is the fact that the extent of any individual's capacity to make a decision is not a static, unchanging state of affairs, but something which is contingent on a whole range of different factors. It is crucial for those carrying out non-instructed advocacy to be aware of these factors and the potential impacts they may have on decision making.

Discussion point

Making difficult decisions

The following exercise explores the processes of decision making and the sorts of things that influence it.

I want to look at this point at some of the factors that influence the choices we make and how we make them, by thinking more generally about decision making. Consider the following list of decisions that we all might have to make:

- What clothes to wear
- Where to go on holiday
- Whether or not to get married
- What car to buy
- What to have for lunch
- Whether or not to accept a job offer
- When to retire
- Which programme to watch on TV
- Whether or not to get divorced
- Whether or not to move house
- Where to invest savings

Now think about how straightforward it is to make the decisions described here. Which decisions do you think are hardest to make? One way of thinking about this is to rearrange the list into a hierarchy with the decisions which are most straightforward to make at the beginning and those which are hardest at the end. We will all have our own personal lists, but I would guess that decisions about what clothes to wear, what to have for lunch, and what to watch on TV are likely to be relatively easy to make, whilst decisions about marriage and divorce, moving house and accepting a job offer or retiring are going to be much more difficult to make. It would be worth pausing at this point to consider decisions that you have had to make in your own life, whether they have been hard or difficult, and why that is.

Returning to our list think about those decisions that you identified as being most difficult to make. Why do you think that these decisions are difficult?

Again you will have your own list of reasons, but I would suggest that some or all of the following may be on it.

Familiarity

One important factor which has an influence on decision making is familiarity. We have to make decisions about what to have for lunch every day, but make decisions about where to live and whether to move home very rarely.

Complexity

The decision about what clothes to wear can be a relatively straightforward one (unless like *The Great Gatsby* I have 'shirts piled like bricks in stacks a dozen high' (Fitzgerald

(continued)

1926 p89)). The decision about whether or not to retire may be much more complex, and involve the consideration of a wide range of different factors.

Emotion

'There is increasing recognition of the role that emotion plays in choice behaviour and our response to choice' (Hardman 2009 p89). Some decisions have few emotional ramifications, my choice of TV programme for example. However, others, whether or not to marry or divorce for example, are emotionally charged with rational and effective elements intertwined. The impacts of emotions can also affect our capacity to make decisions. So if we are stressed decision making will be more difficult.

Consequences

Where I go on holiday is important but its long-term consequences are probably more limited than a decision I make about where to invest the limited money that I have.

So we can see how these elements: familiarity, complexity, emotional context and consequences are all important in decision making. However the picture is more complicated than this. Underlying psychological traits such as decisiveness and impulsivity will also have an impact and the social context of the decision also needs to be considered. For example we may know nothing about cars, but having an expert friend who can guide us, a source of support in the decision making process, may help make the decision much more straightforward. What this exercise shows us is that individual differences in social context and psychological make-up can impact upon one decision being more difficult to make than another.

We have seen how challenging decision making can be in relation to the sorts of choices we can face day to day and, most importantly, how a number of things can impact upon the ease with which any decision can be made. In work with people who find making decisions difficult it has long been recognised that a range of factors over and above those directly pertaining to the decision itself (its complexity, emotional context and familiarity for example) can also have an important impact. I now want to look at some of these factors in more detail.

Strengths and resources   Every individual who comes to a point where capacity is an issue for them does so by way of their own particular narrative or biography (Kitwood 1993, Killick and Allan 2001) and with a particular set of social supports, which make them more or less able to engage with decision making. Kitwood (1993, 1996) argues that 'biography', a broad concept which describes the history and consequent social resources that an individual brings to the process of dementia, and that process's social psychological context have an important impact upon any individual's ability to communicate. Within a holistic practice model of dementia (Kitwood 1997) capacity is therefore not a static thing but something which varies with social context. So, for example, 'a person with dementia may, in the afternoon, feel exhausted by the effort of coping and managing and respond very differently in the morning after they have had a chance to rest' (Phillips et al. 2005 p115).

Context of care   The nature and scope of care available to an individual can clearly have an impact on their capacity to make decisions. A clear care planning process based around person centred principles can be important. Having meaningful relationships with key staff members can be facilitative of choice. For those in residential care engagement with the outside world can also be important (Commission for Social Care Inspection 2006a).

Communication strategies   Communication and the context of care are clearly areas that are linked, with successful care dependent upon the adoption of effective communication strategies by carers. We will address communication in more detail later on in this chapter. At this point it is important to note that in communicating with people who may find decision making difficult advocates need to be aware of a range of different communication strategies (Marshall and Tibbs 2006). Practical knowledge of hearing impairment (Allan et al. 2005) or the impacts of medication, for example, needs to be combined with an understanding of more specific communication strategies, around narrative and life story work for example (Killick and Allan 2001, Wells 2006). A flexible approach to communication will be important: as Marshall and Tibbs (2006 p97) point out, 'anyone who cannot bear to touch someone else is unlikely to be suitable for this kind of work (dementia advocacy) because so much communication is through touch'.

I want to end this discussion of decision making with two important points. Firstly, all of this underlines the importance of treating individuals in a specific social context. We often group people together under the banner of labels such as learning disability or dementia, but this process of labelling fails to recognise that the assignment of such labels can be determined by a range of social factors (Williams 2006) and that within the categories the labels purport to describe there can be vast differences between individuals. This is one reason why a person centred philosophy ought to be at the centre of the provision of care. Secondly, much of what we have said about individuals' strengths and resources, the context of care and effective communication applies to both advocacy and social work more generally. Advocacy which does not take account of these key factors in care will not be very effective.

There is no single way of 'doing' non-instructed advocacy. In fact most of those writing about this area have identified a range of different approaches which fall within the scope of what we could generally term non-instructed advocacy (Wells 2006, Henderson 2007, Boylan and Dalrymple 2009, Dementia Advocacy Network 2011b).

These approaches have different emphases but are not necessarily mutually exclusive. There is certainly the potential to apply more than one approach at the same time. They are, however, underpinned by slightly differing understandings of the role of advocacy, and the multi-dimensional model of advocacy introduced in the last chapter is again relevant here when trying to tease out the differences between the various forms of non-instructed advocacy.

Before we look at the detail of these different ways of carrying out non-instructed advocacy, I want first to consider a distinction made by Henderson (2007) between what he sees as two core roles that non-instructed advocates undertake in their work, the role of articulate friend and the role of watch-dog/negotiator. The primary concern of the watch-dog/negotiator role is ensuring that the service user has access to 'appropriate services and support' (p4). So the advocate here is concerned with an oversight of what is being provided for the service user, and, if this appears not to meet his or her needs, taking action and negotiating for things to be done in a different way or for additional services to be provided. The articulate friend focuses on the person themselves looking at how far they are content, and also at maximising their autonomy and control. The way that this is achieved is through establishing a trusting relationship, enabling the advocate to comment on their preferences and intentions. Archetypically this would involve a long-term relationship between service user and advocate over an extended period of time (rather in the mode of citizen advocacy, which we looked at in the last chapter). One key distinction between these two roles is in the degree to which their focus (following the multi-dimensional model) is instrumental or expressive. This as we will see is an issue which permeates much of the debate about the different ways of undertaking non-instructed advocacy.

Forms of non-instructed advocacy

There are a number of different varieties of non-instructed advocacy, each with its own particular philosophy, shared in differing degrees by other approaches. I am going to start by looking at rights based and person centred approaches. There are two reasons for starting here. Firstly, the greatest contrast lies between these two forms of advocacy and the balance between instrumental and expressive focus is most in evidence. Secondly, there is almost universal agreement in the literature about their importance. In relation to the other areas we will consider – questioning models, observation/witness and substituted judgement – there is less unanimity about their importance, but each approach has the potential to add something to the tool-kit of the non-instructed advocate.

The rights based approach

At the heart of this model sits the idea of citizenship. All people, whether or not they have capacity, have rights as citizens (enshrined within human rights legislation). The rights based (sometimes called 'human rights based' (Henderson 2007, Boylan and Dalrymple 2009) approach has as its primary purpose speaking up for those not able to give voice themselves and scrutinising services that may be provided against clear independent standards. The first source of these independent standards comes from human rights and associated legislation. However, advocates applying a rights based approach will be familiar with a whole range of legislation and guidance which might impact upon the lives of service users they are supporting, and be familiar with mechanisms to challenge and change the behaviour and decisions of professionals. The role of the advocate is 'to ensure using a variety of means that the basic human rights of the service user are promoted, defended and where necessary used to take affirmative action on behalf of the service user' (Henderson 2007 p12).

The rights based approach is quite closely linked to legal advocacy, which we looked at in Chapter 1, and it has a similar instrumental focus and generally an individual scope although it can be used to address collective issues at times. Boylan and Dalrymple (2009) argue that this rights focus can provide a counterbalance to the 'best interest' orientation of many health and social care professionals.

The person centred approach

This approach contrasts with human rights, placing the relationship between advocate and service user at the centre of the process of advocacy. This approach is about 'building up a picture of that person: their likes, dislikes, values, beliefs, history, lifestyle' (Dementia Advocacy Network 2011b p1). Through this process the advocate begins to find out what the individual's views and wishes might be. The way this is achieved is through the establishment of a trusting relationship, enabling the advocate to comment on their preferences and intentions. (We can see that this approach is quite close to citizen advocacy, which we looked at in Chapter 2.) The person centred approach to advocacy can complement a person centred orientation to health and social care practice (Koubel and Bungay 2008). Adherents of this form of advocacy would argue that the approach offers a very effective way of 'maintaining a person's well-being, upholding their personhood and ensuring that they are respected as an individual with individual needs' (Wells 2006 p35). It is generally acknowledged that person centred non-instructed advocacy works best as part of a long-term intervention, but it is an approach which could inform briefer advocacy based interventions

The observation/witness approach

I want to move on now to look at other forms of non-instructed advocacy. I am going to start with the observational/witness approach. This approach involves the advocate acting as a 'witness to the way in which services interact with the service user' (Henderson 2007 p14). Typically the advocate would spend time in the person's environment observing their daily routine and noting how they respond. It is an approach that is particularly applicable in residential or group care settings. The premise on which this form of non-instructed advocacy is based is that in responding to their environment the individual is revealing something about themselves. Preferences, likes, dislikes can all be revealed through observation. So one goal of observation is to learn about the service user. The other aspect of this approach is to look more generally (informed by the information gathered from observing the service user's behaviour) at the care being provided. Observation here may extend to scrutiny of care plans (Dementia Advocacy Network 2011b).

One thing which can help when observing is a framework around which to structure observation. The Care Quality Commission's SOFI (**S**hort **O**bservation **F**ramework for **I**nspection) (Commission for Social Care Inspection 2006a) is one example of a tool specifically designed to do this. It takes the process of observation and witness a stage further, by allowing advocates to adopt a systematic approach to this area of practice, and, by virtue of the key domains identified within the framework, to develop an empathetic understanding of the service user's perspective. The SOFI tool covers three key aspects of the service user's experience – emotional well-being, engagement and the style of staff interaction – and identifies a range of indicators which allow those inspecting care facilities to evaluate care across the three domains. Interestingly one goal of the detailed process of observation undertaken using the SOFI tool is to empathise with the person with dementia and to understand the world from their perspective. This approach, where observers attempt 'to take the standpoint of the person with dementia and make a subjective assessment of what they are experiencing' (Capstick 2003 p13), an idea which originates in Dementia Care Mapping (Baldwin and Capstick 2007), has something in common with the next form of advocacy we are going to look at, substituted judgement.

Substituted judgement

Substituted judgement involves trying to make the choice that the person would make but which they are unable to communicate. There are obvious difficulties with this approach. Joyce (2007) looks at the case of Joseph Saikewicz, a 67-year-old man with profound learning disabilities living in institutional care in the USA. Mr Saikewicz was discovered to be suffering from acute leukaemia, for which chemotherapy was a possible treatment. Using substituted judgement as the basis for decision making a court-appointed guardian decided that Mr Saikewicz should not receive treatment, on the basis that this would be his view if he were able to voice an opinion. Those criticising the judgement in this case argued 'that it was impossible to try and make the decision that a person who had never been competent, and never expressed a view would have made' (Joyce 2007 p7). There are many similarities between best interest approaches and substituted judgement. Both involve 'an element of someone else making a decision based partly upon what they know about the person and partly on their own judgement' (Wells 2006 p39). Both are beset with the problem that potentially they move advocacy too far in the direction of making decisions on behalf of others, rather than trying to ensure that any decisions that are made take full account of the service user and their experience.

Questioning models

Finally we come to questioning models of advocacy. We are going to begin with a discussion of the use of questions in non-instructed advocacy and then move on to look at a specific example of this approach: the ASIST watching brief approach, which is often seen as the archetypical questioning model (Henderson 2007, Boylan and Dalrymple 2009, Dementia Advocacy Network 2011b). Questioning approaches share some common ground with the other approaches to advocacy we have looked at so far. In fact a questioning approach, where a key part of the advocate's role is to ask those making decisions about a service user a systematic set of questions, is a strategy that can be applied in several different forms of advocacy. The systematic use of questions can be important in exploring the process of decision making and in investigating the rationale for any decisions made. Boylan and Dalrymple draw upon Mercer's work (Mercer 2008 in Boylan and Dalrymple 2009), identifying a list of questions an advocate might use when adopting a rights based approach. Here are some examples:

1   'Have the decision makers taken every effort to ascertain the wishes and feelings of the person?'
2   'How have the opinions of carers, friends and professionals regarding the person's wishes and feelings been taken into account?'
3   'What efforts have been made to ensure the participation of the person?'

These questions are essentially process focused, trying to ensure that the person's rights are respected throughout the decision making process.

The questioning model can also be applied in trying to understand the impacts of any decision on the quality of life of a service user. The best example of this is the *watching brief* approach from ASIST (Advocacy Services in Staffordshire). This approach 'centres around eight quality of life domains which are used as the basis for a series of questions that the advocate can put to the decision maker on behalf of the service user' (Henderson 2007 p13):

- Competence
- Community presence
- Continuity
- Choice and influence
- Individuality
- Status and respect
- Partnerships and relationships
- Well-being

In relation to each of these domains the advocate asks questions of the decision maker. So in relation to competence, for example, the advocate might ask 'how the proposal will promote the person's independence' or 'support them to develop new skills and maintain existing ones' (ASIST 2007 p10). In relation to individuality the advocate could ask how the proposal will 'address the person's preferences' or 'offer opportunities to express preferences' (ASIST 2007 p11).

These questions are not designed to be confrontational, but rather to create the opportunity for dialogue between advocate and decision maker, through which the appropriateness of any action can be addressed with the service user at the heart of the decision making process. The importance of dialogue in this model is one of the key things which distinguishes it from the more rights based approaches to questioning. However, it does share features with the structured observational approaches, the use of the SOFI tool for example, which uses a somewhat similar domain based way of evaluating quality of life issues. However, the overall emphasis is on the interaction between advocate and decision maker rather than observation.

Practice example – Robert

Robert is a 74-year-old man, a former bus driver, who lives with his 82-year-old partner, James, who used to be a nurse. They have been living together for the past 30 years in a one bedroom flat. James has recently finished treatment for throat cancer which involved radiotherapy and chemotherapy. About 3 months ago Robert collapsed in the supermarket and was taken to hospital. It turned out that he had had a stroke, which has left him with limited movement down the left side of his body and has made it much harder for him to think clearly and logically, and to pay attention to things. The stroke has had an impact on his speech and memory. A lot of the time he appears confused and irritated. Robert is now on an elderly ward in hospital and he and James are thinking about the options which are available to them. They speak with Phillip, the social worker attached to the ward. A number of issues emerge from their discussions.

- Over the past month or so Robert has shown some small improvements. He has been speaking more and some movement has returned to his left side. It also seems to James that he is a little more coherent. The amount of physiotherapy he receives on the non-specialist ward where he is is quite limited, however.
- James feels that because of this Robert should move on to a specialist neurological rehabilitation unit where he can get more intensive help, and that if this were to happen then Robert might improve further. The medical team on the ward have said that this is not an appropriate course of action as Robert is too old and the nature of his impairments too severe to support this. James has read some recent material in the nursing literature which appears to contradict this point of view.
- Robert has repeatedly said during his stay in hospital that he would like to go home. Although it can be difficult to follow the sense of quite a lot of what Robert says he has been very clear about this. He has many supportive friends who live nearby and who visit him regularly and push him round the hospital grounds in a wheelchair. However, James thinks that he would need a lot of help if Robert were at home. They live in a basement flat accessible only by stairs, and James' cancer treatment has left him with limited energy.
- The team treating Robert on the ward think that he should go into a specialist nursing home for people who have had a stroke or brain injury as the next stage. However, Phillip knows that there isn't a nursing home with these facilities anywhere near where James and Robert live and so a specialist placement would be many miles away. A non-specialist home could be found nearer, but the other residents would be much older and there would be no specialist skills in working with someone like Robert.

This is quite a complex situation and there are roles here for advocacy. Firstly, there is the question of the treatment Robert should receive in hospital, and advocating for

James' views to be taken into account, and about Robert's rights to treatment. Secondly, there is the question of Robert's wishes and how they can be fed into a process of decision making around his future.

Discussion point

Think about this case and about the models of non-instructed advocacy we have looked at so far. Consider, a *rights based approach*, the *person centred approach*, *observation witness approaches* and the *watching brief approach*. Now, for each form of non-instructed advocacy, look at the strengths and weaknesses of each model as applied to the case. One important thing to consider is whether different approaches could be combined here, an eclectic approach to advocacy, or whether a single consistent model is more appropriate.

Communication and non-instructed advocacy

It is important for non-instructed advocates to be aware of issues around communication in their work. Obviously the use of signing, where appropriate; awareness of the impact of physical difficulties on communication, muscle control or hearing, for example; and the use of talking mats and prompt cards can all be significant in this area (Marshall and Tibbs 2006, Wells 2006, Williams 2009). I want to focus here on dementia advocacy where specific communication and engagement strategies can be helpful. Working with people with dementia communication can be challenging. Service users can give inconsistent messages, and Wells (2006) argues for the use of observation, listening and reflection as three keynotes in communication, when looking for consistent narratives in what can seem incoherent talk (Killick and Allan 2001). Creative communication strategies are particularly important as part of a person centred approach, where the relationship between advocate and service user is an important part of finding out about the service user's world. Wells (2006) sees befriending and spending time with a person as they undertake day to day activities as an important part of this work. She also identifies life story and reminiscence work as a potentially powerful way of making connections with a person. This approach can make a person feel valued, and help to build a relationship. It also has the benefit of giving the advocate a sense of the nature of the person, in that it reveals the types of choices that have been made and information about preferences and values.

Discussion point

One final thing to consider before we move on to look at statutory advocacy roles is to return to the case of Robert and James. Think about Robert's difficulties with communication: what sorts of strategies might help in communicating with him?

Statutory advocacy roles

The Mental Capacity Act – Independent Mental Capacity Advocates and statutory non-instructed advocacy

The role of the Independent Mental Capacity Advocate (IMCA) is a relatively new one. It came into being as part of the 2005 Mental Capacity Act. The aim of this legislation was to try to bring into a statutory framework the previous legal arrangements in relation to people who lacked the capacity to make decisions. The common law was the primary legal reference point in relation to mental capacity prior to the 2005 act, although the 1983 Mental Health Act provided elements of statutory regulation. However, most substitute decision making took place within a common law framework, increasingly shaped by the concept of best interest (Redley et al. 2006). The complexity of the legislative position before the 2005 act was compounded by what has become known as the Bournewood case. This 'case' involved the detention of a 49-year-old man who was autistic and not able to speak, and who ended up effectively detained in Bournewood Hospital. Legal action by his carers led to an eventual decision by the Court of Appeal that in these circumstances detention in hospital was illegal, as he was not able to agree or refuse treatment. Although the House of Lords subsequently overturned this decision, the European Court of Human Rights ruled that in the use of common law and the principle of best interest in what we might call substitute decision making, where a person lacked the capacity to make a decision themselves, 'there was an absence of procedural safeguards to protect against arbitrary deprivation of liberty' (Brown and Barber 2008 p91). The Mental Capacity legislation introduces this framework of safeguards around decision making, one aspect of which was the creation of the IMCA role: a 'late addition' (Brown and Barber 2008) to the Act.

So what is the role of the IMCA? A full discussion of substitute decision making under the auspices of the Mental Capacity Act is beyond the scope of this book. However, it will be helpful to touch upon some of the key elements of and overriding principles behind the legislation, in order to understand the place of advocacy within it. The Act essentially defines what is meant legally by someone lacking capacity and then goes on to identify a legal framework for decision making when this is the case. This framework is grounded in best interest, allows the making of unwise decisions, and has regard to following the least restrictive course of action. Within this framework those making decisions on behalf of another, commonly referred to as 'decision makers', are required to consult with close relatives, friends or others who take an interest in the person's welfare, best interests and wishes, and their feelings beliefs and values in relation to the proposed course of action. The IMCA role is primarily about providing advocacy for those who lack anyone able or willing to represent them in this way, or where decision makers are unable to contact an appropriate person, and feeding back information to the decision maker in a report. There are three key circumstances when (in the absence of others) IMCAs must or may become involved in decision making.

- In two key areas of decision making – in the provision of serious medical treatment, and new accommodation, either by the local authority or an NHS body

- In adult protection cases in certain circumstances (and in some care reviews)
- In relation to Deprivation of Liberty assessments where the person who lacks capacity has no representative or where that person needs support or cannot be accessed immediately

The role of the IMCA is made up of several elements. The Department of Health's overview of the role (2009a) identifies four separate components:

- The first and perhaps most important part of the role is to ascertain the 'views, feelings, wishes, beliefs and values' (Department of Health 2009a p31) of the person who lacks capacity and to ensure that due account is taken of these in the decision making process. This is very much advocacy from the perspective of 'giving voice'; making sure that the person about whom decisions are being made is not lost or ignored.
- Investigation of the circumstances surrounding the decision is also important and crucial in supporting the first part of this process. Exploring the perspective of the service user involves making every effort to communicate with, and gather information from, anyone who knows about him or her. It also means looking at any records that relate to the person and using these to inform the IMCA's view on the situation.
- The Department of Health (2009a p31) also identifies a role they call non-instructed advocacy. The IMCA task here is to try and represent the views of the service user in the decision making process. This has a strong rights focus. One element of this part of the work of an IMCA is asking questions on behalf of the service user about the proposed decision; the choices and options available need to be explored as part of this process. It is also important that the IMCA finds out what steps the decision maker has taken to make sure the service has been actively involved in plans around treatment or accommodation.
- This element of the role is supported through what the Department of Health (2009a) describes as 'auditing the decision making process' (p31). The IMCA here is ensuring that the decision being taken is consistent with the Mental Capacity Act and its principles, and taken with due regard for the service user's best interest.

Safeguarding vulnerable adults – the IMCA role

The extension of the work of statutory independent advocacy in the sphere of adult safeguarding represents both a development of previous roles and a move into new territory. The new role involves providing social services authorities and the NHS with the power to instruct an IMCA in circumstances where safeguarding measures are being put in place to protect a vulnerable adult, and where it appears that the person could lack the capacity to consent to those measures.

In these circumstances, and unlike other roles that IMCAs undertake, the IMCA role is not restricted to circumstances where the person who lacks capacity has no family or friends to support him or her. So an IMCA may be appointed in adult protection even though the service user has a supportive family. The other major difference between this role and others undertaken by IMCAs is that the local authority has some discretion within adult protection as to when they involve an IMCA. There is a statutory obligation within decision making in adult protection to *consider* the appointment of an IMCA in all circumstances. However, there is no obligation to appoint in all cases and the local authority has to be satisfied that it would be of benefit to the person to appoint an IMCA (Department of Health 2010a). In fact the evidence is of considerable differences between authorities in their use of IMCAs in adult safeguarding (Department of Health 2010b). The IMCA role in these circumstances is to support people not able to make decisions about their protection by obtaining 'relevant information about their views, wishes and beliefs', which can contribute to the decision making process, and ensuring that the protective measures considered do not excessively restrict their liberty' (Redley et al. 2011 p4)

In practice what local authorities have done is to draw up guidance to staff as to when a referral to an IMCA service would be appropriate (Department of Health 2010a). Typically such guidance focuses on risk, particularly those circumstances where risk is highest, circumstances where a family may not have the interests of the person lacking capacity at heart (perhaps where they have been implicated in the abuse), conflicts of interest between decision makers and serious financial abuse. Redley et al. (2011), although acknowledging the generally positive view of professionals working in adult safeguarding about the introduction of IMCAs into this area, do caution that integration between IMCA services and adult safeguarding 'requires more than good guidance and training; it also requires the development of mutual understanding and trust' (p8).

Independent Mental Capacity Advocacy is an important statutory service which does build protection of the interests of the most vulnerable people into the mental capacity legislation and beyond (into safeguarding adults). It is interesting that advocacy in this role is driven by both a rights based and person centred agenda. Advocacy interventions by IMCAs are short lived; they average 8 hours' work per client (Redley et al. 2010 p1821). Redley et al.'s research (2010) reveals a strong person centred orientation amongst IMCAs, yet in such brief interventions a person centred approach is hard to sustain, requiring as it does a relationship between advocate and service user. The Department of Health guidance on the IMCA role (Department of Health 2009a) also clearly envisages there being a strongly rights based aspect to their work. Here a rights based or watching brief questioning model might be an important way of interrogating the decision making process in a systematic way. Redley et al. (2010) describe this combination of the specific and rights orientated advocacy underpinned by person centred practice as 'decision-led but client focused' (p1821) (a description coined by an advocate interviewed in their study), which helps sum up what is at the heart of this role.

Independent Mental Health Advocacy

The introduction of the 2007 Mental Health Act came at the end of a process of much debate around restrictive and community based treatment and the place of advocacy within the mental health legislation. That advocacy became part of the legislation was something of a triumph for those lobbying for amendments to the legislation to make it less focused on coercion (Mental Health Alliance 2007). The statutory advocacy role in mental health, the Independent Mental Health Advocate (IMHA), is less specific in its remit than the Independent Mental Capacity Advocate (IMCA) role we have just been looking at. Obviously, unlike the IMCA role this is not non-instructed advocacy. IMHAs are available to support specific groups of 'patients' in a range of areas to do with their rights in relation to treatment.

So who is eligible for the IMHA service? There are three groups of people with mental health problems who are eligible for support from an advocate within the legislation. The first group is those detained in hospital. Everyone subject to detention under a section of the Mental Health Act qualifies for support from an IMHA, except those detained on a short-term basis in an emergency situation. The second category of eligible people is those living in the community but receiving treatment within a statutory framework. So this group includes people who are subject to guardianship or supervised community treatment (a Community Treatment Order). The final (much smaller) eligible group is those who are discussing certain specific types of treatment (in relation to which the legislation includes some special safeguards), neurosurgery or the implantation to hormones to reduce the male sex drive, and ECT when under the age of 18.

The role of the IMHA covers three areas, all of which are linked together.

- **Helping people understand information** IMHAs have an important role to play in explaining the Mental Health Act and how it affects people. So the IMHA can explain which parts of the legislation apply to a particular service user and any restrictions to which they are subject.
- **Helping people exercise rights** An IMHA can help service users in pursuing their rights under the Mental Health Act, supporting someone through the process of applying to a tribunal to review their treatment, for example. They can also offer support in challenging treatment decisions and pursuing complaints.
- **Helping people participate in decisions about their care and treatment**

Helping people make their views heard by supporting them in ward rounds and meetings with professionals is an important part of the IMHA role. Ensuring that professionals explain treatments and assist service users to consider the options available to them is also a key part of enabling people to participate in their care.

Practice example – Jeremy

Carmen is a social worker in a Community Mental Health Team (CMHT). Over the past six months she and a fellow member of the team, Valerie, a Community Psychiatric Nurse, have been working together with Jeremy, a young man in his late twenties, white, originally

(continued)

from Ireland, who is studying at a local university (although he has not been attending classes with any regularity in the past year). Jeremy was referred to the CMHT by a housing officer. Jeremy lives in a housing association flat, in a large Victorian house now broken up into a number of separate flats. His neighbours had spoken to the housing officer expressing some concerns about Jeremy. He is in arrears with his rent and facing eviction at some point. Jeremy's flat is on the ground floor and he has covered all his windows with silver foil, including the windows and glass door from his flat to the communal garden. He can also be heard at night shouting and arguing with himself. Since Jeremy's referral to the CMHT, Valerie has been his key worker, seeing him on a weekly basis and trying to monitor his taking of medication prescribed by his GP for depression. Inside Jeremy's flat there is very little food and Jeremy has been getting thinner. Jeremy's sister, his closest relative, has contacted the CMHT and spoken with Carmen, expressing concerns about him and wondering whether he shouldn't have some time in a psychiatric hospital, which happened in Ireland before they both moved to England. Carmen and Valerie make a number of efforts to see Jeremy but he is either not at home or not letting them in. On one early evening visit they hear Jeremy inside the flat shouting loudly. Eventually they manage to see Jeremy and he agrees to come and spend some time in hospital. After one night he leaves, however. This pattern of trying to keep in touch with Jeremy and then his coming into hospital repeats itself on two further occasions. Eventually following further expressions of concern by Jeremy's sister he ends up coming into hospital under a section of the Mental Health Act for 28 days.

In hospital Jeremy refuses to speak to staff or to take medication. He is referred to an Independent Mental Health Advocacy service, and will not come to meetings with the consultant, sending his advocate instead. He also makes complaints about Valerie for harassing him in the community, and Carmen for the part she played in his compulsory admission to hospital and for speaking to his housing officer to stop any eviction until he is out of hospital. He appeals to a tribunal to have his compulsory detention lifted. His sister contacts the team to express concerns about the fact that, when she has contacted the hospital on the phone, Jeremy has refused to speak to her and she has had to speak to his advocate instead, who she feels has been 'taken in because Jeremy can seem normal' and is trying to get him out of hospital. Valerie brings up these issues in the CMHT. So far the team have not been actively treating Jeremy with medication; they have been trying find out more about him and his behaviour. Valerie suggests giving him medication against his will (permissible under the Mental Health Act) to try to ensure greater cooperation with treatment.

It would be naïve to think that professionals and advocates will always coexist in some kind of seamless harmony. This case illustrates some of the conflicts which can surround the whole area of independent advocacy within a statutory framework. Professionals can feel as though advocacy is undermining their roles in care and treatment. However, it is crucial that professionals work in a way which is consistent with respecting Jeremy's rights whilst a patient. It is not always straightforward to make decisions about compulsory admission to hospital, and in Jeremy's case it has clearly been a complex decision taken over a long period of time. It is important in these circumstances that professional judgements are subject to scrutiny, through tribunals for instance. Social workers have a responsibility within multidisciplinary teams to support the rights of service users in such circumstances. The advocacy of the IMHA has a representative purpose; it is about enabling people to speak when they can and speaking for them when they find this difficult. The perspective is very much about ensuring the service user's voice is heard. This is something which cannot always be achieved without conflict.

Supporting self-advocacy

So far the focus of this chapter has very much been on working with individuals. However, as we know, advocacy is an activity which has the potential to link the individual with the group, to address wider collective issues and needs, and to be a force for social justice and change. In Chapter 2, when we looked at self-advocacy, we confined our discussion to look at those advocating for themselves as individuals. I want to develop and expand that discussion a little at this point and explore self-advocacy as a group approach, with a focus on work with people with learning difficulties, as well as considering how social work practitioners can support this form of advocacy.

In this area of practice self-advocacy is construed in a much wider sense. Simons (1992) points out that self-advocacy has two meanings: 'it can refer to a process of individual development through which a person comes to have the confidence and ability to express his or her feelings and wishes'. However, it can also refer to 'the process by which groups of people get together and give voice to their common concerns' (Simons 1992 p5). These two elements of self-advocacy can be interlinked in a positive way: groups can support individuals to develop skills and confidence to advocate on their own behalf; those individuals can then use their skills to contribute to and develop the group. Over and above the two constructions of self-advocacy we have looked at so far is a third idea, self-advocacy as a social movement pushing for social change and a means of securing goals of greater social justice for people with learning difficulties. The idea of advocacy as a 'new social movement' (Larana et al. 1994) very much akin to the Green Movement, Disability Rights or Gay Rights Movement, has been evoked in this context (Bersani 1998). The definition of self-advocacy by Rhoades, in Brandon and Brandon's book *Advocacy Power to People with Disabilities* neatly sums up this perspective (Brandon and Brandon 1995a). It sees self-advocacy as having the following characteristics:

- A new social movement organised and controlled by people with learning difficulties assisted by advisers
- The promotion of equality, independence and recognition for people with learning difficulties as fully fledged members of society
- Working to protect the legal and civil rights of people with learning difficulties
- The promotion of the rights of people with learning disabilities to participate and influence the care services they receive

Self-advocacy as a group practice has a relatively long history, which we can see shares some of the characteristics of the other new social movements we have identified. The convergence of a number of different organisations working towards supporting and representing the views of people with learning difficulties in the establishment of People First (initially in the USA), at the end of the 1970s and early 1980s, marks a key point in its development (Dywab 1996, Williams 2006, Boylan and Dalrymple 2009). People First started in the UK in 1984 following the attendance of a group of people with learning difficulties at a conference in Tacoma, Washington, USA (Whittaker 1995, Buchanan and Walmsley 2006). This nascent movement was consolidated by the oganisation of an international conference held in the UK in 1988 (Williams 2006). Self-advocacy has subsequently spread across the UK with the establishment of a wide range of groups, some generic, some specific to a particular service.

Walmsley (2002) argues that the conception of self-advocacy aligned directly with the disability rights movement is not straightforward to sustain and that self-advocacy 'sits in many ways uneasily within the disabled people's movement' (p31). However, although self-advocacy may lack the theoretical underpinnings of the disability rights movement and 'minimise rather than rejoice in difference' (Walmsley 2002 p31), offering 'a compensatory rather than positive assertion' (Szivos 1992 p127) of its value, it has undoubtedly had a major impact in raising awareness of the views of people with learning difficulties and has influenced the design and delivery of services. The emphasis placed on people with learning disabilities having a voice in and control over the services they receive, in Valuing People, the white paper on services for people with learning disabilities, is in substantial part a result of the influence of the self-advocacy movement (Boylan and Dalrymple 2009).

I want to turn at this point to the question of how social workers can most effectively support service users in self-advocacy. As we look at this area, the division between micro and macro advocacy roles, which we introduced in the last chapter, provides a helpful framework for our discussions. I am going to start by considering the micro level.

Supporting self-advocacy at a micro level

As Williams points out, 'many social workers are involved in self-advocacy' (Williams 2009 p131). This involvement encompasses a range of activities at a micro level. Self-advocacy provides social work with a model of how work with individuals can be undertaken in a way which is consistent with the principles of valuing people, and supporting choice and autonomy. This can be achieved in a very practical way, by supporting service users in making links with self-advocacy groups and building their confidence to become involved, particularly where this may be difficult. It is often the case that service users living at home with their families are less likely and able to access self-advocacy (Simons 1992), and social workers can facilitate access for this group. However, it is also important to consider how social work can be carried out in a way which fits with the principles of self-advocacy. Brechin and Swann (1989) argue that 'the self-advocacy movement offers a model of growth and development against which professional assumptions and approaches can be tested' (p49). They present a

Table 3.1 Self-advocacy compared with professional support

Key elements of self-advocacy	Features of the support offered by professionals
Growth and confidence	Enhancing mastery and control
Trust	Learning to be on their side in seeing problems
Self-valuing/pride	Learning to enjoy and know people
Identity	Believing in people
Determination	Commitment
Responsibility	Accentuating positive qualities
Ability and knowledge	Sharing skills and information
Sensitivity to others	Monitoring own communication
Developing a voice	Learning to assist without control or power

(Adapted from Brechin and Swann 1989)

model of practice which looks at the features of help offered by professionals measured against key elements of self-advocacy. Table 3.1 shows how the model might work in practice.

It is worth thinking at this point a little more about this list. What challenges does it present to the practitioner and how might professional practice address this set of criteria drawn from self-advocacy? What sorts of constraints could the organisational context of practice place on this? It is also worth considering whether there are elements of self-advocacy not covered by this list. It is probably important to remember that, whilst self-advocacy is about cultivating autonomy, a sense of identity and confidence, it is also concerned with creating real changes in the way in which services are delivered.

Social workers can support self-advocacy at a micro level in their dealings with other professionals. An understanding of how the principles of self-advocacy can be reflected in professional practice is an important part of this. Simons' research (1992) shows that, despite generally positive attitudes from staff, some professionals can be reluctant to embrace the aims and principles of self-advocacy. He identifies a number of ways in which this can happen.

- Professionals can lack a commitment to service user involvement and not accept service users' rights to be involved in self-advocacy
- They can be reluctant to practise in a way which is consistent with self-advocacy and be resistant to person centred approaches to care
- They can pay lip-service to self-advocacy and even try to manipulate self-advocacy groups
- They can lack knowledge and not properly understand what key concepts, autonomy and independence for example, mean

The role of the social worker in this context is two-fold. Firstly, they have an ambassadorial role to try to improve understanding of this area and explain how self-advocacy works. Secondly, they have a responsibility to challenge negative percep-tions of self-advocacy.

Another area where support for self-advocacy can be important is in group care set-tings. I want to return at this point to the case example which we looked at in Chapter 2, the Rose Terrace advocacy service. To recap, Rose Terrace is a small voluntary-sector-supported living project, comprising support accommodation and a drop-in centre. Over the past few months the management committee of Rose Terrace has been con-sidering the establishment of some kind of advocacy scheme within the project. After much deliberation they have decided that a self-advocacy group would be the most appropriate form of advocacy. Emma is a qualified social worker employed by Rose Terrace to manage the services there. She has been given responsibility for establishing the group and helping it get going. Rhoades' definition of self-advocacy acknowledges the important role that 'advisers' play within self-advocacy. Advisers or supporters are non-disabled people whose role is to foster and sustain self-advocacy groups. 'This role involves a delicate balance between helping the group and not controlling it' (Williams 2009). Emma's role at this stage is that of adviser or supporter. Simons' research on self-advocacy (Simons 1992) identifies a number of different elements of this role, three of which we are going to focus on now.

Providing practical help and support

The adviser's role is primarily concerned with this area. Advisers help with writing letters, recruiting new members, and preparing newsletters and presentations. Problem solving and planning can be an important part of this. They are also involved with the provision of information: for example, making links with other groups or identifying the best way of presenting the group's views to service providers.

Ensuring everyone's voice is heard in the group

In Simon's research advisers describe this aspect of their work as acting as a 'referee'. However, the scope of this element of the adviser role extends beyond intervening in interpersonal conflicts within the group, and involves establishing ground rules and group decision-making procedures (voting for example).

Clarifying/summarising/recalling

Simon's research reveals that this is an aspect of the adviser role which service users value. Clarifying involves 'putting issues or arguments in context' (Simons 1992 p62), summarising recapping arguments and the different points of view expressed, and reminding group members of discussions in previous meetings.

Emma's role in supporting this group is more complex than merely working within the parameters we have just laid out. Imagine that you were Emma reporting back to the management committee after the first couple of meetings of the group. What sorts of issues regarding the group do you think it might be important to highlight to them?

I think Emma might legitimately have concerns about the service context within which this group has been established. Firstly, there is a question about its independence. The group is reliant on Rose Terrace for a place to meet and resources to help it run. Secondly, if self-advocacy is about ensuring the voices of service users have an influence on the services they receive, then members of the self-advocacy group should also be on the project's management group. If this is not the case then it is not clear how this aspiration can be fulfilled. Finally, there are wider questions about the group's independence. How far is it legitimate for Emma to manage the service and to be adviser to the group? The management committee may want to consider whether there are conflicts of interest here.

In this case example we can start to see that there are particular difficulties attendant upon service specific self-advocacy. Working within a particular service can restrict the scope of advocacy and move its focal point away from a concern with the civil rights, equality and independence of people with learning difficulties, towards consumerism and the evaluation of the specific services provided by the organisation (Aspis 1997).

Thus far we have been looking at group advocacy on the micro level from the perspective of practitioners working within group care settings. However, self-advocacy in group care is also an important consideration in the purchase and monitoring of care packages. One key aspect of the social work role in relation to self-advocacy groups is ensuring that it is available to service users in day and residential care settings and critically reviewing services where they do exist. Emma's questions to her management committee will be relevant here. The issue of independence, external advisers offering support, and how self-advocacy can influence the practice of the care provider are all important ones for a social worker undertaking this role.

Supporting self-advocacy at the macro level

Supporting self-advocacy is not just something which happens at the micro level, with specific individuals or particular groups. Social work practitioners and managers can also support self-advocacy at the macro level, developing services, campaigning and supporting civil rights. There are two important ways in which this can happen.

Enabling self-advocacy to become more demanding

Simon's research suggests that from the perspective of service providers self-advocacy groups could be more assertive in their demands and take a more active role in shaping services. It is a real challenge for services to enable this to happen and to some extent the personalisation agenda is driving change in this area. Service users' and carers' views can often be marginalised in forums such as partnership boards (Carr 2004). Service users' involvement in, and control over, the evaluation of services has again been limited (Whittaker et al. 1991). In *Supporting Self-Advocacy*, Lawton (2007) looks in general terms at how to give self-advocacy groups a greater impact on service provision. The SCIE report identifies four areas which service providers should address to try to encourage more participation: an agenda set by service users, honesty about who controls what, a thoughtful approach about the most effective methods of communication, and giving time to the process.

Pursuing a rights agenda

Alliances between local groups, and links into national campaigns and causes, are very important in the pursuit of social inclusion, civil rights and equality. In supporting self-advocacy social workers need to encourage this engagement with wider social issues. Wilson (2009) identifies the Elfrida Society Democratic Participation as an interesting example of a rights focused and case based approach. The project – which encouraged voter registration, increased awareness of politics and elections, and enabled people to vote – attempted to begin to address the exclusion of people with learning difficulties from the political process. There is some indication it may have had some impact (Brody 2010).

Key learning points

- Advocates undertaking non-instructed advocacy approach their work in a range of different ways. The most important of these are the *person centred*, *rights based*, *observational/witness* and *watching brief* approaches. However, in practice advocates may combine different elements of these forms of advocacy in their work
- *Non-instructed advocacy* ought to be undertaken in a way which takes account of the individual needs of service users, their strengths and resources, the context of the care they receive and the nature of the decisions they face in their lives
- Adopting a flexible approach to communication when service users find it difficult to express clear preferences is a key element in the non-instructed advocacy role
- *Statutory advocacy* roles within the Mental Capacity Act and the Mental Health Act offer opportunities for social workers and advocates to work cooperatively, in relation to safeguarding for example, but also possible sources of conflict
- *Self-advocacy* groups are a growing feature of many service users' lives, and social workers can adopt a range of strategies to support these developments at both the micro and macro levels

Further reading

Brown, R. and Barber, P. (2008) *The Social Worker's Guide to the Mental Capacity Act 2005*, Exeter, Learning Matters

Department of Health (2009a) *Making decisions: the Independent Mental Capacity Advocate Service*, London, Department of Health/Office of the Public Guardian

Lawton, A. (2007) *Supporting Self-Advocacy*, London, Social Care Institute for Excellence

Marshall, M. and Tibbs, M. (2006) *Social Work and People with Dementia*, Bristol, Policy Press

Walmsley, J. (2002) 'Principles and Types of Advocacy', in Gray, B. and Jackson, R., *Advocacy and Learning Disability*, London, Jessica Kingsley

Wells, S. (2006) *Developments in Dementia Advocacy: Exploring the role of advocates in supporting people with dementia*, London, Westminster Advocacy Service for Senior Residents.

4 The Value Base of Advocacy

Introduction

Advocacy is an area of social work practice where values are central to practice, with 'ethical issues . . . inseparable from the principles of advocacy' (Parrot 2010 p103). This chapter is concerned with a range of such ethical issues which can arise within advocacy and explores how advocacy fits within the types of ethical frameworks which have traditionally been used to help social workers understand and resolve the dilemmas which practice so often presents. Any discussion of advocacy and values must also take account of the fact that advocacy is 'significant in developing a practice which is anti-oppressive' (Parrot 2010 p104). With its rights orientation and strong focus on empowerment, advocacy has the potential to further the goals of anti-discriminatory practice, something we will touch upon in this chapter and explore in more detail in Chapter 5 when we consider empowering models of practice in advocacy.

At first sight independent advocacy can appear to be a world into which ethical dilemmas do not intrude. The role of advocates is to represent the views of their clients and this makes three demands upon them. Firstly, that the advocate be skilful: able to engage with service users and succinctly present their views to decision makers. Secondly, that the advocate be knowledgeable: aware of the legislative and policy frameworks within which they operate, and the rights and entitlements of those they represent. Thirdly, that the advocate be conscientious and diligent, committed to being an honest and effective representative. Behaving ethically would for independent advocates therefore involve embracing professional virtues of respecting and voicing the views of others, a commitment to developing and sustaining expertise, and diligence in the pursuit of professional responsibilities.

For social workers the ethical world of advocacy is more complex. Although they are committed to the values which underlie independent advocacy their responsibilities extend beyond those of their independent peers, and as a consequence there is sometimes scope for conflict between the role of advocate and other professional responsibilities. The aim of this chapter is to explore the challenges faced by those acting as advocates as part of a wider professional brief, and most importantly the conflicts that can arise between the best interests of service users as they themselves perceive them and as viewed by professionals. The chapter also looks at the tensions that can exist within professional practice between social workers' views of the right course of action and the constraints their employing organisations can place on these.

We began with an outline of the values underpinning independent advocacy and I will explore these in more detail later when looking at the UKAN code of practice. However, although there is undoubtedly a distinction to be drawn between independent advocacy and the advocacy carried out by social workers within their professional roles, it is probably a more diffuse distinction than might at first sight appear. To illustrate this point I want to begin the discussion of advocacy and values by looking at some of the issues and dilemmas faced by independent advocates.

Values dilemmas in independent advocacy

- A user of an independent advocacy service asks her advocate to speak to a relative who 'knows everything about her' to help make a decision about her future care. The advocate is concerned that the service user is a bit intimidated by her relative and is not sure that the relative has the service user's best interests at heart. Is it appropriate for the advocate to take instructions from the relative as this is clearly what the service user wants?

- A client of an independent advocacy service within a psychiatric hospital wants to let the psychiatrist treating him 'have a piece of his mind' and 'let him know what the patients think about him' at a planned review at which his advocate will be present. The service user has indicated that this will involve him behaving angrily and swearing at the psychiatrist. The advocate knows that this will sour the relationship between the service user and the psychiatrist and make things worse for her client. How far should this choice by the service user, perceived as unwise by the advocate, be supported?

- An advocate is working for a service user who drinks heavily and when drunk can be aggressive and violent towards his neighbours, and is facing eviction. The service user is always intoxicated when he sees the advocate and never gives a clear indication of what he wants to do. The manager of the advocacy service has suggested to the advocate that she cannot continue this work without a clear sense of what the service user wants as there are many demands on the resources of the advocacy service. How should an advocate proceed in this situation?

- A service user with physical disabilities has requested assistance from an independent advocacy organisation after being refused a service from a social care provider. The service user has been offered personal care services, but will not accept an Asian care worker. How far should an independent advocate voice the views of a service user in his situation?

Discussion point

Think about the above examples and the sorts of dilemmas they might present to an advocate. Remember that a dilemma is best described as a choice between options both of which have unwelcome consequences. What might the underlying issues be here?

(continued)

How could you use principles to address these dilemmas? Think about the GSCC Codes of Practice and how they could help you here:

1   Protect the rights and promote the interests of service users and carers
2   Strive to establish and maintain the trust and confidence of service users and carers
3   Promote the independence of service users while protecting them as far as possible from danger or harm
4   Respect the rights of service users while seeking to ensure that their behaviour does not harm themselves or other people
5   Uphold public trust and confidence in social services
6   Be accountable for the quality of their work and take responsibility for maintaining and improving their knowledge and skills

We can see a number of key issues emerging from these dilemmas.

- The tensions which can exist between service users' desires and intentions, and their adoption of courses of action which at first sight might appear counter-productive or even damaging to their welfare in some way. The second of these dilemmas is an example of this.
- The desirability of the outcomes sought through advocacy and the question of whether this should influence the process of advocacy. This raises questions as to the role of advocacy and how far advocates should subscribe to the causes for which they are advocating. Social workers, for example, have an obliga-tion to address the wishes of service users and to work within the broader precepts of anti-discriminatory practice. Our last example concerns this question.
- The potential conflicts which can exist between services users and those clos-est to them. How far should the views of relatives influence the process of advocacy and how should their views be most effectively represented and ad-vocated for in planning care for vulnerable individuals? This question lies at the heart of our first example.
- The demands of the organisational context of advocacy: how far should ad-vocates' actions be influenced by the requirements of the organisations for which they work? This a question our third example raises.

Discussion point

These are dilemmas for independent advocacy but, interestingly enough, social workers face similar dilemmas in their practice when undertaking advocacy roles. It is worth thinking about how a social worker would approach them as part of their professional role and what the similarities and differences might be in the approach adopted.

The ethical foundations of social work and advocacy

Social work is a value laden activity, one in which there is a constant tension present between respecting the autonomy of service users and protecting them from damaging themselves and others. Discussions about the function of social work, its dual welfare and protection role, have existed since the profession's inception (Jones 1983). Advocacy as such an important part of social work practice is not immune therefore from such debates.

In trying to understand the underlying ethical foundation of such debates most writers on social work ethics have taken as their starting point the contrasting ethical systems of utilitarian consequentialism and Kantian deontology (Clark 2000, Becket and Maynard 2005). This has become the prevailing ethical framework for understanding how these conflicts between care and control manifest themselves in practice; 'debates about ethics within the professions have tended to be characterised in terms of a tension between deontology and utilitarianism' (Hugman 2005 p7). A brief account of these two approaches to moral philosophy will therefore be useful at this point, before we begin to look at how these systems of moral thought can be applied to the role of advocacy. Kantian ethics is based around the idea that we have moral duties to one another. It adopts a deontological approach, where the moral value of any action is judged by looking at the extent to which it conforms to a moral rule. Kant argues that we can arrive at such rules through a process of reasoning. At the heart of his moral philosophy lie two interrelated ideas. The first is perhaps best summed up by the dictum that we should treat people as ends and not means. In other words we should not set aside a person's humanity even if mistreating them in some way might bring a perceived benefit. So for example torture would always be wrong whatever the benefit it might bring (Beckett and Maynard 2005). In order to behave in a way which remains consistent with this principle we also need to apply moral rules universally. This is the second element in Kantian ethics. So if we had a moral rule which required us to be honest then we could not make an exception to this, if in a particular set of circumstances dishonesty might be seen to bring a greater benefit.

Consequentialist approaches to ethics in contrast focus not on the inherent rightness or wrongness of any action, but, as the name suggests, on its consequences in the world. In utilitarianism, the most well-known and developed version of this approach, the moral worth of any action is judged by its capacity to generate happiness, following the principle of utility that faced with an ethical choice we should purse that action which produces 'the greatest happiness for the greatest number' (Mill 1972). So for a consequentialist an act such as lying, which within deontological ethics would be considered morally wrong, might in certain specific circumstances be morally acceptable if it were to generate more happiness in the world than truth-telling. The 'just war' argument, where war is justified because its long-term consequence would be the alleviation of greater suffering, is a classic example of this type of ethical thinking.

When we consider the value base of advocacy both these ethical perspectives come into play. A Kantian approach emphasises the importance of the service user's self-determination and the social worker's role in facilitating that person's wishes.

A utilitarian approach to considering the consequences of any action lays greater stress on the best interest of the service user as it is perceived by the social worker.

The other important element in the social work value-base is the profession's commitment to the goals of social justice, in which anti-discriminatory practice plays a central role. So whilst being attentive to the tensions between deontological and consquentialist perspectives in ethical decision making, social work also needs to operate within a value framework which addresses these principles.

Practice example – Cheryl

The following case study illustrates how some of these issues manifest themselves in practice

Cheryl is a 16-year-old woman who has spent much of her life looked after by the local authority. Over the past four years Cheryl has lived with her aunt, Corrine, in a kinship care arrangement supported by the local authority following periods of time spent in children's homes and in shorter term fostering arrangements. Cheryl was removed from her mother's care aged 11. Her mother, who had had persistent problems throughout her life with drug and alcohol use, had moved to live with a new partner who behaved violently towards her and to Cheryl.

Cheryl is supported by Sandra, a social worker with the leaving care team. Recently Cheryl has been talking to Sandra about leaving home and about moving to her own independent accommodation. A friend of Cheryl's who goes to the same care leavers group run by the local authority has recently moved into a semi-independent bed-sit run jointly by a housing association and a voluntary organisation which provides social support, the Moving On project. Cheryl left school aged 16 and is currently not undertaking any kind of full-time education or training. She has applied to a local further education college to do a course in car mechanics, but her application for this course has been rejected.

Quite a lot of the time Corrine struggles to cope with Cheryl's behaviour at home. She often stays out late at night sometimes not returning home. She has a much older boyfriend who has been verbally, and her aunt suspects physically, abusive towards Cheryl. On one occasion recently Corrine found her in the early hours of the morning slumped outside her front door in the rain, obviously under the influence of drink and possibly drugs. Corrine took her to the local accident and emergency department, where she had her stomach pumped.

Sandra knows that places in the Moving On project rarely come up and that when they do there is a lot of competition for them. To get a place for Cheryl Sandra will have to produce a lengthy report arguing Cheryl's case and to present this to a panel. Without Sandra's active professional support it will be much more difficult for Cheryl to secure a place in the project. Cheryl is adamant that she wants to do this and that she has a right at her age to live independently. Corrine feels she is very vulnerable and will not manage away from home. She is completely willing for Cheryl to live with her for as long as she wants.

Cheryl's situation presents a dilemma for Sandra. She has to choose between two possible options. She can support Cheryl's desire to live independently and wholeheartedly pursue a place for her in the Moving On project, advocating strongly for this course of action. Alternatively she can make a professional judgement that

Cheryl is not at the moment ready to live independently. She may be very vulnerable and even at some risk if she goes to the project. It would therefore be better that Cheryl at this stage in her life does not pursue this option, although it would obviously be a possibility at some point further down the line.

When these two options are considered in the context of deontological and consequentialist ethical frameworks, the first seems more in keeping with a rights based approach to practice. Advocating for a place in the project is consistent with the pursuit of Cheryl's rights to self-determination. Our second option fits better with a utilitarian approach. If Sandra opts for this course of action she is more focused on the consequences of what happens than on the principles underlying her choice.

Another way of thinking about these sorts of dilemmas is by considering the idea of need. Bradshaw in his discussions of the taxonomy of need (Bradshaw 1972) outlines four different ways in which we might understand the concept of need:

- Normative need – what experts, professionals or the agency with power over resources define as need
- Felt need – equated with what we want
- Expressed need – another side of the felt need coin, the demand for a service, or felt need turned into action
- Comparative need – need defined by comparing people in similar circumstances

Sandra is essentially making a judgement in this dilemma about the best way of meeting Cheryl's expressed need, her request to use the Moving On project. Sandra is making a normative decision about what course of action to take and thinking about whether Cheryl's needs are best met through the project. In doing this she is also thinking about issues of comparative need, about the demands for places in the project which outstrip supply and how choices between potential candidates for the project should be decided. So how she advocates on Cheryl's behalf will depend upon her understanding of the issue of need. Schneider and Lester (2001) argue, using a version of the Bradshaw formulation of need, that for social workers there is the potential, by focusing on self-determination and on strengths, to ally the needs of service users and the perspectives of service users. This is an area we will return to when we look at rationing resources later in the chapter.

Representative and subscriptive advocacy and desirability

We have looked elsewhere at the issue of the different ways of understanding advocacy, at the extent to which it is about giving voice, making space for the service user's perspective to be heard, and the extent to which it is about persuasion (promotional advocacy). An analogous distinction also applies to the ethics of advocacy. Audi (1995) argues that there are two types of advocacy: representative and subscriptive advocacy. *Representative advocacy* is archetypically the advocacy that a lawyer might provide for a client. Here the lawyer is voicing the perspective of another person and presenting a case, but not motivated by personal commitment to the position being advocated.

In contrast *subscriptive advocacy* involves a commitment to the cause being pursued. The archetype of this approach would be the concerned citizen lobbying for change of some sort with politicians or policy makers, motivated by a belief in the benefits this would bring. The ethical constraints that apply to each perspective are different. For the representative advocate the primary focus is on the process of advocacy itself. For the subscriptive advocate the object of the advocacy and the moral value/worth of the cause being pursued are of central importance.

Practice example – the hospital advocacy project

An advocacy project based within a large psychiatric hospital deals with a range of issues raised by patients within the hospital. The project is run by a mixture of service users and professionals, and its focus is on self-advocacy. Within the hospital there is a rehabilitation unit which supports patients who are going to be in hospital for longer periods of time with the eventual aim of their being discharged into the community. The independent advocacy service have worked with a number of patients within the unit who have raised concerns about what they see as the over-use of medication, the number of patients receiving ECT and the length of time patients stay on the ward before their eventual discharge. Over the past few years the advocacy service have represented the interests of a number of patients supported by the rehabilitation team and have also made representations to the management of the hospital about the general running of the service.

The advocacy project has been approached by Gerald. He has been in hospital for three years and on the rehabilitation unit for the past two. The rehabilitation team have put in place a plan for Gerald's discharge, which involves him moving to a supportive hostel staffed 24 hours per day and having his medication reduced. Gerald, however, is very resistant to this plan of action. He feels he needs more time on the unit in order to be ready to live independently and, although coping fine with his current level of medication, is anxious that the psychiatrist treating him is not giving him enough medication to ensure he stays well. Gerald is an articulate and able person who worked for a number of years as a solicitor before his mental health problems began about 15 years ago. He has already written to the hospital chief executive and to his MP to raise his concerns. He feels his 'campaign' as he calls it would benefit from input from the independent advocacy service. Interestingly, at a recent meeting between the advocacy service and a group of senior managers within the hospital where the criticisms of the rehabilitation team's policies on discharge and medication were raised, the chief executive of the hospital did point out that this was far from being the consistent view of patients within the service.

This case is a good example of this division between subscriptive and representative advocacy. The hospital advocacy project has an obligation to represent the views of Gerald to those responsible for his care. The work ought to be undertaken in a diligent way. However, it is much more problematic for the hospital advocacy project to subscribe to Gerald's perspective on his treatment in hospital. In fact there is evidence that Gerald's views on his treatment have had a negative impact on the cause based representations the advocacy project has been making to the hospital authorities about the general treatment of patients. Audi (1995) argues that ethical principles that govern these two positions, representative and subscriptive, are different. The focus of representative advocacy is on the service user's rights to have their voice heard and their perspective considered in relation to discussion about medical treatment, and is an important counterbalance to medical paternalism (Thomas and Bracken 1999). The ethics of subscriptive advocacy are governed by the nature of the cause being advocated and for the benefits it might bring. Audi uses the idea of desirability to encompass this idea. For social workers advocating on behalf of service users, desirability principles are important. Where there is congruence between professional perspectives on service users' needs and goals and the aims of the service user themselves, advocacy is a relatively straightforward activity. In circumstances where the primary focus of the work is to enable a service user's voice to be heard and where there is divergence of perspective about how a service user's best interest is served, it is sometimes more difficult for a social worker to undertake an advocacy role. Problems might also exist where what is being sought though advocacy is not consistent with social work values, particularly in relation to anti-discriminatory practice. Some of these issues will be explored further when we look at the relationship between social workers and independent advocates later in the chapter.

Advocacy codes of practice

There are a number of sources to which we need to turn in considering the ethical guidance for advocates. I am going to look at two areas primarily: codes of practice for independent advocates and Bateman's idea of principled advocacy, both of which give value frameworks within which it is suggested that those undertaking advocacy roles should work. My starting point is Bateman's work (Bateman 2000). He identifies six principles which he argues together provide a code of ethics for health and social care professionals acting as advocates. The place of principle within Bateman's overall account of advocacy is crucial. Bateman recognises some of the challenges that social care professionals face when they act as advocates within their broader professional roles. The adoption of a clear value base plays a pivotal role in this aspect of their practice. The crux of his argument is that if professionals are to undertake these roles (which Bateman believes strongly that they should), then they need to do so from a base of principle. Values need to be at the forefront of professionals' analysis and judgement. This goal of Bateman's in outlining a principled approach to advocacy is identified succinctly by Boylan and Dalrymple (2009) as 'trying to get as much as possible for service users without colluding with the oppressive elements of the system' (p13). The principles which Bateman outlines are as follows:

1   Act in the client's best interest
2   Act in accordance with the client's wishes and instructions
3   Keep the client properly informed
4   Carry out instructions with diligence and competence
5   Act impartially and offer frank independent advice
6   Maintain client confidentiality

Bateman's code of practice is interesting in that, like the professional codes of practice covering social work (and other professions like nursing), it addresses both the principles that an professional acting in an advocacy role might use to resolve ethical dilemmas and the expectations we might have professionally of a good advocate. So, loosely, the first two principles address issues to do with service user interest and autonomy or how we might begin to navigate our way through this complex area, the final four cover acting in ways which are in accordance with what we might expect of a competent professional advocate.

I want to begin with the first two elements where Bateman's focus is primarily on general principles guiding practice. We can immediately see here a tension which exists between, on the one hand, principles of autonomy and respect for the wishes and instructions of the service user, and, on the other, the service user's interest. Brandon and Brandon (2001) are highly critical of this aspect of Bateman's principled advocacy arguing that 'the advocate has no business playing about in areas of assumed divinity' (p58). However, Bateman is acknowledging in his code of practice the real tension that practitioners experience within their work, a tension interestingly enough that the examples at the beginning of this chapter illustrate, is not just confined to those undertaking advocacy roles as part of a broader professional brief. However, Bateman's principles do only amount to a statement that both of these factors are germane to ethical decision making in advocacy, without any elaboration of how one might decide between them in circumstances where they are in conflict. It is not clear what factors we should consider when deciding which is the dominant principle: should it be risk, the strength of professional judgement, or the vulnerability or resilience of the service user? However, these two principles are operating in the same territory as elements three and four of the GSCC Code of Practice, which provide a slightly firmer foundation for decision making.

Elements 3 and 4 of Bateman's model focus on diligence and open communication. Here the concern is with how to do advocacy well (or the virtues perhaps of an ethical advocate (Banks 2009)). Finally, Bateman considers impartiality, independence and how to maintain confidentiality.

The distinction between subscriptive and representative approaches to advocacy is worth thinking about when considering Bateman's principles of advocacy. We can see that the first two principles in Bateman's list relate to desirability of outcome and a subscriptive approach. The final four are more orientated towards the question of how to effectively represent the views of others.

The Action for Advocacy's Advocacy Charter provides a code of practice for advocates (Action for Advocacy 2006) which addresses five key areas of principle:

- Clarity of purpose – the boundaries and scope of the advocacy role and the importance of not going beyond these
- Independence – the issue of how to avoid potential conflicts of interest
- Putting people first – not giving advice or making choices on behalf of the service user
- Empowerment – recognising service users' existing skills and supporting people in their development. Ensuring organisations undertaking advocacy have

a commitment to the involvement of the users of their services in their wider
activities.
- Equal opportunity – respecting difference and working within equal opportunities policies

The focus here is much more on a representative model of practice. The concern is
not primarily with the potential conflict between needs and wishes (although the
charter does not always completely distinguish between the two; 'advocates should
ensure advocacy support is appropriate to the service users' needs and/or wishes'
(Action for Advocacy 2006 p8). The Action for Advocacy Charter concerns itself more
with the process of advocacy: how advocacy is effective in a way which is consistent
with a clear value base. For social workers acting as advocates this can be a challenge and
organisational constraints can impact upon the capacity of social workers to operate
effectively as advocates. It is this area which I want to explore now.

The organisational context of social work advocacy

Diligence and the challenges of working in a bureaucracy

Social workers often face a tension between working speedily and efficiently, and operating within a system of bureaucratic rules. The following case example serves to
illustrate some of the issues this raises.

Practice example – the Lawler family

The Lawler family have lived in London for many years but came originally from Glasgow.
Their two children, now 10 and 11 years old, have always had difficulty with school
attendance and sometimes with their behaviour once there. Their parents have experienced
ongoing problems with dependence on drugs and alcohol. As a result social workers have
been periodically involved with the children over a long period of time, although things at
home have been considerably more stable over the past 18 months or so. The local social
services office has been contacted by an advocacy and advice service which the children's
mother has approached, for assistance with a specific issue. Her twin brother has recently
died in Glasgow of a heart attack and she is concerned about the impacts this might have
on the family and on herself and her capacity to cope. He had spent some time living with
the family in London where he'd come to work and the children had got to know him
well. His death has had a substantial impact on the whole family. The parents have already
approached the social services department themselves, but been informed that their case
is not a priority. However, this has been looked at again in the light of the concerns raised
by the advice service and an appointment for assessment has been arranged with a social
worker. The social worker looks with the parents at a range of strategies they might use
in order to support themselves emotionally and helps them to access some appropriate
services. The family have also asked whether it might be possible to get any help with
the costs of the journey to Glasgow for the funeral, planned in a couple of weeks' time.
The social worker is aware that the social services department cannot provide direct help

(continued)

with this request, but is able to approach a local charity which might be able to assist. An application is made to the charity and they are able to provide a cheque covering a substantial part of the travel costs reasonably swiftly. However, the local authority's finance department will not release the money until the cheque is cleared. There is a standard period for this of 10 days. But the funeral is now due to take place in 3 days' time. The local authority remains steadfast in its adherence to this rule, despite representations by the social worker and the advice and advocacy service.

This is an example of bureaucracy within social care organisations, which Malcolm Payne describes as: 'excessive compliance with procedures and regulation so that organisations' purposes are not achieved efficiently' (Payne 2000 p3). In discussing a similar case to the one which we have described he argues that 'any official in any organisation will have gone through something like this' and it is certainly the experience of social workers that bureaucracy can get in the way of the most appropriate outcomes for service users (Evans and Harris 2004). The codes of practice of advocacy set great store by workers operating diligently and efficiently. However, bureaucratic systems working within social care have the potential to restrict their capacity to do this. This is a good example of how difficult it can be to act ethically in circumstances where the scope for independent autonomous decision making is limited (MacBeath and Webb 2002).

The problems that bureaucratic systems can create for social workers can throw up complex practice dilemmas. Payne (2000) examines the ethical choices social workers face in situations similar to the case scenario we have looked at and argues that there may be circumstances in which circumventing bureaucracy, even if this might mean a social worker breaching organisational rules, would be justified. In relation to nursing, Bandman and Bandman (2002) describe this approach as 'guerrilla advocacy' and although important needs to be allied to broader approaches to change the way systems work. Payne goes on to argue that only a social work which is 'citizen responsive' and 'user involved' (Payne 2000 p85) offers the potential of an escape from what are essentially counterproductive bureaucratic systems. If this is to be achieved then social workers individually, and the profession as a whole, need to move practice in this non-managerial and more open direction. We can again see here the link between the experiences of social workers with individual service users and wider concerns to do with the nature and direction of professional practice. This underlies the importance of making the link between cases and causes and the duty that social workers have to lobby for change at all levels as part of an advocacy orientated approach to practice.

Whistle-blowing

All of this does not mean that social workers have to accept the perspective of the organisation for which they work in relation to their practice. The GSCC Code of Practice states that social workers must 'use established processes and procedures to challenge and report dangerous, abusive, discriminatory or exploitative behaviour and practice' (GSCC 2002 p5). As we shall see, doing this is often far from straightforward, and when internal mechanisms for reporting and dealing with bad practice are exhausted social workers have an ethical duty to take their concerns outside their organisations and to 'blow the whistle' on what is going on.

Whistle-blowing and obedience

Milgram's obedience study and the Stanford Prison experiment

In the 1960s social psychologists became increasingly interested in obedience. The horrors of the Nazi and Soviet genocides, where acts of almost unimaginable brutality were carried out by ordinary people obeying orders, in part prompted this interest. The Vietnam War's My Lai Massacre also served to focus attention in the USA on this area. Milgram's prototypical experiment (Milgram 1963) on conformity has attracted more attention than perhaps any other in social psychology and has been replicated on many occasions in a range of cultural contexts (Wade and Tavris 2000). The aim of the experiment was to investigate how willing people would be to behave unethically if ordered to do so by an authority figure. Participants in the experiment were told that they were taking part in an investigation into the impacts of punishment on learning. They believed that subjects in the experiment had been randomly assigned to either the role of teacher or learner. In fact learners were confederates of Milgram and part of the experiment. Teachers in the experiment were instructed to give learners (who were seated in a separate room and attached to electrodes) a shock, by operating a lever, when they made errors in reciting pairs of words they were meant to have learned. Their instructions came from an experimenter, dressed as a scientist in a white coat. Teachers were instructed to give increasingly severe shocks, ranging from a level marked slight shock to danger, severe shock and finally 435–450 volts. As the level of shock increased learners had been instructed to cry out in pain and ask for the experiment to be stopped. 62.5% of those involved in the experiment were willing to carry on and give shocks at the 450 volt level.

   In the Stanford Prison experiment (Hanay, Banks and Zimbardo 1973) student volunteers were randomly assigned the roles of prisoner or guard in a mock prison created by the Stanford University psychology department. Prisoners wore prison uniform and guards military khaki. Under these experimental conditions prisoners became increasingly passive, demoralised and apathetic, and guards more abusive and authoritarian. After 6 days the experiment was abandoned because of the psychological impacts it was having on prisoners. Both of these experiments illustrate the power of social situations and their capacity to invoke obedience to authority and make people behave in ways that are clearly wrong. Being able to assign responsibility for our actions elsewhere, to an authority figure, is one classical element of obedience. The routinisation of morally reprehensible behaviour, focusing on doing the job of getting the experiment done or helping the prison run efficiently, also enables people to shut out the ethical concerns they may have about it. Finally, we often lack the skills to break the complex sets of social rules which push us towards obedience.

   When whistle-blowing takes place professionals who reveal bad practice of whatever sort are giving voice to issues facing the most vulnerable. Pilgrim (1995) argues that it is those who are least valued by society and most isolated within the health and social care system that are often caught within what he calls 'layers of isolation' and are most vulnerable to abuse and neglect. This contention is supported by some of the research that exists into the experience of abuse by multiply disadvantaged and excluded groups; children with disabilities for example are particularly isolated and particularly vulnerable (Utting 1997). We can therefore see whistle-blowing as part of the continuum of advocacy, in that it can play a crucial role in giving voice to concerns of service users and carers when other channels of communication have failed and either where those service users are unable to voice concerns or where those concerns have been ignored. Hence, Mike Cox argues that we should see whistle-blowing as an essential social work function and that 'whistle blowing and accountability in the annals of social work training are located around the tradition of advocacy' (Cox 1998 p189). Brandon and Brandon (2001) identify whistle-blowing as a key part of social work advocacy at the macro level.

An eye cast over the extent of institutional abuse within social care in recent years (particularly of children placed within supposedly safe environments (Levy and Kahan 1991, Kirkwood, 1993, White and Hart 1995, Waterhouse 2000)) can only generate a sense of profound disquiet with the inability of social work to protect the most vulnerable (Corby et al. 2001). For all those of us who have devoted our professional lives to social work it must be a source of sadness. Institutional environments have always left vulnerable people prey to abuse (although in the more distant past such abuse has often been kept hidden (Smart 2000)). However, the issue of whistle-blowing when faced with poor practice is about more than the most obvious examples of the abuse of users of social care services. Preston-Shoot (2000) argues that social workers operate in environments where their professional judgements are subject to ever increasing oversight and control, the product of greater financial constraint and a managerialist approach to practice. In these conditions the pressure on social workers to go outside of their employing authorities to seek to resolve important ethical issues about the quality of services increases all the time. One slight source of professional solace in the face of these catalogues of abuse and bad practice is the role social workers have undertaken in whistle-blowing.

There are many recent instances of whistle-blowers within social work being dealt with severely by employers. Mark Hunter (2009) cites the cases of a number of social workers who have been dismissed by employers, most notably Simon Belwood and Nevres Kemal, despite their disclosures clearly being in the public interest and the subsequent vindication of their action. The case of Alison Taylor, who was sacked for revealing evidence of child abuse in North Wales children's homes, provides an interesting model of how whistle-blowing impacts upon the practitioner and how organisations respond to it (Taylor 1998). Taylor, the manager of a home run by Gwynedd Council, approached the police in response to 'wide spread allegations about the abuse of children in care' (Taylor 1998 p41) which had come to her attention, after attempts to raise the issue with her superiors had led to no action being taken. Taylor's experience is typical of that of many whistle-blowers (Hunt 1998). Utting (1997) identified the risks to staff who had taken their concerns beyond the boundaries of their organisations: 'Where staff have pressed complaints they risked ridicule in some cases ostracism and worse' (Utting 1997 p157). This was very much Taylor's experience, treated initially as a maverick and then quickly as a troublemaker. The denial with which her claims were met is also typical. Cox (1998) offers an explanation for the resistance with which whistle-blowing is met within social care agencies. He argues that social workers have lost 'the profound reforming stance of nineteenth century practitioners' (p189) and that lines of accountability have moved increasingly from accountability to professional role to accountability to organisation. This is in part a response to the diminution of social workers' professional autonomy (Preston-Shoot 2000). The culture therefore within organisations is for staff to be seen not as professionals with a duty to uphold professional values, but as employees whose primary responsibility is to the organisation which employees them. These organisational attitudes and values make it more difficult for adequate support to be given those who want to reveal bad practice and abuse.

Milgram's work underlines the challenges that whistle-blowing presents to professionals and the profound difficulties which going against organisational policy can represent. Psychologically our natural response when confronted with bad practice can be to acquiesce and we need to be aware of this tendency. The Public Interest Disclosure Act (1998) has established a legal framework for whistle-blowing, protecting workers from reprisals in circumstances where they raise concerns about malpractice, both within and beyond their employing organisations, where the disclosure is in the public interest. Malpractice under the Act includes breaches of the law, and dangers to health, safety and the environment, a definition broad enough to include the types of serious concerns a social worker might have about their employing organisation. Preston-Shoot (2000) looks at some of the key factors that those contemplating whistle-blowing might appropriately consider over and above the Act itself. Whistle-blowers need to be aware of the law and policy and practice guidance. These can be a potential source of objective standards against which malpractice might be judged. The research base of practice might also be an important guide to when disclosure might be appropriate. Hunter (2009) emphasises the importance of maintaining an accurate record and audit trail in relation to malpractice. Prospective whistle-blowers would also be well advised to seek support from trade unions and bodies with a specific remit to support whistle-blowers: Public Concern at Work and Freedom to Care for example.

A recent GSCC poll (GSCC 2009) shows that most staff within social services are still fearful of the professional consequences of whistle-blowing. Yet its importance particularly in the context of inquiries into residential child care cannot be underestimated (Berridge and Brodie 1996). A consistent theme of inquiries into institutional abuse has been the importance of establishing clear mechanisms to allow staff to raise matters of concern:

> Every local authority should establish and implement conscientiously clear whistleblowing procedures enabling members of staff to make complaints and raise matters of concern affecting the treatment or welfare of looked after children without threats or fear of reprisals in any form.
>
> (Waterhouse 2000)

There is clearly some distance to go before this aspiration becomes a reality.

Whistle-blowing is a rather extreme example of the problems of working within bureaucratic systems. However, being an advocate as a social worker presents a range of other challenges. The sorts of bureaucratic rules that can exist within local authority social service departments can have an impact on the capacity of social workers undertaking advocacy to fulfil this role completely effectively. We are going to examine two of these areas in greater detail: the impacts of bureaucratic rules and the issue of rationing in social care. In both these situations there are potential clashes between the values of social work and advocacy, and constraints imposed by organisational systems and rules.

Advocacy, rationing and the management of resources

One key area where social workers face challenges from external advocates is in relation to decisions they make around the rationing of services. A good example of the role played by disability advocacy services is the Gloucester Judgement, where disabled service users successfully challenged a local authority decision to withdraw services they were receiving. Resources within social work, whether in the statutory or voluntary sector, are of necessity finite, and as a consequence managing such limited resources will mean that some of those who approach social services for assistance will be refused help. The role of social workers within this system is interesting. At first sight it can appear that responsibility for rationing is divided between social workers and the organisation for which they work. So social workers might be seen as having a primarily bureaucratic role in evaluating need. The establishment of a mechanism for judging between the varying demands of different cases and deciding which should be funded could be seen as lying with managers. In this account of rationing social workers are primarily bureaucratic functionaries.

However, this is perhaps a rather simplistic way of thinking about of the rationing process in that it suggests that frontline social work staff do not have a major role to play in rationing. There are two main problems with this version of rationing. Firstly, this view of social workers underplays the ways in which 'the face-to-face communication that workers experience can have a high impact on decision making' (Payne 2000 p48). Their specific knowledge of the precise circumstances of the service user is particularly influential where rationing decisions are being made. Even at the point of initial assessment of need social workers can exclude potential services users from service (Baldwin 2000). Secondly, to assume that social workers merely provide information on cases and managers then decide whether the case meets some sort of abstract criteria for the receipt of a service ignores the broader professional responsibilities that social workers have. It is the reality of social care that resources are finite and judgements will have to be made between competing demands on budgets. It seems an abdication of professional responsibility for social workers to limit their role in this process. After all it is they who know the service user best and who will have devoted their time and professional expertise to careful assessment of the service user's situation incorporating a full record of his or her perspective. As Payne (2000 p48) points out it is not uncommon for professionals to be actively involved in these types of decisions. Both doctors and lawyers commonly ration the resources available to them and this is seen as an integral part of their professional role.

If we accept, as I think we have to, that there is a social work role to play in rationing then this in itself generates some important dilemmas for practitioners, between the competing demands of advocacy and fairness. In relation to rationing, the position of the social worker is far from clear and can generate some complex practice dilemmas. Is the role of the social worker to advocate on behalf of all clients to maximise the chances of a service user obtaining the resources they want, or should social workers accept that they need to also take account of issues of fairness and acknowledge that some of those approaching social services for help will be denied services and that this will be an ethical decision? The first of these courses of action is most consistent with a rights based approach to practice, a largely Kantian approach, where decisions are looked at largely on their immediate merits rather than through scrutinising their broader consequences. The second is more in keeping with the principles of utility, which seeks to maximise well-being through the most effective distribution of a limited resource. A social worker appears to have two duties here, to 'advocate for service users and contribute towards her agency being fair and non-discriminatory', which potentially 'pull in different directions' (Becket and Maynard 2005 p97).

Becket and Maynard point out that advocating for every service user assessed can be a difficult course of action for social workers (Becket and Maynard 2005). It could for example lead a worker to exaggerate the level of risk a family faces in order to access resources. However, this could lead to families being labelled as, say, 'child protection cases' through a social worker's pursuit of resources to meet their needs. They argue that social workers have a duty of realism in relation to their work. Essentially this commits social workers to pragmatic responses to the needs of service users with which they are presented in the course of professional practice. This duty as it relates to advocacy means that the decisions to advocate for resources that social workers make need to be considered within the context of the needs of service users and guided by the principles which govern the fair allocation of limited resources.

However, it is important to remember that social work has a 'global concern to remedy the defects of resources and social relations in the sphere of everyday life' (Clark 2000 p77) and there are as a consequence two sides to questions of advocacy, rationing and social justice. On the one hand social workers' decisions about advocacy on the behalf of individuals ought to be consistent with Becket and Maynard's principle of realism. Running alongside this, however, there is also a professional responsibility to draw attention to the broader impacts of rationing decisions as they relate to whole communities of need. Social workers have a duty to advocate collectively for the collective needs of service users, who are excluded from access to services because of rationing (albeit rationing carried out according to principles of fairness). This is consistent with a progressive view of social welfare (Rojek et al. 1989, Mullaly 1993) and with the principles of anti-discriminatory practice, where social work is viewed as more than just a mechanism for providing services to meet the needs of consumers, but rather as an activity with the potential to also drive social change. So cause advocacy at the macro level, undertaken by social workers in relation the service users they work with, is also a key element in social workers' professional practice as advocates (Brandon and Brandon 2001).

If we return to our earlier case study, Cheryl's case, then we can see how this might work. Sandra has an important role in determining access to the Moving On project as her recommendations will influence the decisions made as to who gets a place in the project and who does not. She is also aware of issues of fairness in making decisions about how she undertakes this advocacy role; places in the project are limited and ought to go to those who are most likely to make a success of placement there. However, Sandra (and her colleagues in the leaving care team) will also be aware of the overall demand that exists for independent supported accommodation for young people who have been through the care system, and the need for more accommodation providing a wider range of support. This offers an opportunity for her and her colleagues to lobby decision makers within the local authority and voluntary sector, for an approach to this service user group which better meets their needs and which is adequately resourced. Service users, social workers and their independent advocates have common interests at this level and their combined efforts have the potential to change the nature and extent of service provision.

Our discussions up to this point have both identified some of the ethical dilemmas which social workers and independent advocates can face in their practice and some of the common ground that they share. We have also looked at some of the constraints that the professional context of advocacy can place on social workers. One thing this serves to underline is the importance of independent advocacy in the working lives of social workers.

Working alongside professional advocates

Working with carers' advocates: confidentiality and best interest

We have already looked in some detail at the challenges presented by differing conceptions of best interest and the place this plays within advocacy. However, one interesting way in which dilemmas in this area can play themselves out is in the interactions between advocates representing the views of carers, and professionals with responsibility for supporting the cared-for person. Disparities in the views of carers and service users can exist in all areas of social work and, as Gorman points out in relation to older people, 'carers' needs may differ from service users' needs and there is a potential for conflict' (Gorman 2009 p94). It is perhaps in the area of mental health where issues about the place of carers' participation in care and treatment are most problematic. One key finding of the Clunis Inquiry Report (Ritchie et al. 1994), which reviewed the care and treatment Christopher Clunis received from psychiatric services following the death of Jonathan Zito at his hands in 1994, was that mental health professionals paid insufficient regard to the views of carers and relatives in their decision making. As Tony Maden points out 'although he (Christopher Clunis) had a caring and supportive family with whom he maintained contact throughout, services made no attempt to involve them in his care' (Maden 2007). There continues to be evidence that many mental health professionals continue to disregard the views of carers (Hervey and Ramsay 2004, Rapaport et al. 2006b) and that carers are involved peripherally in decisions about care if at all (Rethink 2003). The main reason that professionals give for with-holding information from carers is confidentiality and 'a particularly testing issue is when the service user objects to the family's involvement although their inclusion appears to be justified to professionals' (Rapaport et al. 2006b). A scenario with which many mental health professionals will be familiar is the call from an advocate on be-half of a close and caring relative, expressing concerns about how well a service user is coping in the community. However, the worker has clearly been told by the service user that they do not want their father/mother/sibling playing any part in their care. There are no straightforward answers to the dilemmas these circumstances can create, but it is of value to explore both the ethical underpinnings of this situation and the practical approaches that can be taken to address it.

How does keeping service user information confidential from carers relate to the classic Kantian/utilitarian ethical divide within social work, the starting point for this chapter? Principles to do with respect for service users' wishes and autonomy, and respect for confidentiality as an overriding principle have their source primarily in the Kantian view of ethics. However, the dilemma for professionals here is that they are bound both by this respect for service user autonomy embodied in the principle of confidentiality and a need to serve the best interests of the service user, which might be best addressed by a more active consideration and engagement with carers' perspect-ives. Carers of people with mental health problems themselves identify advocacy as an important way of ensuring their voices are heard (Rethink 2003). The experience of independent advocates supporting carers can be a very difficult one. They can face a wall of silence or only a simple acknowledgement of the fact that concerns they have raised have been noted. Professionals themselves may be working in circumstances where service users have specifically asked that their families are not involved in their care. There are however ways of working through this apparent impasse. Social workers need to be aware of the limits of confidentiality, of when pursuing the best interests of the service user overrides its strictures. In mental health (as in other areas of social work) there are legal structures which enable the voice of the carer to be considered in certain specific circumstances. The Mental Health Act (1983) makes provision for the nearest relative of a service user to request a formal assessment under the act of the service user's mental health. Social workers have a professional obligation to ensure that they make carers' advocates aware of this provision. Rapaport et al. (2006b) emphasise the importance of carers' involvement throughout the process of care planning, and one part of this is engagement with carers' advocacy from the start when all parties involved are most receptive to this idea. It is important also that a full multidisciplinary discussion takes place of concerns raised by carers when risks have been identified, and that it is incorporated into formal plans for risk assessment and management (Morgan 2000). This enables a stronger sense of where thresholds around confidentiality might lie in relation to risk which can then be made explicit to all.

As I argued in Chapter 3 independent advocacy is now a much more pervasive presence within social care. The greater focus on children's rights and the new agendas around personalisation in adult care have increased the need for advocacy services. For social workers and other professionals this raises the increasingly important question of what sorts of values should govern social worker's dealings with independent advocacy services. As we have seen, the interactions can be challenging to social workers and other professionals and at times frustrating for independent advocates particularly given the common interests in positive outcomes for service users which they share. The following (far from exhaustive) list constitutes an outline of some of the key principles which govern this area.

Principles for working with independent advocates

Understand and be aware of the limits of your own skill

One crucial decision which social workers have to make when contemplating under-taking an advocacy role is when they should do this themselves and when they should pass this role to an independent advocate. This is an area which was addressed to some extent in Chapter 2. One key factor social workers need to be aware of in respect of this question is the extent to which they are competent to carry out an advocacy role. This is a professional responsibility for practitioners to 'recognise when outside help is required and know the limits of their expertise' (Bateman 2000 p56). However, it does not mean that practitioners have carte blanche to ignore advocacy altogether. As we will see, building expertise and skills in advocacy is another facet of becoming an advocacy friendly practitioner.

Do not advocate where there is potential for conflict of interest

One difficult decision that practitioners need to make is identifying circumstances where there might be some conflict between the broader professional social work role and the role of an advocate which could be undertaken within it. Brandon and Brandon (2001) draw attention to the challenge that advocating within a broader professional role can present for social workers and the possibilities which exist for conflicts of interest. The concept of role consistency (Audi 1995) is quite a useful one here. Where there is a consistency between professional role, perspective and what is being advo-cated, when advocacy is subscriptive, then the issue of conflicts of interest is much less likely to intrude. However, a range of possible conflicts do exist (Boylan and Dalrymple 2009). As we have already argued, service users and social workers can have differing perceptions of how the service user's best interests are most effectively addressed. In these circumstances it is important that service users have access to independent advo-cacy to ensure their voice is heard. There is also the potential for organisational issues to impact upon the capacity of social workers to act as advocates. As we have seen in our discussion of whistle-blowing it is not always straightforward for social workers to advocate for courses of action which run contrary to the policies of the organisations for which they work.

Be open and honest in dealing with advocates

Dealing straightforwardly with service users is as we have seen something that is em-phasised strongly in the codes of practice of independent advocacy. It is also important that social workers adopt the principles of open communication when working with advocates. This can be difficult to achieve where the organisations for which they work are threatened by independent advocacy and wish to restrict the information available to independent advocates in order to protect their own interests. The tensions between commitment to one's organisation and the professional values of openness and honesty can be a potential challenge for social workers endeavouring to work in an open way.

Recognise and support the need for independent advocacy

Independent advocacy impacts upon the professional world of the social worker in two ways. Firstly, advocacy is part of the social worker's day-to-day professional life. Social workers operate alongside advocates all the time and their practice and the decisions they make are subject to the scrutiny which independent advocacy brings. Secondly, the organisations which employ social workers, most importantly local authorities, do themselves have broader policies and strategies directed at advocacy services which they fund. Social workers have a part to play in supporting, promoting and shaping these services. Social workers who want to support independent advocacy in their practice need to embrace two approaches which relate to these two elements of their work. In their everyday work they need to adopt what I would call advocacy sensitive practice. In the ways in which they relate to their organisations they need to promote what could be termed a culture of advocacy (Henderson and Pochin 2001).

Commit to developing knowledge and skills in relation to advocacy

We know from Chapter 1 that advocacy is a key element of social work practice. Yet there is a danger that it can be seen as a peripheral part of the social work task, which can be passed over to separate independent advocacy services to undertake, despite the commitment within the professional practice standards to an approach to social work where advocacy plays an integral role. One of greatest strengths of social work is that it offers the potential for a holistic approach to supporting people. Advocacy can play an important role in empowering practice as an element of a more broadly based intervention. To make effective use of independent advocacy social workers need to commit to developing their own knowledge and skills in this area. So, for example, appropriate referral to welfare rights services requires a knowledge of this area, of the limits of the practitioners own skills and of the resources available to address the specific needs of the services user.

Establish mechanisms to ensure the views and perspectives of service users are recognised within their organisations

Despite the fact that there is an increasing recognition of the importance of service users' views in shaping social work practice, progress towards the establishment of methods to enable this aspiration to be realised is slow (Croft and Bresford 1993, Bresford 2001). Boylan and Dalrymple (2009) acknowledge the link between individual advocacy and wider strategies to ensure that the voices of service users are able to influence practice and policy. Brandon and Brandon (2001) argue that there are two elements to social work advocacy: the first is the direct representation of service users' advocacy at the micro level; the second is engagement at the macro level with the broader organisational and political spheres to support the goals of advocacy. An advocacy friendly approach to practice is supportive of the establishment of participatory mechanisms within organisations, 'particularly targeting people who are excluded at present, those who are hard to reach or seldom heard' (Adams 2008 p145).

Support and lobby more widely to help the collective views and needs of service users to be recognised

Finally an important part of supporting advocacy is engagement with local campaigning and lobbying. Beresford and Postle (2007) argue that social work ought to be 'citizen-based' and its aims allied with the principles of participatory democracy. For social workers this means work with individuals in social need, supporting wider goals of social inclusion and social justice. This perspective is consistent with Brandon and Brandon's (2001) idea of advocacy encompassing work with service users indirectly at the macro level through local community based campaigning. This broader concept of advocacy Beresford and Postle argue is a crucial part of the social worker's role consistent with 'building capacity with groups of people using services and thus enabling them to work autonomously' (Beresford and Postle 2007 p155). Thus advocacy ought to have the capacity to move social work towards what Mayo terms a 'transformational' stand point where communities are empowered to 'develop strategies and build alliances for social change' (Mayo 2002 p 164).

'Because social work's particular specialism is working with groups of people who are oppressed, discriminated against or marginalised by society it is particularly important that social work values should emphasise a commitment to social justice' (Beckett and Maynard 2005 p81). One way in which social work can pursue this aspect of its ethical base is through advocacy grounded in a broader project centred around an engagement with wider social issues.

Key learning points

- One central dilemma that social workers face when undertaking advocacy is managing the tension between service users' desires and wishes and their own professional view of service users' best interests.
- Advocacy can be both a subscriptive and representative activity. *Representative advocacy* involves the presentation of the perspectives of others to those making decisions. The best interests of those involved are not central to this process. In *subscriptive advocacy* there is a consistency between the service user's and the social worker's perception of best interest. It is more straightforward in ethical terms for advocates in general and social workers in particular to operate with a subscriptive framework.

- Working within large organisations presents a number of challenges to social workers undertaking advocacy, particularly in relation to bureaucratic constraints on practice, managing the rationing of resources and ultimately whistle-blowing.
- Working alongside independent advocates can be challenging for social work practitioners and generate a range of ethical dilemmas. Carers' advocacy is one area where differences of view between carers and service users can present ethical dilemmas. Some key principles ought to govern the interface between social work and independent advocacy. Advocacy is a part of social work practice which is consistent with the principles of social justice, and effectively engaging with independent advocacy services is an important way in which social workers can begin to address the goals of social justice within their work.

Further reading

Action for Advocacy (2006) *The Advocacy Charter*, London, Action for Advocacy

Bateman, N. (2000) *Advocacy Skills for Health and Social Care Professionals*, London, Jessica Kingsley

Brandon, D. and Brandon, T. (2001) *Advocacy in Social Work*, Birmingham, Venture Press

Hunt, G. (ed.) (1998) *Whistleblowing in the Social Services*, London, Arnold

Milgram, S. (1963) Behavioural Study of Obedience, *The Journal of Abnormal and Social Psychology*, 67(4), 371–378

Parrot, L. (2010) *Values and Ethics in Social Work Practice*, Exeter, Learning Matters

5 Advocacy Practice Models

Introduction

One helpful way of understanding advocacy is as a process and it is perhaps not surprising therefore that most of those who have written about advocacy and social work have produced models of this process. This is I think partly a hangover from advocacy's legalistic roots. Advocacy is often seen a lay version of legal process and consequently needing a similar formalised structure. However, working within the parameters of a clear process is often very helpful for both service user and social worker. Social work is an activity where issues of power are very much to the fore. Those in whose lives social workers are involved are often very disadvantaged and disempowered. As Sheppard (2006 p40) points out: 'The space occupied by social work is defined by its position in the interface between the mainstream and the marginal in society. It can be no surprise therefore that social work involves those that are poorest most disadvantaged and marginalised.' Social workers' practice needs to be carried out within a framework that is sensitive to issues of power. Advocacy is no exception to this and, as an area that is often seen as having the capacity to empower, needs to address empowerment within its processes.

This chapter therefore starts with an exploration of current process models of advocacy and proposes a simplified more fluid account of the process, in which the concept of mutuality is addressed. It goes on to explore powerlessness and the concept of empowerment and at how it can be incorporated into models of the advocacy process. Advocacy's importance within social work is in part because it offers a very direct way of pursuing the aims of anti-discriminatory practice through empowerment. This chapter explores the relationship between these two concepts and the process model presented here shows how advocacy can be used to work towards anti-discriminatory goals. The potential of task centred approaches to social work to act as a vehicle for advocacy is looked at, before finally a consideration of models of cause advocacy.

Models of the advocacy process

Process models are very useful in social work. Within social work theory there exist a number of process models of practice. Crisis intervention (Caplan 1965, Roberts 2005) for example is informed by an underlying understanding of crisis as a process in which a new and unfamiliar set of circumstances impact upon the person seeking help, disrupting their emotional and cognitive equilibrium. Managing the crisis involves a staged process the end point of which is the development and implementation of an action plan and the return to a more balanced psychological state. Similarly in the closely related area of working with loss and grief a staged model helps both social work practitioner and service user work towards some sort of resolution of the immediate distress caused by the loss (Currer 2007, Weinstein 2008). Later in this chapter we will look at task centred work which again follows a particular standardised process of intervention and as we shall see shares some common ground with advocacy (Doel and Marsh 1992).

Brandon and Brandon (2001) and Bateman (2000) both regard advocacy as a staged process. Bateman presents us with a six stage model comprising the following elements:

- The presentation of the problem
- Information gathering
- Research
- Interpretation and feedback to the client
- Active negotiation and advocacy
- Litigation and appeals

Brandon's model incorporates similar stages:

- The presentation of the service user's situation. At this stage in the advocacy the process itself is outlined and the service user describes the problem they have. The advocate explains the context of the problem, and 'relevant systems, complaints procedures appeals machinery . . . relevant legislation' (Brandon and Brandon 2001 p68).
- An investigation and information finding stage. Here further information is sought and the parameters of the problem explored.
- A process of negotiation.
- (Depending upon the outcome of the negotiation), litigation and recourse to formal means of address.
- Finally, an evaluation of the process as a whole.

Brandon and Brandon build into their model the rather legalistic idea of the advocate taking instructions at two points: after the completion of the first stage, and again once the investigation and information finding stages of the process have been completed.

The strengths and weaknesses of current process models

There are a number of reasons why an established process is helpful in social work in general and in advocacy in particular. Firstly, having a process gives clarity to an intervention. Both service user and social worker will be aware of how things will proceed and the expected timescales within which the stages of the process will be accomplished; 'agreeing deadlines to achieve goals is more effective than open-ended time-scales' (Doel and Best 2008 p47). The positive impacts of timescales are one reason for the relative effectiveness of task centred practice in social work (Reid and Epstein 1972, Doel and Marsh 1992). Process, however, provides more than just a clear time-frame. It gives both worker and service user a common basis for understanding the nature of the intervention and a clear sense of what the end point might be. This can be empowering for the service user. Advocacy is a systematic activity involving quite complex tasks and often requiring some strategic planning. Clarity of structure helps the worker with these processes. One of the strengths of Bateman, and Brandon and Brandon's models is that both are relatively simple and straightforward to understand, which aids transparency. Furthermore, having an idea of possible outcomes is an important part of evaluating the impacts of advocacy with individuals. So a process gives both social worker and service user a clear sense of the nature and purpose of an intervention and of its boundaries.

As we have seen there are real strengths to an approach to advocacy which is built on a clear and easily understood process, and both the models we have considered achieve this. However, when we think about advocacy within the context of social work practice, we can begin to identify some of the weaknesses of the two (quite similar) models we are considering.

A good starting point for this is the distinction between the representative and enabling models of advocacy practice. To recap, a *representative model* of advocacy is based upon the idea of the advocate speaking for the service user presenting his or her views to a decision making forum. An *enabling model* aims to work towards the goal of the service user being supported to make representations on their own behalf. If our goal in advocacy is to enable then we may need a model of advocacy which is consistent with empowerment and there is scope to look at the process of advocacy in a way which is a little more consistent with this goal.

In social work advocacy often forms part of a broader intervention. Social work and health care professionals' perspective on service users is a holistic one. In addition to the goals of advocacy a social work intervention will be concerned with psychological well-being and social interaction. At the centre of this process is the idea of partnership working, which is such an important part of the ethos of social work (Stevenson and Parsloe 1993, Braye 2000). Interestingly independent advocates do have to adopt a broader perspective in certain settings. Best interest advocacy undertaken within the framework of the Mental Capacity Act involves the IMCA looking beyond interactions with an individual, and the adoption of a wider more holistic perspective on the individual to ensure their best interest is addressed (Brown and Barber 2005). In Bateman and Brandon's work the idea of partnership is present but could have a more explicit role in the advocacy process model. The emphasis is on the expert knowledge of the advocate, and within it the role of the service user is rather passive. It is the advocate who at the first stage of the process brings their expertise to bear, and knows where to go to undertake further research and what type of research might be appropriate. This mimics the structure of our interactions with legal representatives. If we consider an archetypical legal intervention then it follows a similar pattern. We pay to engage a lawyer. The lawyer looks at our case and makes an initial judgement as to what the best course of action to follow is and takes initial instructions. There follows investigation on behalf of the lawyer and then further instructions from the client, and a formal legal process in which the lawyer leads. This is a traditional approach to the law in which 'the lawyer is an autonomous agent whose task is to take control of the client's social problem and translate it into a legal one and resolve it' (Maughan and Webb 2005 p141). There are a number of difficulties with this expert/client approach:

- For the client in this framework they only develop their own skills in a limited way. They learn something about accessing a solicitor and how to seek help, but I am not sure how far they develop skills and knowledge to manage their problem more effectively in the future.
- This is a process with an individualistic orientation and does not make links between the difficulties faced by an individual and the wider collective interests of groups and communities.
- The goal of enablement can get lost within the process.

For a social worker advocating on behalf of a service user this process can seem a very linear one. Social workers are often advocating on behalf of people who lack confidence, particularly when dealing with complex bureaucracy, in situations when they are very likely to feel disempowered. For someone in these circumstances the importance of consultation and feedback as part of the advocacy process cannot be overestimated. The outlines and definitions of problems which serve as the starting point of advocacy can often be unclear and need further definition and refinement. It may be that service users' understandings of the problems they face may change as the process of advocacy unfolds. Advocacy within social work also takes place within a practice context where supervision is an important mechanism supporting practice.

Mutuality

A key concept used by Schneider and Lester (2001) to capture the nature of this social work advocacy role is mutuality. They use the idea of mutuality to describe the relationship between service user and social worker in advocacy. Schneider and Lester (p167) explain the ethos of mutuality in the following way: 'social workers should understand that they are obligated to advocate not only for clients but with them as well'. Mutuality describes the nature of the relationship between social worker and service user. Schneider and Lester argue that the relationship should be:

- Reciprocal
- Interdependent
- Equal
- Joint

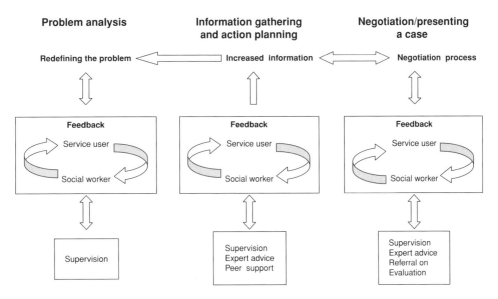

Figure 5.1 A process model of advocacy

It should also involve a sharing of 'collaborative responsibility' (p166) between service user and social worker.

As I have already argued it is obviously important to have a clear structure within which advocacy is undertaken. What would an approach to the process of advocacy which incorporated the idea of mutuality look like? The essential elements of Bateman and Brandon's accounts of the advocacy process can be seen as: problem analysis; investigation, information gathering and action planning; negotiation; and potentially seeking formal redress. Looking in more detail at each of these stages we can begin to see what mutuality might mean at each of them.

Figure 5.1 shows a process model of advocacy which attempts to incorporate the idea of mutuality and to focus upon partnership working. As we can see the model is a simplified three stage approach to the advocacy process, with scope at each stage for service user and social worker to feedback to one another and to go back to a previous stage if necessary. At each stage of the model additional reflective tools and resources for both service user and advocate are identified, including supervision, expert advice, peer support, referral to specialist services and evaluation.

Problem analysis

At this stage in the advocacy process the social worker is considering three key areas. Firstly, she or he is interested in the nature and scope of the problem itself. How amenable is it to an intervention based around advocacy? Is the social worker the best person to undertake this advocacy, do they have sufficient expertise, are there any potential conflicts of interest in their role? What is the background history to this problem and how far has the service user been able to address it themselves?

Secondly, the social worker will be focusing on communication and facilitating a dialogue with the service user. The process of advocacy will be discussed and made explicit and the social worker will help the service user tell their story, which is crucial in obtaining a full picture of the problem for which they are seeking help. Help-seeking itself can be a challenging undertaking for anyone and the social worker needs to be attuned to the challenges this can present.

Finally, at this stage the social worker is looking with the service user at their strengths, their previous positive experiences of successfully sorting out problems in their lives, and resources available within their social networks which could help support them in advocacy. Approaches drawn from solution focused approaches to social work can be helpful in this context (Parton and O'Byrne 2000). Service users seeking help from social services can feel quite disempowered and certainly techniques such as exception finding, looking at previous circumstances where service users have negotiated similar issues successfully, have a value in relation to advocacy.

Investigation, information gathering and action planning

Traditionally investigation and information gathering roles have been viewed as something the advocate undertakes, reporting back to their client once this process is complete and then being instructed by the advocate client whether and how to proceed. Within an advocacy process informed by the principles of mutuality, the social worker would look at which tasks he or she should undertake and which are best undertaken by the service user. When this information is brought together the process moves into an action planning phase, which looks forward to negotiations to come and at the roles service user and social worker will play within it.

There is a danger in advocacy that feedback can be seen as a one way process, with the advocate reporting back on progress made and seeking affirmation from the service user that the advocacy is moving in a direction which is consistent with their wishes. The idea of mutuality involves a greater sharing of tasks and feedback in both directions, from service user to advocate and vice versa.

Presenting a case and negotiation

Finally, in negotiation itself it is important to consider whether the aim for the social worker and service user is that the service user's views be represented by another person or that the social worker works to enable the voice of the service user to be heard. There may of course be circumstances where both of these things happen. This is a stage at which peer support may also be important in underpinning the process of negotiation. Once the outcome of the negotiation is known, there is the potential for the case to be referred on into a more formal process of litigation, for example, or if a satisfactory resolution of the problem is achieved at this stage then the intervention will need to be evaluated, a reflective process involving service user and social worker. At this point the links between individual issues and collective causes can also be explored.

Advocacy and empowerment

The connections between advocacy and empowerment are something which a number of writers on empowerment have highlighted (Braye and Preston-Shoot 1995, Brandon 1995a, Payne 2005, Adams 2008). As Adams points out 'all aspects of advocacy and self-advocacy are potentially empowering' (2008 p13).

In social work the term empowerment is used in two ways. Firstly, empowerment can be seen as an aspiration, a goal or end point of a social work intervention, or indeed of social work as a professional activity as a whole. Secondly, empowerment can be regarded as a process (Fook 2002), where certain social work approaches are employed in order to 'help clients gain power of decision and action over their own lives' (Payne 2005 p295). Obviously these two ideas about empowerment are linked together. So the approach to their work that practitioners adopt influences outcomes for service users. Social workers themselves and the organisations they work for can be very powerful (something we will examine later in this chapter), and the way this power is shared and used influences the experience service users have of social work intervention. One other aspect of empowerment it is important to think about at this stage is the distinction between structural and psychological empowerment. Structural empowerment means the removal of barriers preventing access to material benefits, changes in the world which improve people's lives. So access to better housing, increased income, jobs and education would all be examples of structural changes in people's lives. Psychological empowerment describes the way in which our psychological state can change, with greater confidence and a stronger sense of self-esteem, when we gain access to real material improvements in our lives. Any approach to advocacy which is centred upon empowerment needs to address this conceptual framework.

Discussion point

Vulnerability, powerlessness and help-seeking

It is often quite difficult to understand what it is like to feel disempowered, particularly from the perspective of a service user who is seeking help with a problem. Having to seek help in itself can feel like an acknowledgement of failure, an admission in some sense that you haven't been able to manage your life independently. Often when social workers are acting as advocates they are confronted with people who are in crisis and who are struggling to cope with things which others appear to manage successfully day to day. A useful three part exercise can help us to empathise and understand the circumstances of those who are seeking help from us.

All of us have at some point in our lives sought help from another person with a problem which we have had and which we can't sort out on our own. One useful exercise for advocates is to think about what this experience is like. It's important when doing this to focus on the feelings that help-seeking can generate. One way of doing this is to think about a specific example from your own life and then to consider the impacts it had on

(continued)

you. Think about the emotions help-seeking invoked in you (both positive and negative) and list them.

The next part of this exercise involves thinking about advocacy itself. Advocating on our own behalf or being supported by someone else is again an experience we all have in common. Many of us will have for example employed a legal representative, made a complaint about goods or services, sought assistance with a problem in the work place, school or college from another person, complained to a local council, or written to a councillor or MP. Thinking about these experiences can also help us be more sensitive to the perspectives of service users when we are advocating for someone else. The next stage of this exercise is to think about the feelings both positive and negative generated by this process. It is again worth listing these and also listing what was positive and what more difficult about the experience.

Finally, consider a situation where you successfully pursued or were supported to pursue a complaint or issue of some kind. It could be something quite simple like returning goods which didn't work properly or being overcharged for something. The final piece of reflection is to consider what this experience was like, again reflecting on your feelings at the time.

As we can see from this exercise, when seeking help from an advocate or advocating on someone else's behalf we can feel quite vulnerable and our sense of our autonomy can be affected.

Powerlessness and service user empowerment

Why is empowerment given such emphasis and importance in social work? To address this question it is helpful to look at why and how people who use social services are themselves disempowered, before going on to consider how advocacy might be linked to processes of empowerment.

No one who has worked as a social worker can fail to have been struck by the fact that social work is an activity undertaken almost exclusively with those who are poor (Corrigan and Leonard 1978, Sheppard 2006). Poverty, and the social disadvantage associated with it, is a pervasive feature of the lives of those who use social services, 'a central feature of social work practice because it affects most of the people social workers engage with' (Oak 2009 p51). Oak continues as follows: 'poverty...is strongly associated with the absence of power, autonomy and social and political influence' (p51). We can also now start to see, when we consider poverty and disempowerment, the links between the psychological and the structural. Townsend (Townsend 1996), looking at the impacts of unemployment, underlines the links between the material deprivation that unemployment brings and its psychological impacts, the damage to the sense of self and self-esteem which results from exclusion from the world of work.

Although poverty is a useful starting point when trying to understand the nature of disempowerment, it is by no means the whole story. A range of other important factors also contribute to disempowerment, which in social work have often been viewed through the lens of anti-discriminatory practice (Dominelli 2002b, Thompson 2006, Okitikpi and Aymer 2010). The terms anti-discriminatory and anti-oppressive practice are sometimes used interchangeably in social work, but they do represent two related but distinct perspectives on social work empowerment. Our earlier distinction between empowerment as a goal for social work practice and empowerment and a process can give us a sense of this distinction. Anti-discriminatory practice is an approach which focuses on how social workers can ensure that their own social work practice is carried out in a way which is consistent with not discriminating against those from disadvantaged groups. Anti-oppressive practice goes beyond this and envisages a broader goal for social work, to work towards the types of social change which would help greater power go to those who currently have least.

The models of anti-discriminatory practice which have been most influential in social work have in the main been what we could loosely term social strata models (Dalrymple and Burke 1996, Keating 1997, Thompson 2006). A feature of these models is the link they draw between the personal experience and feelings of the individual, their immediate cultural environment, and wider social and political forces. Thompson (2006) sees these elements – the personal, cultural and structural – as being interconnected with prejudice at one level feeding into discrimination at another, and individual change therefore as having an impact on wider social structures.

When we return to the question of how service users are disempowered, Thompson's strata model provides us with a generic account of how discrimination in relation to a wide range of different areas – culture, ethnicity, religion, sexuality, age, disability and gender, for example – can restrict opportunity and disempower. Pervading ideologies built on notions of difference feed into discrimination, the impacts of which are felt in material terms, through the restriction of their life chances by those discriminated against. However, one weakness of the Thompson model is that, although it describes the relationships between different levels within the social structure and the operation of discrimination at each level, its account of the processes of discrimination and how oppression is developed and sustained is less fully developed. In order to get a sense of this we need to turn to Keating's and Solomon's accounts of discrimination.

Keating (1997) acknowledges that oppression operates on different levels, but also that it has different dimensions at each level. So for example at the socio-cultural level oppression is mediated by language. He argues that at the individual level if we are to understand oppression and powerlessness we need to look at 'how people experience oppression subjectively and at how the basic dimensions of life are violated' (Keating 1997 p40). This way of thinking has close affinities with the work of Barbara Solomon. Solomon (1976) presents a model of empowerment which relates to the experience of black communities, but which can be applied more generally to social work with those who are disempowered (Payne 1997). Powerlessness, she argues, springs from 'a complex and dynamic relationship between the person and his [sic] relatively hostile social environment' (pp16–17). She sees powerlessness as a product of the negative valuations from the wider society to which individuals and groups in black communities have been subjected, 'to such an extent that powerlessness in the group is pervasive and crippling' (p12). The impact of Solomon's model is that it acknowledges that powerlessness is both a feature of individual experience, with some individuals 'having been exposed to negative valuations so intensely that they accept them as correct or inevitable and do not make any effort to exert any power' (Adams 2008 p51), and of social structures. This is very much akin to the concept of internalised oppression used by Braye and Preston-Shoot (1995). Empowerment therefore needs to operate at the psychological/individual level and in respect of wider social structures and cannot be an effective strategy unless pursued in relation to group and community as well as individually.

Professional power in social work

The dual caring and controlling role of social work is well documented as is the obvious use of power by social workers in their direct interventions in people's lives (Russell-Day 1981, Jones 1983, Okitikpi 2011). However, power in social work is a complex issue. Sheppard (2006) provides us with a very useful outline of the coercive use of power in social work practice which attempts to capture some of the nuances of this complexity. Sheppard argues that power can be understood in two different ways in social work. The first of these is what we could call overt coercion. Overt coercion describes the use of power to intervene in people's lives in a directive way to ensure that a service user does what the social worker requires. Overt coercion involves the use what we could call legitimate power; power which comes through the application of the law. It is easy to think of examples of social workers using power in this way. Using the Children Act to remove a child from a home where they were at risk, or the use of the Mental Health Act to take a person presenting a risk to themselves or perhaps to another person to a psychiatric hospital are examples of this type of power. Sheppard also talks about something he terms latent coercion. The threat of the use of the powers we have just been describing is one part of latent coercion. However, social workers are also powerful because of their professional expertise and because of key aspects of their roles, the allocation of resources to help people manage with their problems for example (something discussed in Chapter 7).

I think we can also add to this another way of understanding power in social work. This is the power which comes from the bureaucratic structures within which social work operates. This is what Smith (2008) calls 'power as process'; the complex mechanisms of assessment in which the professional knowledge of social workers is applied to service users to categorise them and make decisions about resource allocation, in themselves serve to exclude those using services and give power to professionals (Evans and Harris 2004).

Participation

As we know, powerlessness is not only a product of service users' social circumstances. The coercive nature and bureaucratic structure of social care agencies can themselves disempower service users. One important goal of empowerment therefore is to empower service users in relation to the organisations whose aim it is to help them. Wilcox's (1994) five-stage model of participation is a helpful framework for understanding how the process of advocacy can enhance participation. Wilcox based his model on Arnstein's ladder of participation (Arnstein 1969). Arnstein's ladder looks at the degree to which citizens are able to participate in public projects. She argues that there are 'significant gradations of citizen participation' ranging from power holders behaving in a tokenistic way to full citizen control. The focus of Wilcox's work is mainly on the participatory elements of Arnstein's model. Arnstein's ladder begins with two non-participatory positions, 'manipulation' and 'therapy', which 'enable power holders to educate or cure participants' (Arnstein 1969 p217). The next stage of her model, where participation starts, is 'informing' and this is the starting point for Wilcox's model. Wilcox argues that participation involves the following dimensions.

- Giving information – ensuring that people are as fully informed as possible
- Consulting – providing a range of choices and options
- Deciding together – a shared approach to finding the way forward
- Acting together – a partnership approach to joint working
- Supporting independent initiatives – giving control to people

Participation is a key component of the empowerment based model of advocacy and an issue any model of the advocacy process ought to address.

A model of advocacy and empowerment

Advocacy has the potential to address both the psychological and structural components of empowerment. It can also address the goal of empowerment through encouraging greater service user participation in services. The process model we discussed earlier in this chapter sees advocacy as essentially made up of three stages: a problem analysis stage; an investigation, information gathering and action planning stage; and a final stage of presenting a case and negotiation. Table 5.1 shows the links between the process of advocacy we outlined earlier and the principles of empowerment, and provides us with a practice framework for advocacy which is more consistent with principles of anti-discriminatory practice.

Empowerment is a central feature of this model. At each stage in the process there is the potential for empowering practice which will build on service users' psychological strengths and link into wider support networks and to bigger causes. There are a number of ways in which advocacy can help empower.

Developing self-confidence and skills

This means recognising and building upon skills that exist already, concentrating on strengths, and providing access to information. The focus in this area is on the psychological aspects of empowerment. At the problem analysis stage it is essential to identify service users' strengths when exploring the nature of the problem and to draw attention to past successful problem solving. It will also be helpful to identify the service users' existing support networks and to think about how they might provide support on a psychological and practical level. As advocacy progresses advocates can work with the service users to develop skills and knowledge around the advocacy task. The use of scaling questions can be very useful here (Parton and O'Byrne 2000). They are often used in solution orientated approaches to practice as a way of both measuring service

Table 5.1 Empowerment and the advocacy process

	Problem analysis	Information gathering and action planning	Presenting a case and negotiation	Continuing involvement
Developing self-confidence and skills	Strengths focus – previous successes self and social network	Evaluation and affirmation of progress made and increased confidence Developing skills and knowledge Scaling questions	Developing skills, rehearsal and preparation, assertiveness	Working with groups, helping to develop skills and passing on knowledge
Linking into networks of support	Identifying extended formal support systems	Supported self-help, peer expertise	Speaking out with peer support, sharing experience with others	Offering peer support to others
Engaging with bigger issues	Exploring the wider social and community context of the problem	Links with support groups and cause advocacy	Setting case in the wider context and making links to other cases	Active campaigning
Moving from passive to active roles	Identifying shared tasks	Undertaking shared tasks Shared consultation with expertise	Focus on enabling to speak and not speaking for	Participation in user led advocacy services

Increasing participation and control

users' increasing confidence and affirming to them the progress they are making. In relation to case presentation and negotiation, preparation is important with an emphasis on assertiveness, and on rehearsing difficult situations, developing the social skills needed to present an effective case.

Linking into networks of support

This means identifying, using and becoming involved with supportive structures in the community. There are a number of ways in which this can happen with different degrees of formality. It might be as informal as a young looked after person having a friend present in a review. It might be more formal: a person with mental health problems attending a peer led training course on the process of DLA review. By accessing these broader networks of support service users are developing a greater sense of their own capacity to manage problems and also starting to get an idea of how social structures impact upon their own disempowerment. So a social worker will be supporting a service user at an individual level and also helping to link them into self-help and peer-support mechanisms.

Engaging with bigger issues

This means becoming actively involved in collective lobbing for change and helping others with advocacy in the future. Advocacy at the individual level is of paramount importance as it can directly impact upon the material circumstances of individual service users. However, it is often the case that many people may face similar sorts of problems and there is the potential for advocacy to work both individually and collectively. Over and above this service users often face discrimination and oppression which, as we have already argued, may impact upon their psychological sense of powerlessness. There is clearly scope for advocacy to set individual issues within a broader community and social context and begin to address social change (Fook 2002).

Moving from passive to active roles in advocacy

This means taking greater control of the advocacy process and representing oneself rather than being represented by another. For social workers and service users, advocacy is a collaborative process shaped by the idea of mutuality. Therefore tasks are shared, consultation with experts is a joint process, and the goal is, as far as it is possible, to enable service users to speak for themselves. A long-term aim is, following Wilcox's participation model, to help service users become involved in advocacy services over which they have power, moving from partnership and acting together to support for independent initiatives.

I want to look at this point at a case study to illustrate how this empowering approach to advocacy might work in practice.

Practice example – June

June is a 46-year-old white British woman who lives in a two-bedroom flat, rented from a large housing association. Her 23-year-old daughter Wendy and her 6-year-old granddaughter live nearby.

About six years ago June was diagnosed with osteoarthritis. This affects her hip, making it hard for her to walk a great distance, and her hands, making it difficult for her to undertake intricate tasks. She has good days and bad days with her arthritis: sometimes walking is not too much of a problem; sometimes she can't go far at all. June was divorced about a year before the diagnosis and moved into her current accommodation at this point. Before her divorce June worked sporadically for an employment agency in a variety of secretarial

(continued)

and administrative roles. She also had a number of periods of depression and was once admitted as a voluntary patient to psychiatric hospital. About 18 months ago Wendy's husband was killed in a motorcycle accident. This was a terrible blow for the whole family and June became very upset and not able to sleep. Her GP prescribed her Valium to help with her anxiety and sleeping.

Over the past 6 months June has become more depressed and withdrawn, and has not felt able to work. She spends much of the day watching the television. She has become very anxious about going out of the flat. Her daughter has taken on more responsibility for running the household and pops in to see her several times a day. June is still taking Valium and feels it is contributing to the way she is feeling. When she tries to cut down her dose she gets very anxious and weepy. She is worried she has developed a dependency on these drugs. June has spoken to the GP over the phone about stopping, but he has advised against this and suggested that a gradual plan of withdrawal over 6 to 8 months would be the most sensible plan. June feels it would be much better to stop altogether. Wendy's view is that her mum should follow the course of action the GP is suggesting and they have had a number of arguments about this. June would like him to come out to see her to discuss things, but he has told her that home visits are only for emergencies and that she should come into the surgery.

June has problems with damp in her bedroom and a smell from the drains at the back of the block of flats in which she lives, which a number of her neighbours have also commented upon. Her flat is on the fourth floor and recently the lifts have often been out of order. She has spoken to the housing association about these problems, but nothing has been done. She has now requested a move to another property, but at the moment the housing association say that this is not possible, as she wants to remain close to her daughter. June has been referred to the local authority adult services team by a tenant liaison officer from the housing association, who feels that she needs more support at home.

June's situation is one where advocacy could be adopted as an approach in relation to a number of different aspects of her life. June has a series of problems with her housing:

- Access to her flat because of the repeated problems with the lift
- Problems with damp inside the flat
- Drainage problems
- Her request for a transfer to more suitable accommodation
- Finance and benefits

In addition to this there are difficulties with the support Judith is receiving from her GP, which leaves something to be desired.

How would June's situation fit with the empowering model of the advocacy process outlined here? Firstly, it is clear that June lacks confidence in her capacity to deal with the problems she faces. However, it is important to focus early on in the advocacy process on her skills (her work experience might be important here), and on identifying the support mechanisms she has available to her in her immediate family and social sphere. There might also be other support networks available to her. Are there tenants' organisations that could be of help? Internet self-help groups exist for those dependent upon prescription tranquilisers. National organisations representing the needs of people with disabilities, specifically arthritis, could be a valuable resource. All of this may help June develop a wider sense of the context of her problem, in relation both to her immediate community and the community of people with disabilities. At this stage a clear problem inventory could be developed, prioritising which problems to deal with first and identifying clear service user and social worker tasks.

At the information gathering and action planning stage both social worker and June would be involved in a series of investigative tasks. The social worker might make contact with the tenant liaison officer, June with the tenants' association. The online forum may have suggestions to make as to how best to address the GP about tranquiliser dependency. Bigger issues may begin to be addressed: the over-prescribing of tranquilisers, or the inadequacies of housing agency's responses to the needs of people with disabilities for example. It might be appropriate for both the social worker and June to meet with an independent housing advisor to get more information about her rights, a process of joint consultation.

In the case presentation and negotiation phase emphasis would be on adopting a joint approach to presenting a case, the focus of which would be on enabling June to play as active a part as possible in this. So the social worker might help June to write to the housing association or perhaps write a supporting letter. Meetings with the housing association could involve June and the social worker with June taking the lead, and possibly with a representative of the tenants' association in attendance to offer support. This might emphasise the collective nature of the problems with the lifts and drainage. Preparation and rehearsal might be an important part of this process.

The end point of this type of shared process might be that June becomes more involved in the tenants' association or is able to pass on her experience to help others dependent upon prescription tranquilisers. She may become more aware of the way in which discrimination can limit the opportunities available to those with disabilities. Finally, it is important to remember that advocacy in this case may form only one aspect of a more wide ranging intervention, which might involve emotional support for June, work with her daughter, a wider assessment of her support needs and the provision of other services or direct payments.

Task centred work and advocacy

The task-centred approach is unique in social work. The theoretical approach and practice methods adopted by social workers have generally had their roots in other disciplines. Psychology is the source of psychodynamic and cognitive/behavioural interventions. Solution-focused approaches have their roots in brief counselling techniques. Systems theory has provided the basis for systemic practice. In contrast the task centred approach is a home-grown practice model. The origins of the approach lie in research undertaken by Reid and Shyne (Reid and Shyne 1969) comparing brief task focused interventions with the more open ended psycho-dynamically orientated case work which dominated practice up until the 1970s. The research demonstrated the effectiveness of a briefer more practically orientated model and, through a process of further research, a structured method of intervention was developed (Reid and Epstein 1972, Reid 1978).

It is possible to see advocacy as a discrete and separate activity in social work, which falls outside generic approaches to practice. I think this is a mistake. As we have already argued social workers undertaking advocacy can draw on a range of social work theory to inform and shape their practice. Furthermore advocacy is so often a key component of the overall social work task, so separating advocacy from theory weakens the holistic focus of any intervention, which is such an important element of the overall ethos of social work. Perhaps because of its pragmatic origins within social work, the task centred method is an approach which has a close fit with a number of different aspects of social work practice. As Ford and Postle point out in their discussions of the application of the approach to the case management process, 'it is a clear and practical model which can be adapted to a wide range of interventions' (Ford and Postle 2000 p52).

How relevant is the task centred approach to advocacy? The two core elements of the approach, its focus on problem solving and commitment to time limited interventions, are both consistent with advocacy. Reid (1978) identified a range of different problems in relation to which the task centred approach is effective. These include problems with an emotional focus: interpersonal conflict, difficulties with social relationships, reactive emotional distress, and problems in social transition. Included also, however, were problems of a more practical nature, difficulties in role performance, inadequate resources and problems with formal organisations, all areas where advocacy might be an important element in an intervention. Finally, task centred work is most effective when problems are identified by service users, are clearly defined, and at least to some extent amenable to solution by service users themselves undertaking supported independent action.

If we look at the task centred approach to practice in more detail then we can see how it could provide a structure for intervention which is consistent with advocacy. There are five important elements of task centred practice which are relevant to advocacy.

A staged systematic approach to practice

Task centred intervention normally involves progress through a series of stages. Although there are a range of different accounts of the approach (Reid 1978, Doel and Marsh 1992, Marsh and Doel 2005), they share a common general account of the structure of intervention which goes along the following lines.

- A process of problem exploration or definition
- An agreement as to which areas need to be prioritised
- The formulation of objectives and goals
- Undertaking and achieving tasks
- Review and ending

The first striking thing about this process is that it clearly fits in many ways with the model of advocacy outlined in this chapter (and in fact with other versions of the advocacy process we have looked at, Bateman's model for example). This is particularly true of the problem definition aspect of task centred work. This involves identifying and prioritising the problems which the service user brings to the social worker. The role of the social worker here is not to be directive, but to facilitate the service user's exploration of these issues and to challenge beliefs that the difficulties faced are unresolvable. The purpose of problem exploration is to move to a point where agreement can be reached on the way forward and on which problem should be prioritised.

This initial part of the process of task centred work is very similar to the problem analysis which is the starting point of the advocacy model presented here, although there is less emphasis placed on information gathering and obtaining expert advice. The shared concern with partnership, however, is also an important area of common ground. Task centred interventions are often made up of a number of intertwining strands, with a range of different and sometimes interrelated problems addressed. It is often the case that advocacy forms one strand of such interventions. Even within presentation of a case and negotiation, particularly where tasks are shared between advocate and service user, aspects of the task centred approach can be applied.

Starting with the problems identified by the service user

This common principle is one that influences both advocacy and task centred methods. Both operate within a largely voluntarist framework, with the service user taking a leading role in identifying what the focus of the intervention is going to be.

A focus on empowerment and building skills

One important benefit of task centred work is that it gives service users a positive experience of problem solving, and builds confidence and skills, which can be applied to future problems. This increases the motivation of those who have been through the task centred process to engage with future problems and to seek help. These positives apply to advocacy as well. However, one limitation of task centred work is its focus on the individual and lack of attention to structural disadvantage and 'deep-seated problems of poverty and social inequality' (Payne 2005 p117).

Results orientated

One key principle of task centred practice is that it is very outcome orientated. The original rationale for the model's development was that it offered a more effective approach to social work intervention than had hitherto been available to practitioners.

That emphasis on outcome measurement has remained an important aspect of the model ever since. The structured nature of the intervention offers practitioners the opportunity to review progress throughout the process and then evaluate final outcomes. Brandon (1995a) stresses the importance of ensuring that advocates review and evaluate their practice.

Before we leave task centred practice it is worth thinking about some of its limitations. Although it provides a structured approach to intervention, as we have already highlighted it can downplay the role of structural factors in the problems service users face. It is important that social workers adopting this approach to intervention are aware of how their own professional power can manifest itself in realtionships with service users if it is to address empowerment effectively.

Cause advocacy

When we think about advocacy in social work we normally have in mind a one-to-one relationship between social worker and service user working together to gain access to resources and secure rights. Social work is generally conducted in an individualised case based way. In our discussions of empowerment we have looked at the relationship between advocacy for individuals and wider collective concerns. The model of the advocacy process we have looked at starts to address this issue, with one of the potential end points of the advocacy process being service user involvement in organisations providing advocacy and peer support. However, the idea of collective responses to shared issues and problems can be taken a step further. Social workers can involve themselves in actively lobbying for the needs of groups of service users. This is essentially what we could call cause advocacy.

Cause advocacy – the battles for carers' rights

A good example of cause advocacy in the field of social care is what is often termed the carers' movement. There are two important and distinctive strands within the movement I want to examine. The first concerns the struggle to recognise the needs and rights of carers generally. The second is the movement for greater recognition and support for the needs of young carers.

When we look at the carers' movement overall we can see the processes of cause advocacy at work. Before the middle of the 1960s those undertaking caring responsibilities would not have defined themselves as carers or 'thought of themselves as distinctive in the sense of belonging to a special category of people'; the category was 'created through the interplay between individual experience and various interest groups – policy makers, researchers and pressure groups' (Bytheway and Johnson 1998 p241). One key catalyst for the movement was the work of Mary Webster. Mary had spent the previous decade caring for her elderly parents and in 1963 began a campaign for the greater recognition of what had hitherto been a hidden issue, the difficulties faced by single women caring for dependent relatives at home (Cook 2007). She wrote to the newspapers highlighting 'the difficulties single women face with earning the family living and caring for the home, the sick and the elderly'. This was the starting point for the formation of a coalition of interest. She was soon in contact with hundreds of women in similar circumstances with similar

(continued)

---

experiences of caring. The focus of this coalition's concerns was two-fold. Firstly, it aimed to draw attention to the emotional demands of caring. What this is like is perhaps best described by a carer. The following quote takes us towards the heart of the caring experience: 'I can't remember the last time I had a holiday or didn't sleep here. Caring is lonely, it's the isolation' (MacDonald and Bailey 2008). Mary Webster's description of carers as being 'under house arrest' (see Lansley 2010), struck a chord in the public imagination. Secondly, this coalition of interest highlighted the financial disadvantage and difficulties carers faced. In 1965 the National Council for the Single Woman and her Dependants was formed, the first organisation lobbying for the interests of carers. The evidence that this group presented to politicians was largely experiential. Caring, although a feature of women's lives for centuries, had only just become a phenomenon recognised in the public domain, and its excluding impacts were only starting to be explored. However, representations made by the organisation began to change attitudes and raise awareness and led to the first legislative change related to caring: the introduction of the 1967 Dependent Relatives Tax Allowance (Cook 2007).

As the movement developed two factors became more influential. Formal research into the extent of informal caring began to have a greater influence on policy and the carers' lobby found powerful allies within the rapidly developing feminist movement concerned with women's rights more generally. Finch and Groves' (1980) work, which served to 'emphasize the financial emotional and career losses that women faced when they took on the caring role' (Dalley 1996 p66), was an important staging post in the development of a feminist analysis of this area. The 1985 General Household Survey revealed the extent of formal care. By this stage Invalid Care Allowance, the first carer specific benefit, had been introduced, and the Impacts of Caring report produced by the National Council for the Single Woman and her Dependants (NCSWD 1977) had led to the first protection of state pension benefits for carers.

The National Council for the Single Woman and her Dependants eventually merged with other carers groups to form the Carers National Association, now Carers UK. The result of the activities of these pressure groups was the range of legislation relating to carers that we have today: the Carers (Recognition and Services) Act 1995, the Carers and Disabled Children Act 2000, the Carers (Equal Opportunities) Act 2004 and the Work and Families Act 2006. This legislative framework placed duties on local authorities to formally recognise the full range of carers' needs and their capacity to provide care when assessing the cared for person, and on employers to enable carers to work flexibly.

The primary focus of the carers' movement had been on older carers. However, in the 1990s recognition was increasingly being given to the roles children were playing in supporting ill or disabled parents at home. The Carers National Association played a role in the development of this awareness, but unlike the movement for the recognition of the rights of adult women carers, where at first much of the evidence of the problems they faced was anecdotal, research was a key driver in the development of the young carers' movement. From the start the coalition of interest which developed around this issue involved both the carers' movement and the Young Carers Research Group at Loughborough University (Becker, Aldridge and Dearden 1998). Their work served to raise awareness of

(continued)

this issue and in parallel local groups for young carers began to be established, providing support for young people and advocacy on an individual and collective basis. The 2004 Young Carers Report by the Young Carers Research Group (Dearden and Becker 2004) draws on information obtained from these groups and on the 2001 census data, to paint a comprehensive overview of the extent to which young people were involved in caring and the nature and impacts of these roles.

Before we leave our example of cause advocacy, the carers' movement, it is important to reflect upon the potential of cause advocacy and upon some of its limitations. Ann MacDonald and Sue Bailey's study of Suffolk Family Carers (MacDonald and Bailey 2008) highlights a wide range of positive impacts the service has on carers (including support through individual advocacy). However, it also reveals the limitations of advocacy, whether for individuals or for a cause, on which the following reflections on the emotional costs of caring, from carers, serve as a reminder:

'Just the silence is what I find so hard. He doesn't talk; he's got no interest in anything, so there is no conversation.'

'You lose friends very quickly when you're caring for older people. As the older people come through the front door the friends go though the back!'

The term cause advocacy has its origins in the advocacy traditions within the USA. Schneider and Lester (2001) view cause advocacy as a natural endpoint to advocacy undertaken with individuals. Social work's fundamental concern is not just with the internal psychological world, but with the dynamic interaction between an individual and their environment, the 'person-in-the-environment' model as they term it, underpins this approach.

Schneider and Lester's model of cause advocacy addresses three central issues: why cause advocacy is important, the nature of representation in cause advocacy and the application of the concept of mutuality. Schneider and Lester identify a number of reasons why cause advocacy is an important element in the overall approach adopted by social workers to advocacy. They see it as a logical extension of work with individuals consistent with the social work value base with its emphasis on the pursuit of social justice. The process of linking 'client to cause' works along the following lines: 'social workers may notice similarities in the type of problems individual clients have, and after repetition after repetition, they determine to act to effect change in policies, laws or practices affecting specific groups or large numbers of people' (Schneider and Lester 2001 p196). It is interesting to note here that the ultimate goal of cause advocacy is very often to change the law and policy. (We will return to this theme a little later on.) There are good reasons for adopting such collective approaches. Advocacy with individuals may offer only limited scope to secure change. Working with a group for a cause may be the best way of accessing resources for service users and pursuing issues of social justice. Schneider and Lester also draw attention to issues of effectiveness and efficiency in advocacy. They argue that making a multiplicity of individual representations regarding the same issue wastes resources. A single approach to a common problem allows advocates to pool resources more effectively, and as a single process rather than many is more efficient.

However, synthesising the views of a number of people and determining the views of an entire group is often a challenging task: 'acting exclusively on behalf of the group or cause is complicated because it is so difficult to determine clearly the exact point of the entire group' (Schneider and Lester 2001 p199). The question of representation, of how a collective approach can represent a multiplicity of perspectives, is an important one for cause advocacy and for service user involvement more generally (Croft and Beresford 1993). One useful idea when thinking about this area is the distinction between representative and participative democracy (Hill et al. 2004). The archetype of representative democracy is politics and the choice though the voting system of political representatives. Participatory democracy is focused much more on ensuring that the structures and processes for bringing people together in the pursuit of a cause allow the participation of as many of those involved as possible. Interestingly struggles around causes where legal process is involved are generally focused on individual test cases; the success of Jackie Drake's case in the European Court of Justice, which extended the right to Invalid Care Allowance to married women, is a good example (Walker and Walker 1991).

Mutuality is also an important aspect of seeking to pursue a common cause. This involves advocates adopting 'a willingness to be criticized, to listen to group concerns and be humble in the exercise of judgement' (Schneider and Lester 2001 p201). Working in a way that is consistent with the social work value base, particularly self-determination, plays an important part in mutuality as it relates to cause advocacy. In cause advocacy the advocate is often not just working with a group of service users, but also with other advocates, and again those relationships need to be based upon the principles of reciprocity and equality which underlie mutuality.

Building on Schneider and Lester's work it is possible to begin to develop an account of the process of cause advocacy, which has many similarities with our earlier analysis of advocacy on an individual basis.

Creating links between service users, advocates and others – a coalition of interest

Cause advocacy is all about identifying a common problem and then approaching this as a collective issue. This process works better if there are mechanisms to connect together those involved in advocacy. Having effective forums in which shared common concerns can be voiced is important in this. They provide inter-organisational mechanisms, which enable service users and advocates to meet and begin to move towards change of some sort. Often it is workers on the front line of service provision who recognise an injustice or the fact that the needs of a particular group are not being met. Seeking sources of support and partnership beyond the local, and the involvement of politicians and policy makers, can also be an important part of this process.

Gathering evidence and undertaking research

Having good evidence backed by research, and knowing the extent of the problem that you face when advocating for a cause, is an important part of the process of cause advocacy. Evidence can be both experiential (which can have a great impact) and gathered through more formal research. Seeking support from those who have skills in research can also be helpful at this stage, and is part of building a broader coalition of interest in cause advocacy (Brueggeman 2002).

Clarifying and achieving goals

Cause advocacy often has two distinctive sets of goals. The first are to do with consciousness raising, drawing attention to an important issue and raising professional and public interest. The importance of this type of activity cannot be underestimated and may be an end in itself for cause advocacy. One good example of this would be the influence of the Women's Aid movement in the late 1960s and early 1970s (Pizzey 1974) in bringing to public attention the problem of domestic violence, which hitherto had remained private and secret. Innovative provision of services for excluded groups has often gone hand in hand with cause advocacy. The second set of goals relate to changes in three interrelated areas: practice, policy and the law. This is something which is very distinctive about cause advocacy; its goals are both the improvement of individuals' circumstances and changes to wider social structures.

I want to consider an example of cause advocacy at this point which demonstrates the links between these areas on a local level. We have already looked at the role of collective advocacy in the development of services for carers. Dearden and Becker (2003) provide us with an interesting example of the development of practice and policy in relation to young carers in education in Lewisham in the 1990s, which demonstrates some of the impacts of cause advocacy within a particular area and specific context. The starting point of this work was the identification by school nurses of a number of young people who appeared to have caring responsibilities within Lewisham Schools. Supported by the voluntary sector organisation Carers Lewisham, the nurses undertook a more formal survey of caring responsibilities amongst school children, which revealed a surprisingly high number of young carers in the local authority's schools. Eventually funding was obtained for a schools development project supported by the Princess Royal Trust for Carers, and guidance and materials produced for local schools, which made them aware of young carers' rights and enabled them to meet the needs of young carers more effectively.

In this example we can see several key elements of the cause advocacy process we have just outlined. A coalition of interest developed, with Carers Lewisham providing a collective forum in which shared concerns about the well-being of young carers in the education system could be shared. This was a group whose needs had not been properly recognised at this stage. More focused evidence gathering and research was undertaken and, with the involvement of the Princess Royal Trust for Carers, a wider coalition of interest extending beyond Lewisham was created. The importance of innovative projects as catalysts for change can be seen in the final development of materials for schools, which helped to change practice and policy, if not at this stage the law.

As we have seen a lot can be achieved through cause advocacy at a national level and at a local level, but the approach has its limitations. A useful exercise is to think more generally about how effective public protest movements are in instigating change and more broadly about what they can achieve.

Discussion point

Think of a public movement which you admire. It could be a protest movement or drawing attention to some sort of injustice. It could be in your local area or a national or international movement. Now consider:

- what it was able to achieve, and
- what it couldn't change.

Remember, achievements might include:

- Practical successes in changing legislation and policy
- Raising awareness of an area which has previously been ignored
- Creating a sense of solidarity
- Inspiring others now or in the future

It is important to remember that there are some things that cause advocacy cannot change. Legislation and policy changes may greatly improve the lives of carers, for example, but they cannot entirely remove the burden of the caring role. There are also benefits to pursuing a cause, in the inspiration it may give to others and the sense of solidarity it may give to those involved, which are not directly related to the success or failure of the enterprise.

Key learning points

- Models of the advocacy process help to give clarity and a common framework to help social workers and service users to understand the advocacy process.
- The idea of working in partnership is a key element in Schneider and Lester's concept of mutuality and gives the basis for a model of the advocacy process with a stronger focus on a collaborative approach, which is more consistent with the goal of empowerment.
- Task centred approaches to social work practice can also provide a helpful framework for social work interventions centred around advocacy.
- Cause advocacy enables advocates to move beyond work with individuals to address collective needs. A coalition of interest between service users, advocates and others can work to raise awareness of issues and to change policy and legislation.

Further reading

Adams, R. (2008) *Empowerment, participation and social work* (4th ed), Basingstoke/New York, Palgrave Macmillan

Bateman, N. (2000) *Advocacy Skills for Health and Social Care Professionals*, London, Jessica Kingsley

Brandon, D. and Brandon, T. (2001) *Advocacy in Social Work*, Birmingham, Venture Press

Schneider, R. and Lester, L. (2001) *Social Work Advocacy: a New Framework for Action*, Belmont CA, Brooks Cole

Sheppard, M. (2006) *Social Work and Social Exclusion*, Aldershot, Ashgate

6 Advocacy Skills: Presenting a case

To act as effective advocates social workers need some core skills. This chapter aims to examine the skills associated with presenting a case and looks at a number of circumstances where social workers do this, presenting a case to a funding panel or for example a charity. Some key ideas about strategies for presenting a case are explored and the chapter looks at cause advocacy and some of the essential skills it requires.

Exploring and understanding problems

It is widely acknowledged that assessment lies at the heart of social work (Milner and O'Byrne 2009). Coulshed and Orme (2006) see assessment as an ongoing process within social work practice, where changing circumstances often require that a problem be looked at afresh. Assessing service users' advocacy needs is an important part of this process. For the social worker, addressing the problems that service users present which relate to advocacy demands the adoption of a systematic approach and sensitivity to the emotional and social world of the service user. It will often be the case that the social worker is finding out about issues relating to advocacy whilst at the same time exploring a number of other areas in the service user's life. In recent years social workers have tended to shy away from the term 'problem'. Approaches to practice focusing upon strengths (Saleebey 2009, Teater 2010) and solutions (Parton and O'Byrne 2000) have moved social work away from problem orientated approaches to practice.

However, there is a clear benefit for those using advocacy skills in adopting an approach which acknowledges the practical (and external) nature of the sorts of difficulties that service users face, and that are amenable to an approach based around advocacy. Bateman's distinction between 'bounded' and 'unbounded' problems is quite useful here (Bateman 2000). Bounded problems, he argues, are discrete and can be treated as a separate matter, with both problem and solution clear. In contrast, unbounded problems are far less certain and more difficult to disentangle from their contexts. The exact nature of the problem and of its solution will be less clear. Bateman suggests that it is bounded problems which are most straightforwardly addressed by advocacy. Bateman himself perhaps overplays the value of this distinction.

Advocacy around the withdrawal of disability benefits (for example) might require aspects of both practical and emotional support, and be tangled up with a range of other contextual issues. However, it does have heuristic value and gives us a sense of what is distinctive about the advocacy role, perhaps supporting the point that advocacy is more practically orientated than other parts of social work. We will therefore draw on both problem orientated and strengths perspectives in our approach to analysing problems in advocacy.

There are two parts to addressing problems in advocacy. The first involves identifying and analysing what the key issues and problems are. The second is to identify the strengths and resources the service user possesses, in order to begin the collaborative approach to advocacy. A good starting point for this discussion is the type of problem analysis used in task centred approaches to practice. We looked in the last chapter at the potential of task centred work in advocacy. Within task centred work a range of strategies are adopted in order to address problems systematically, many of which are applicable to advocacy. One helpful way of considering problems is to think about them in terms of two dimensions, breadth and depth. By the breadth of problems I mean their extent, how they link to other problems and issues in a person's life. By depth I mean how entrenched they are, how long they have been going on and the extent of the impact that they have. If we think about a very common problem which families often ask social services for help with, living in over-crowded conditions, we can see how this distinction would work. When we think about the breadth of the problem we are thinking about its impacts upon the children's social relationships and education, the challenges it raises for parents and perhaps the links with other over-crowded families on the same estate. When we think about the depth of the problem we are considering how long it has been going on for and how difficult it has been to address, measuring the emotional impacts it has and looking at whether it is getting worse. This distinction is akin to the idea of headline and subsidiary problems we find in task centred work (Doel and Marsh 1992) and can give us a framework for a problem scanning process. This also allows us to prioritise the focus of our advocacy efforts. What O'Connor et al. (2007) term analytical questions are important here: looking at who the problem affects, how it is viewed by those it affects and why it is having an impact now. A detailed account of problems is important in advocacy as it will form the basis for presenting an effective case, an area we will move on to cover later. It enables the social worker to make judgements about the case and with the service user decide what is to be done, the final stages of Milner and O'Byrne's (2009) account of the assessment process.

The second part of problem analysis involves identifying strengths and resources. Kondrat (2010) describes a multi-dimensional strengths approach covering a wide number of different areas in a service user's life, and identifying strengths applied in one area and applying them in another. In relation to advocacy it is important at this stage to be starting to try to identify service user strengths and to show how these might be important in a collaborative approach to the advocacy process. It is particularly important to identify previous successful efforts to address similar problems. This is very much in keeping with the exception finding approach which is so important in solution focused work (Parton and O'Byrne 2000).

Presenting a case

Advocacy is different from many other areas of social work practice in that when social workers are undertaking advocacy they are to varying degrees partisan. Although they have to behave honestly and be accurate, there is still scope for them to organise and present material in ways which can sway the opinions of others.

I am going to look generally at three different ways in which material can be organised and then consider the different approaches in relation to disability living allowance. The first approach I want to consider is what we might term problem analysis. This looks at addressing some core questions about a situation in the material that is presented. What, why, when, where, how and who questions are addressed. There are many advantages to adopting an approach to case presentation which deals with these questions. It focuses on detail and on analysis and fits well with the assessment approach that has been outlined. The second way that we might consider organising material is chronologically. This gives a detailed account of the history of a problem. It has the potential to show something getting worse and changing over time. The third approach that could be adopted is the narrative approach. Essentially what is happening here is that a story is being told. Some of the detail that problem analysis captures might be lost by doing this, as might elements of the history, but this approach might be able to provide a more accurate sense of the impacts of the problem personally. There is nothing to stop a case being presented in a report using all three of these approaches simultaneously. So for example a chronological presentation of events might include some problem analysis and perhaps finish with more narrative elements.

Discussion point

The following example (adapted from one used by advicenow.org) shows these different approaches in action. This is the supporting statement of someone who is appealing a decision to award her a lower rate of Disability Living Allowance. As you will see it includes all three of the approaches we have just outlined.

    I am writing to explain my condition and to appeal against the award of a low rate of DLA for care. I am appealing the decision because I believe I am entitled to the middle rate of care. I have ulcerative colitis and severe depression.

    Here we see what is wrong, why she is appealing and what she wants – so very much a problem analysis approach.

    My depression started about 15 years ago, and although treatment was quite successful at first, things have got worse over the years. Five years ago I spent some time in a psychiatric hospital. Although I improved a little after this things have got worse over the past 18 months or so.

    This is a chronological approach – looking at events in order and trying to show how the present is connected with the past.

(continued)

Because of my depression I often can't face the day. I am shaky on my feet and need to go to the toilet frequently. Afterwards I feel sick and exhausted. I tend to feel worse in the morning. When my sister is with me she encourages me to get up. Going in the shower can be difficult because of the pain.

Again we've returned to the problem analysis mode here – so we are looking at when things are difficult, how the condition affects her, who can help when and where things are most difficult.

A couple of months ago I managed to get myself into the shower. However as I reached up to the shower head I fell, bang flat on my back. I lay there for about 15 minutes and just couldn't get up and I didn't know what I was going to do. Then fortunately I heard my sister's key in the door and she helped me.

Here we are using the narrative approach telling a story and using some dramatic devices to engage the reader.

Which of these strategies is most effective?

What sort of messages does each convey?

It is interesting to reflect on the different impacts these approaches can have. Chronological approaches suggest a quite formal and structured approach to the problem and are rather similar to the ways in which doctors present cases, which perhaps gives a sense of gravitas. The problem analysis approach aims to be logical in its attempts to persuade addressing issues and questions before they come up. Narrative approaches engage the reader in a story and may touch an emotional chord.

Advocacy and emotional support, mental health and benefits

One important group of those claiming benefits because of disability are people with mental health problems. This group of claimants are particularly subject to vilification in the popular press. Witness the *Daily Mail* headlines 'Thousands are claiming incapacity benefit for stress in sick note Britain' (*Daily Mail* 2007) or 'Just one in six incapacity benefit claimants is genuine as tough new test reveals two million could be cheating' (*Daily Mail* 2009). Threats to incapacity benefit, for any group that are reliant upon it, can have a particularly damaging impact upon their psychological well-being. For those with mental health problems the issues are particularly stark. Successive governments have been concerned to reduce the growing costs of disability benefits in the UK. There has also been a shift in ethos within the benefits system, towards providing benefits with the intention of moving their recipients towards work. As part of this process the eligibility for benefit of those with disabilities has altered, with the disability tests put in place becoming increasingly orientated towards moving those with disabilities (particularly mental health problems) into the work place by placing more stringent assessments of their situations into place.

This process has led to the introduction of what is now known as the work capacity assessment. This assessment provides a framework for moving those currently drawing incapacity benefit onto one of two proposed benefits: the newly created Employment Support Allowance or Job Seekers' Allowance.

To face this type of assessment is extremely difficult for service users and it is important to consider the challenge it presents. The issue of appearing at their worst is extremely distressing for service users. The work capacity assessment looks at a range of areas of daily living and risk. However, to most effectively represent their needs they have to think about when they are least well and able to cope, when they shun social contact and medication makes them drowsy and withdrawn. When interviewed they may want to create a good expression but will also be aware of the need to demonstrate what they need. They will also have to talk about difficult subjects, suicidal thoughts for example or voice hearing.

Presenting a case to a panel for funding

Presenting a case to a funding panel for resources is an important part of any social worker's life within the statutory sector and is a situation when social workers are putting forward a case for valuable resources on behalf of a service user. Social workers often use the possessive 'my client' or 'my service user' when talking about their work. There are many who would baulk at the sense of possession and ownership this can convey. However, what it also suggests is the powerful feeling of social workers' personal commitment to those they work with, something which is often apparent when they seek resources for service users from within their own agencies. Funding panels in social work exist across service user groups. They are normally led (some might say dominated) by senior managers, with responsibility for the budgets being considered, and are made up of a range of representatives, sometimes wholly from within the local authority, sometimes (and this is often the case with services organised in an inter-professional way) from other organisations, most notably the NHS. The material that is presented to the panel may also vary. Many panels have formal systems where a form has to be completed. Others may have sets of required documentation and a requirement that a report is provided, guidelines for which will normally be available. One thing that they have in common, however, is that generally a social worker faces two hurdles if they want to secure funding. Firstly, they must prepare and present convincing written evidence. Secondly, they must be able to defend the case they are making in front of the panel.

Funding panels have one key responsibility and that is to make the most effective use of limited resources to provide the maximum benefit to service users. (The ethics of this benign rationing are discussed in Chapter 4 and some of the issues it raises for social workers explored.) The extent to which this process is governed by systematic mechanisms for allocating a particular tariff to specific elements or aspects of a service user's situation varies between local authorities. Some of the forms used by local authorities attempt to codify need in a way which appears to do the panel's job in advance. However, there will always be a need for panels to apply their discretion. We have already looked in some detail at the ways in which material may be presented in a report to persuade those making decisions. A social worker preparing a report for panel needs to be aware of how they organise their material and the emphasis they place on problem analysis, chronology and narrative. However, my primary focus in this section will be on understanding the key parameters of the panel process, the determinants of whether a decision is made to fund a particular care package or not. For a social worker presenting a case to a panel it is important to understand the key influences on panel members when asked to speak to a report or ask questions about what has been written. Healy and Mulholland (2007) identify two factors which establish the context for writing in social work, the institutional context and audience. Healy and Mulholland's (2007) emphasis on audience is important to think about in the context of presenting a case in this situation, although presenting a case to a panel mixes presentation and writing together. However, understanding the perspective of the primary audience is crucial.

The starting points for any panel's consideration are the issues of **eligibility** and **thresholds** for service. There are three factors which may influence the panel's thinking in this area. The first of these is whether this person is in sufficient need to merit the service being proposed (a points or tariff system may indicate this). Secondly, there is a question as to whether the service itself falls within the remit of what the local authority is able or willing to fund. Finally, there is the issue of legal obligation and whether the law, the Children Act for example or Section 117 of the Mental Health Act, means the local authority may have some kind of obligation to fund. However, for the social worker it is likely that these areas will have been addressed in the material produced for the panel.

The next preoccupations of the panel will be in two related areas. **Risk** is of central importance in making decisions about spending money. Although ostensibly need is the driving force in making decisions about eligibility, need has begun to collapse into risk, where the high cost decisions of funding panels are concerned.

The panel will also want to know that **alternatives** to the proposed course of action have been explored and that there are reasons why they will not work. It is clearly good practice to try to seek out the least restrictive option for care. So for any service user the panel will have in their minds a kind of hierarchy of care options, beginning with the lowest (and least expensive) level of input. For children this might go something like this (see Figure 6.1).

Placement in family with social work support and/or assistance from family aid/assistant social worker

Family and friend or kinship placement

Foster care

Residential care of some kind

Specialist foster care or residential care

Secure accommodation

Figure 6.1 Hierarchy of care options

The panel would expect that if something at the top of the hierarchy was requested then full consideration had already been given to less restrictive and expensive options.

Panels have something of a dual purpose. They are there to make what are sometimes difficult decisions about funding, but also need to demonstrate that they are doing this transparently with due regard for relevant evidence, by systematically addressing these types of question. It is important that social workers are aware of this type of thinking.

This approach can be viewed in the following way (see Figure 6.2):

Highlighting risk

Identifying alternative approaches

Highlighting their limitations

Identifying the positive benefits of the suggested course of action

Figure 6.2 Questions addressed by funding panels

So far we have addressed some of the most important factors which will shape a panel's decision making. What other concerns might they have?

Next on the list of key areas for consideration come the **views of service users** and how they understand the proposed care package or placement. It is very important that what is written and said conveys a clear sense of the service user's perspective. In my experience of being a member of such panels, common stumbling blocks for social workers are questions which address the service user's views. Good professional practice demands that panels have proper regard for the perspective of the service user. However, they are also concerned with the issue of future placement breakdown and want to get an idea that the placement will work. The social worker is often acting as a sort of conduit to the service user when presenting to a panel. It is important to think empathetically to 'attempt to understand thoughts feelings and experience from the other person's point of view in order to understand how they might be feeling' (Trevithick 2005 p154). What does the package of care mean to the person? How do they see it fitting with their physical, emotional and social development? How are they going to respond emotionally to what is proposed? Panels will be interested in what the service user thinks about the proposed placement, how much they know about it and what sort of information they have received, and their motivation to make the care package work. This is one way of determining what Trevithick calls 'the correct fit between resources being sought and the needs of the service user' (p223). The views of carers can also be important here and a panel may want to explore their potential roles in relation to the package of care.

Panels are often interested in how a proposed care package fits into a broader plan of care for the individual concerned. So any presentation of a case to panel needs to include **a coherent care plan**, which looks not only at the service user's immediate needs, but at any medium- and long-term plans that are in place. The

inter-professional context of practice is important. Any care a social worker is proposing to purchase is likely to be one piece of an inter-professional jigsaw of provision and needs to be presented in this way. Inter-professional support for what is proposed is likely to be extremely important and the panel's attention needs to be drawn to this. Conveying a sense of shared inter-professional commitment is important in relation to this. The views of a child psychologist, for example, that a particular course of action might be of benefit to a child or young person will not carry all that much weight if she or he does not intend to be involved with the service user during and after their proposed placement. In mental health it would be important to underline team support, particularly the psychiatrist's support for a residential placement, and to show how the team will continue their input when the service user is placed and in the longer term when they leave the placement. Panels will want to see consistency between a social worker's plan and the overall inter-professional planning for that person. Obviously the inter-professional context can shape the nature of what is proposed. A particular foster placement might be chosen to sustain a child's attendance at a particular school and continued contact with educational psychology services.

The process of presenting a case to a panel for funding is a challenging one. It is important to remember the panel's essential perspective is a costs–benefits approach. Panel members' overall responsibility is to manage (or we might perhaps say ration) resources equitably and effectively. Social workers need to combine a sense of realism about the service user's situation and what the panel are able to authorise, with an attentiveness to audience, in order to persuade the panel of the strength of their case. Presenting to panel mixes the skills of presenting detailed and accurate information, with an understanding of the motivations and concerns of the panel themselves.

Making a case to a charity for support

Whatever our views of the historical roots of modern social work, charitable organisations and the relief of poverty undoubtedly played a part in the profession's early development. So whether we regard the forebears of current practitioners as being the social activists of the East End Settlement Movement or the hospital almoner arranging charitable support for the needy poor and sick, we cannot escape the connections between social work practice and the charitable relief of hardship.

One key area where social care professionals can support service users is in approaching charities for help and assistance. The whole process requires a specific set of skills. The primary focus of this part of the chapter will be on seeking assistance for individuals although some aspects of institutional and collective support will be explored. The extent to which social workers see supporting and pursuing charitable applications as part of their professional remit varies between practitioners and is also dependent upon a range of external factors including the broader economic picture. There is a likelihood that in times of economic austerity this may become a more important feature of social worker's professional lives (Sale 2009).

Charities have to address a range of charitable purposes as identified by the 2006 Charities Act. These range from the prevention and relief of poverty to the advancement of animal welfare or amateur sport. From the perspective of a social worker the most important and most relevant charitable purposes are those relating to the two following categories.

- The prevention or the relief of poverty
- The relief of those in need by reason of youth, age, ill-health, disability, financial hardship or other disadvantage

Of some relevance but probably less important is

- The advancement of health or the saving of lives

The commission's list of charitable purposes also includes a rather general 'catch-all' category, of 'other charitable purposes' (in keeping with the nineteenth-century Macnaghten doctrine definitions of charity), which can be important in that it addresses the needs of some groups relevant to social work, ex-offenders for example. It is also worth remembering that charitable purposes which at first sight do not appear pertinent to social care may at times be relevant. For example support in relation to animal welfare may be very helpful for a service user in whose life pets play an important role.

Charitable funds can provide help in relation to a wide range of need. The following list adapted from the guide to Grants for Individuals in Need (Johnson and Chronnel 2009) and the Charity Commission guidance on the Prevention or Relief of Poverty for the Public Benefit (Charity Commission 2008) gives a clear indication of the range of help that charitable trusts can provide for the purposes of the relief of sickness and of poverty for the public benefit.

Grants of money   This could include:

- Money to manage crises or disasters of some sort
- A range of expenses associated with travel. Visits to people in hospital residential care or prison are costs that could be met. Travelling expenses relating to travel to residential or convalescence homes might be met. It might also be possible to cover the costs associated with travel, so for example accommodation or child care
- Regular payments over a limited period to cover specific needs
- Money to assist in the payment of utility bills

The provision of items (either outright or on loan)   This could include:

- Furniture, bedding, clothing, food and fuel
- Heating appliances, washing machines and fridges
- Adaptations to the homes of people with disabilities
- Telephone installation

Payment for services   This could include:

- Essential house decorating, insulation and repairs
- Laundering, meals on wheels

- Outings and entertainment, child-minding
- Telephone line costs
- Utilities

The provision of facilities   This could include:

- The supply of tools or books
- Payments of fees for instruction, examination or other expenses connected with vocational training, language, literacy, numerical or technical skills
- Travelling expenses to help the recipients to earn their living
- Equipment and funds for recreational pursuits or training intended to bring the quality of life of the beneficiaries to a reasonable standard

How does decision making work within charities?

Many charitable trusts, particularly smaller trusts, may have a key person who is the first point of contact for those seeking assistance, often described as a correspondent, a secretary or a clerk. This person may have a key role in processing applications, overseeing their progress through the organisation and advising trustees on the approach they should take (although the final say on granting assistance will lie with trustees). The clerk may carry out an initial review of applications for assistance received by the charity. This may involve going back to the person applying for assistance to obtain further information, before the application goes to the trustees for consideration. Within smaller charities the trustees of the charity will often consider all applications. A similar process operates in larger charities although decision making here may take place within a grants panel, including trustees, volunteers and those with professional experience in health and social care. It is important to be aware that some charitable trusts have specific time frameworks within which they operate, when making grants to individuals. In some small charities the trustees may only meet on a limited number of occasions each year and these meetings will shape the pattern of their grant giving. They may not be able to process grants unless a meeting is coming up.

Applying for assistance through charities

Social workers need to work with service users in a systematic way when approaching charities for help. There is a wide range of grant making trusts available and it is important if social workers want to find the right trust that they adopt a structured approach to researching this area. Social workers in the UK are fortunate enough to have access to the Directory of Social Change's Guide to Grants for Individuals in Need, which provides some detailed information about the range of charitable assistance available and the processes of application.

Two general principles need to be addressed before we look specifically at the question of how to go about applying for help. The first concerns the relationship between the funding of charities and the state. Charities will not pay for costs which can be covered by the state. If they were to do this then the money they were paying out would effectively be going to the government and the exchequer rather than the individual. Any social worker supporting a service user in this area needs to be aware that statutory sources of help need to be the first port of call. Interestingly direct payments may complicate the picture of where the boundaries between the responsibilities of local authorities, individuals and the state lie (an area we will explore further in Chapter 8).

The second principle it is important to be aware of is that where charities are working in the area of health, illness and disability applicants do not necessarily have to be poor to benefit from grants. Trusts will focus on a specific set of purposes and aims in their deeds of trust, the legal document which outlines the purposes of the charity. 'Many trusts believe that people should not lose their life savings and standard of living to buy an essential item that they could afford, but that would leave them financially vulnerable for the future' (Johnson and Chronnel 2009 p7).

Criteria to determine eligibility for charitable funding

Charitable organisations have a range of specific criteria which they use in order to decide whether to give grants. They generally serve a particular 'community' (using the word in its widest sense (Stepney and Popple 2008)), either a community based on locality or a community based round common interest.

The following five general areas are often important:

- Geographical area
- Illness and disability
- Work history including service in the armed forces
- Age
- Other general areas

For a social worker looking for charitable support for individuals, one useful piece of advice would be to start locally. Familiarity with local charitable resources can be very important. There are likely to be trusts whose remit is the alleviation of poverty of those with a particular local connection. There may well be other local resources which can be made use of: Rotary Clubs and Round Tables sometimes help with individual need; local churches and hospitals may have access to small charitable trusts. (It is important as well to be aware of local credit unions which might perhaps offer an alternative if it proves impossible to obtain help from a charity.)

The other area where specific knowledge is of great value is in relation to charities which address the particular needs of those with specific types of illness and disability, particular communities of interest. For a social worker consistently working with people who face a particular type of problem, forging links with such charities can be invaluable. So for example a practitioner in a hospital, working on a unit specifically dealing with those who have had a stroke, or a social worker in a voluntary sector agency offering emotional and practical support to stroke victims who have left hospital, might well want to develop strong links with the Stroke Association's grant giving for individuals in need.

Chris Field, head of fundraising and marketing at Aspire, a charity which helps people with spinal injuries, argues that 'Charities need to have greater collaboration with social workers and vice-versa to know what the criteria are for receiving a grant' (Sale 2009). Local charities often seek out connections with social services locally. We have discussed two communities charities relate to, specific localities and communities of interest relating to disability and/or illness. What other criteria do social workers need to look at when making applications to charities?

One key eligibility criterion charities use is occupation. The roots of many grant giving trusts are occupational, so it is perhaps not surprising that they assume great importance where grants to individuals are concerned. So in order to clearly identify sources of support with service users social workers will need to look at their work history (and possibly that of their partner, as family connections can be important) to check for links to a particular area of employment. Particularly important are links to the armed forces, in relation to which a number of well-endowed charitable trusts operate.

Age is also a factor which can determine eligibility particularly for younger and older people. Finally, there are a range of other eligibility factors. Religion is probably the most important of these, but there are also charities aimed at particular types of need (for refugees for example) and particular cultural and ethnic groups.

Other eligibility issues

There are other issues which also need to be considered when thinking about charitable assistance.

- Charities will make stipulations about both income, and savings and equity, which will vary between charities.
- Charities may limit the size of grants available to an upper limit, so applicants need to consider whether this meets their needs.
- There may be limitations on the type of assistance available; charities may not provide money for certain things, the payment of utility bills or rent arrears for example, or restrict their work to one type of support, for example the provision of holidays.
- Charities may require particular types of supporting evidence, from a professional, or perhaps medical evidence.

Practice example – Anna

Anna is a 46-year-old woman. Both her parents were Jewish. Only her mother is still alive, living in Solihull in the West Midlands, where Anna was born and brought up. Anna has three children, all girls, the oldest of whom is 13 years old. Anna was married for 16 years to her husband Andrew, who is an American living in London and the father of the children. About 18 months ago Anna and Andrew separated, because of Andrew's violence towards Anna, which the children had also witnessed. Eventually Anna had to flee the family home

(continued)

and, after a period in a refuge, she moved into her current accommodation. For most of their time together Anna had worked as a civil servant with the Land Registry. However, about 3 years ago she had to give up her job because she was experiencing chronic fatigue, loss of weight and pains in her joints. She was eventually diagnosed as having lupus. The illness is generally managed with anti-inflammatory drugs, although Anna has had to take steroids when her condition has worsened. She is now living on benefits. She and her husband owned a small house, which is to be sold as part of their forthcoming divorce.

About 6 weeks ago Andrew came round to the flat and forced his way inside. Before the police, who were called straight away, arrived he smashed down several internal doors and smashed the TV throwing a coffee table through it. The police arrested Andrew and also contacted social services.

How would a social worker go about seeking help for Anna from a charity to help her fix the damage which has been done to the house? The first thing to think about is her eligibility for support.

When considering Anna's eligibility for support a number of issues might come into play:

- Her current address and geographical area, and in certain cases (relatively rarely), where she was born and brought up
- Issues around illness and disability, but the relevance of these to the grant she is seeking needs to be considered
- Her work history with the civil service
- The fact that she has children whose needs the grant would also address
- Her cultural and religious background

It is also important to consider her immediate financial circumstances and her savings and capital.

Finally, it is worth thinking about any restrictions on what charities approached are able to give grants for, and about what sort of supporting evidence will be relevant or useful.

Social work and poverty

There is an argument that work with the issue of poverty could be a more central concern of social work practice. Chris Jones argues that social work's '... principal long-term concern has been with either the moral education of clients, or where this is impossible with their supervision in order to minimise their nuisance and cost to the state. Material circumstances are considered largely as an external measure of personal and familial morality' (Jones 2002 p43).

Manthorpe and Bradley (2009) argue that although there is a great deal of variation in the way in which social workers view their roles in relation to direct work around poverty, 'one practitioner may conceive their role as close to advocacy, while another may be

(continued)

quick to refer problems on in order to concentrate on underlying pathology' (p206); social workers have a responsibility to concern themselves directly with poverty in their practice.

There are a number of ways in which social workers can directly address poverty in their one-to-one work with service users, some key examples of which I have listed here.

- **Benefit maximisation**
    An awareness of the basic structures of the benefits system helps social workers to signpost service users to the best sources of help, and to provide guidance as to how to effectively ensure that they are receiving the benefits to which they are entitled.
- **Managing debt**
    Debt and budgeting are linked areas; without a clear sense of a weekly budget it is very difficult to get an idea of the impacts debts are going to have. Social workers can provide help and emotional support around these aspects of managing money and again make links with debt advice agencies, keeping people away from expensive loans which will only deepen their debt.
- **Help with budgeting**
    There are a number of strategies which can be used to help with budgeting. Social workers can work with service users around this area, and resources exist within voluntary sector agencies to support those who are struggling to manage.
- **Credit unions**
    Credit unions are cooperative financial institutions owned and controlled by their members (those who use the union), which offer opportunities for saving and a source of credit at good rates, for those on low incomes. They can provide an escape from high-interest loan shark borrowing, which can be such an insidious feature of poorer communities (Mantle and Backwith 2010).
- **Help in kind**
    There are a range of resources which might fall into this category. A number of organisations for pensioners for example run cheap food-cooperatives where food purchased in bulk from, say, the cash and carry is then sold on at cost price, and provides an important resource for those unable to get to out of town supermarkets where food is cheapest. Charity shops will often provide clothes with a letter from a professional. A number of voluntary organisations provide second hand-furniture for those in need, for a minimal cost or for free.
- **Alliance with poverty related campaigning**
    In advocacy it is always important to link work with individuals with wider social issues and to aim for change individually and collectively. This link between individual and cause can be important in relation to poverty. One important way in which social workers can practise in a way which is consistent with combating poverty is to raise awareness of poverty locally and nationally. Looking collectively with colleagues at issues of poverty, and making links with community agencies are an important part of this. Links to local councillors and MPs are also important.

Skills in cause advocacy

In Chapter 5 we outlined a process of cause advocacy made up of three elements, derived in part from Schneider and Lester's (2001) work:

- Creating links between interested parties and the formation of a coalition of interest
- Gathering evidence and undertaking research
- Clarifying and achieving goals

We are going to return to this outline of cause advocacy in this chapter and look at the sorts of skills advocates need in order to successfully pursue a cause.

Developing a coalition of interest

Developing a coalition of interest can be a complex task. We have already looked at the challenges of representing a diversity of views through campaigns around a single cause. This aspect of cause advocacy therefore requires a reflective and considered approach. This challenge is compounded by the fact that a successful coalition of interest is likely to be stronger if its base is broader. However, canvassing a wide range of support by creating greater diversity within the group can itself make the coalition more difficult to sustain. There is a tension here between achieving wide support and sustaining a clear and focused approach to the cause. We are going to examine both of these aspects of cause advocacy, beginning by looking at the issue of broadening the base of support for a cause and then moving to look at specific skills involved in ensuring as wide a range of views as possible are incorporated into any campaign.

Schneider and Lester identify a range of possible strategies that cause advocates can adopt in order to broaden their support. The first of these is to **enlist key influential people**. There are two elements to this in Schneider and Lester's view. Firstly, they argue that cause advocates should firstly 'identify individuals or groups that are already well-established in the community and enlist their support for their cause' (p232). Secondly, in doing this they argue that it is important to be aware of the leadership within the group and specifically seek out leaders, to bolster the leadership of the cause.

Schneider and Lester's second piece of guidance in this area is to **remember that everything is political**. They use the word political in a broad sense here. There are two tasks for any cause advocate: understanding the wider social context of specific local causes and **making links with those working for political change at a national level**. Finally, to do all of this effectively, it is important to adopt as wide a range of strategies for communication within the group and to potential allies as possible, including the use of the **media and the internet** in order to build a coalition.

Networking skills can be very important in this process of extending and strengthening support for a cause along the lines suggested above (Trevillion 1999). For those advocating on behalf of a cause there are three aspects of networking which are worth considering:

- Analysing networks and considering who is connected to each other and in what ways. Consider analysis of formal systems (for example exploring links between organisations, health and social care providers, voluntary sector organisations, churches etc.) and informal networks, talking to service users about the links they make.
- Synergies of interest are important to think about within the network. How far do individuals and organisations have a shared view of the cause being advocated for? What are their differences?
- Finally it is important to think about 'creating new social pathways or "walks" linking disadvantaged individuals' and 'developing networks of empowerment' (Trevillion 1999 p30).

One essential aim of any coalition of interest ought to be to empower those involved in it. In cause advocacy as in work with individuals, empowerment is a potential product both of successfully achieving goals in relation to the cause being pursued and of the process of advocacy itself. Ledwith (2005) makes this link in her discussion of community empowerment: community organising, with its focus on participation and positive action, has the potential to empower those individually involved. For this to happen professionals involved in advocacy need to adopt approaches which are focused on partnership working. Schneider and Lester place quite a lot of emphasis on professional advocates undertaking leadership roles and developing traditional leadership skills. This is in contrast with a number of other writers in this area (Beresford and Croft 1993, Bobo et al. 1996, Butcher 2007), who have viewed the role of advocates in collective approaches to change as being facilitative, assisting in the construction of 'new forms of local democratic governance' (Butcher 2007 p49), with the aim of supporting independent initiatives and giving power to service users (Wilcox 1994).

Biddle (1969) uses the term 'encourager' to try to convey the role undertaken by members of the community, which goes beyond merely volunteering and encompasses the notion of seeking change. I think the term helps to capture something of the facilitative role that professionals ought to be playing in relation to cause advocacy. How can advocates help to construct an effective coalition of interest in ways which are consistent with empowering practice? I am going to look at skills in working with groups in two areas, which may be helpful.

Developing a coalition of interest working with groups

Firstly I want to look at Henderson and Thomas's (2002) non-directive approach to working with groups. Henderson and Thomas identify a range of skills which a worker needs to use in order to facilitate group process without dominating the direction in which the group is moving.

Focusing   This is perhaps the most directive element of Thomas and Henderson's approach. Focusing involves ensuring that the group remains concerned with the task at hand. Sustaining interest by asking questions and supporting group members in expressing ideas and views are important.

Clarifying   Effective group facilitation depends upon clarity about the purposes of the discussion and making sure that comments and suggestions made are understood by all.

Summarising   Summary is a key communication skill in advocacy work with individuals and also when working with groups. It provides the group with an overview of what's been discussed up until that point and has the potential to move discussion forward.

Gatekeeping   Thomas and Henderson use the term gatekeeping to describe any intervention by a worker designed to ensure that every voice in the group is heard, encouraging participants who have said little for example.

Mediating   The resolution of any conflict within the group.

Informing   Henderson and Thomas see a potentially important role for workers as being the provision of information, facts that the group may need to have and the experience of other groups pursuing similar kinds of issues.

Advocates can play an important role in working with groups to enable them to express their views. However, it is important to remember that these relationships 'need to be consistent with people's empowerment on their own terms' (Beresford and Croft 1993 p123).

An issue which was highlighted earlier on in this chapter was that of how a coalition of interest may contain groups with slightly disparate views on what they want from cause advocacy. One way of building consensus within a coalition of interest is to have a series of goals clustered around a particular cause. Schneider and Lester support this strategy as it can enable participants to 'recognise how issues are interrelated' (Schneider and Lester 2001 p233). 'People learn about the many forces affecting them when they work on multiple issues and see their efforts not so much as problem solving, but as social change' (p234).

At this stage it is worth considering a case example.

Practice example – Nkechi

Nkechi is an experienced social worker whose current role is as manager of a local branch of a national charity working with older people, in a small, largely rural, local authority. The charity acts as an umbrella organisation for a number of projects which include a drop-in centre, a volunteer visiting scheme for isolated older people, a lunch club for black elders run in a local church, and an advice and advocacy service. The local authority have recently

(continued)

had their grant from central government substantially reduced and are proposing, as part of a money saving measure, to cut day care provision across the authority. Those most affected are older people, with a proposal to close three day centres. The cuts also extend to a day centre for people with physical disabilities and one for those with mental health problems. The council are proposing that those using the day centres have their personal needs reassessed and where appropriate be allocated a personal budget, so they are able to make their own choices about how they receive their care.

The proposed changes have caused great distress amongst the organisation's members. Many of those who access the advice service and home visiting scheme use the day centres, which cater for some of the most isolated and vulnerable older people in the area.

Within the local authority there is a voluntary services forum, where representatives from across the area meet to discuss common interests. At the forum's last monthly meeting there was a consensus that some action needed to be taken in relation to the day centre closures, and a steering group was formed with Nkechi as a member.

Henderson and Thomas's (2002) idea of what they term banner and sub-goals for cause advocacy is a useful strategy for realising this aim. They suggest identifying a key banner cause and then a series of more specific sub-goals, drawing together a range of views. We can see how this would work in relation to our cause advocacy example in Figure 6.3. (These are just some of the approaches that could be adopted in building a coalition of interest.)

This approach allows parts of the coalition of interest to pursue goals related to their more specific concerns. Undertaking parallel tasks can be a useful strategy here; similar strategies can be used in relation to different aspects of the problem. Nkechi and the organisation she works for might take on responsibility for a range of sub-tasks relating to the impacts of the proposed closures on older people, which would then be fed into the work of the coalition as a whole.

Gathering evidence and undertaking research

I want to move on now to consider the whole area of how evidence and research can support advocacy. It is important to remember that cause advocacy is not a linear process. We saw in the last chapter, when we looked at the carers' movement, that research can drive the development of a coalition of interest and vice versa. Research and evidence gathering may take a variety of different forms, ranging from formal research studies to informal personal testimony. It is important to remember that research and evidence gathering serve two purposes within cause advocacy; they help to inform and they help to persuade. Research and information gathering in advocacy needs to be consistent with the empowering principles which underlie this area of social work practice and to have a participatory focus, coming from and engaging the developing coalition of interest. It is also important to think about the extent to

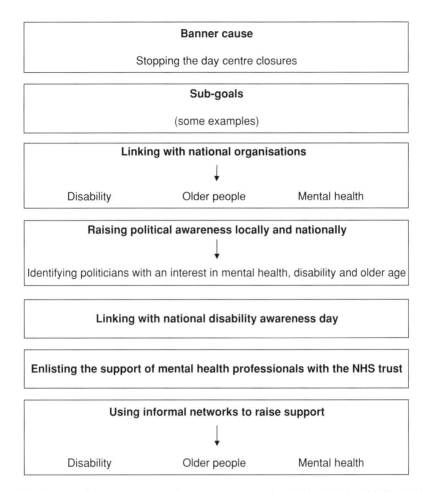

Figure 6.3 A cause advocacy example using Henderson and Thomas's 'banner' and 'sub-goals'

which the background issues underlying any cause need to be researched, and how the specifics of the cause itself should be targeted (VSO 2009).

There are a number of different strategies that advocates can adopt in relation to this area. I am going to start by considering group based approaches and then move onto look at surveys and petitions. Finally, I want to think about personal testimony, including video advocacy.

Most advocacy around a cause involves bringing people together in meetings. This can unite people together pursuing a common cause and galvanise them into action. It can, however, also help to gather information and act as a mechanism to enable those involved in campaigning to express their views. So one helpful strategy for information gathering is to use consultation through meetings. This has a number of potential advantages. Meetings and focus groups allow ideas to develop and people to feed off material that comes from other group members. Beresford and Croft (1993) suggest that a structured group consultation can be a very useful exercise, particularly amongst people who are vulnerable and not used to consultation.

Surveys offer the opportunity to gather information from a wide range of recipients. They can include those not able to attend meetings. They can give numerical information which may influence policy and decision makers. Petitions are also a useful related way of demonstrating the strength of feeling that exists about an issue. They can also help to build a broader base of support, by raising awareness of an issue.

Finally, it is important that evidence gathering does not ignore the personal experiences of those involved. We saw in Chapter 5 the important role that the personal experiences of carers played in raising awareness of the challenges faced by carers, which was crucial in the movement's development. Drawing attention to the sphere of personal experience locates what may seem like a rational and impersonal piece of policy making in the context of the lived experience of real people. Building on our earlier discussion, adopting a narrative approach to this experience can be very helpful, focusing on stories which will stay in the mind of those with the power to change policy.

How might these information gathering and research strategies work in relation to our case study? Firstly, it would be worth considering both broad and targeted research from the outset and begin to gather information available in the public domain before undertaking your own research and information gathering. Broad research would look at overall government policy and at research about the support that day care is able to provide and the impacts of its withdrawl on service users. It might also look more generally at the vulnerability of the groups affected: older people, those with mental health problems and those with disabilities. It would be important to have a detailed knowledge of government policy. Knowing what other groups facing similar issues are doing would also be important. Targeted research would examine the specific context of the day centres under threat, their history, how their work has been evaluated, the populations they serve and the specific details of the reductions in revenue faced by the local authority.

Meetings are an important focal point of any campaign and can be used to gather evidence as well as support the cause. They will help to emphasise the level of support for the campaign to stop the closure of the day centres. They will begin to generate ideas from service users about the impacts of the loss of these services to them. It may well be important to hold large open meetings to lead the campaign, but smaller more focused group discussions may also help to generate ideas and gather evidence on the impacts of the proposed changes.

All of this can feed into a survey. With the information generated from the meetings it ought to be possible to develop a simple survey which will use the experience of service users to investigate the impacts of the loss of the day centres on those who use them.

It will probably also be important to use individual testimony and to think about the way this is presented to decision makers. Writing to outline the personal impacts of the loss of the day centres to local politicians may well be effective. Developing video material looking at individuals' particular stories can be very helpful. This can also be 'instrumental in bringing both individuals and groups together by demonstrating that they share common concerns' (Henderson and Thomas 2002 p122). It is important to use as wide a range of approaches as possible; internet forums addressing local issues can be an important way of getting messages across.

Clarifying and achieving goals

The banner cause/sub-goal exercise is a constructive one to undertake as advocacy around a cause continues. It enables those involved in the campaign to see how they have progressed and to identify achievements. The use of the media can help drive a campaign forward to achieve goals and sustain interest both within and outside the campaign. Schneider and Lester (2001 p205) identify three reasons why this can be important:

1   'Positive reports in the media can influence public opinion and accelerate attention to an issue, putting it on the public agenda.'
2   'The media can increase the knowledge of decision makers and the public about the issues.'
3   'Getting media coverage gives participants a sense of empowerment by seeing their pictures or remarks in the press or on television.'

Even if cause advocacy fails to achieve the changes it seeks, it is still of value, in that it has the potential to forge collective alliances and to empower service users who are involved. If the campaign to stop the day centre closures does not succeed or is only partially successful, for Nkechi it will still have helped to forge stronger links between the voluntary sector organisations involved, and helped older people to work together collectively for change, enhancing their self-esteem and sense of personal agency and empowerment. It may make participants more willing to become involved and to campaign in the future. Evaluation of success is an important end point in this process, but must address both the banner cause and sub-goals, and be attentive to these secondary gains.

Video advocacy

The use of video material in cause advocacy has become increasingly popular in recent years (Gregory et al. 2005). The organisation WITNESS have been instrumental in developing this approach in relation to a wide range of issues across the world (www.witness.org) with a focus on human rights. The Books not Bars campaign run by the Ella Baker Center for Human Rights in California is a good example of this approach. The focus of the Books not Bars campaign was on the proposal for a 'super jail for kids' in California. A coalition of

(continued)

interest developed involving the Ella Baker Center, young people and those with experience of the US juvenile justice system, WITNESS, and the Columbia University Law School.

The Books not Bars video drew attention to the negative impacts of the prison 'indus-try' in the US, particularly in relation to young people. The video addressed the disparities in the treatment of young black Americans within the justice system, and highlighted the relationship between increases in public spending on prisons and decreased spending on education. It also focused on the youth led movement to highlight and combat this policy. The video formed a focal point for a wide ranging campaign which involved a mixture of case and cause advocacy. A family advocacy project provided training and support for the families of young people involved in the California juvenile justice system. A range of teaching materials was developed for schools to enable young people to look at issues of juvenile justice from a human rights perspective and challenge public perceptions of the dangers presented by youth crime. The result of this campaign was that the proposal for a super jail was derailed.

Video materials 'can elicit powerful emotional impact, connecting viewers to personal stories' (Gregory et al. 2005 p5). As our example above illustrates they can also help to build a campaign.

Discussion point

A useful exercise to undertake at this point is to think about our case example dealing with the campaign against cuts in day centres. How could this campaign use video materials?

Think of some examples of how video could be used to support this example of cause advocacy:

- What sorts of video materials could you think about using?
- How would they help in presenting and analysing issues?
- How could they bring people together and build the campaign?
- How could you ensure that they reached as wide an audience as possible?

Key learning points

- Social workers have available a variety of strategies they can use to present problems when acting as advocates. Problem analysis, chronological presentation and narrative approaches all have a potential part to play in this process.
- Different approaches to presenting a case need to be adopted depending on the context of the advocacy role. So presenting a case to a funding panel needs careful reflection on the panel's role and expectations. Similarly, seeking

help from a charity requires attention to detail and understanding of how charities work.
- Cause advocacy requires certain kinds of skill, working with groups and campaigning in order to make the pursuit of a cause an empowering experience for all involved.

Further reading

Bateman, N. (2000) *Advocacy Skills for Health and Social Care Professionals*, London, Jessica Kingsley

Chronnel, C. (2011) *A Guide to Grants for Individuals in Need*, 2011/12, London, Directory of Social Change

Henderson, P. and Thomas, D. (2002) *Skills in Neighbourhood Work* (3rd edition), London, Routledge

Manthorpe, J. and Bradley, G. (2009) 'Managing Finances' in Adams, R., Dominelli, L. and Payne, M. (eds) *Practising Social Work in a Complex World*, Basingstoke, Palgrave Macmillan

Mantle, G. and Backwith, D. (2010) 'Poverty and Social Work', *British Journal of Social Work*, (40) pp2380–2397.

Schneider, R. and Lester, L. (2001) *Social Work Advocacy: a New Framework for Action*, Belmont CA, Brooks Cole

7   Advocacy Skills: Assertiveness and negotiation

Introduction

Social workers operate in complex working environments where adopting an assertive approach to interactions and negotiations with other professionals can be crucial. The National Occupational Standards for Social Work (Topss 2002) identify the 'use of professional assertiveness to justify decisions and uphold professional social work practice, values and ethics' (p57) as a core competence. The primary focus of this chapter is on assertiveness as a basis for effective and principled negotiation within advocacy. The chapter looks at three aspects of assertive negotiation:

- The nature of assertiveness and strategies for negotiating assertively
- Communication skills needed in negotiation
- Models and frameworks for assertive negotiation

These three areas are obviously interrelated. To be assertive requires both the adoption of a strategic approach and the capacity to communicate effectively. These two elements feed into the model of negotiation that we look at towards the end of this chapter. However, treating them as discrete elements can help social workers to adopt a self-aware and reflective approach to these processes.

It is easy to underestimate the importance of negotiation in social work. Jordan (1987 p141) identifies negotiation as a fundamental social work activity: 'Social workers are different [from other professionals] precisely because they characteristically prefer informal negotiation to formal rule bound decision making, and discussion and agreement to solutions imposed by professional authority.' If we begin to explore the types of activity that constitute day-to-day professional social work practice, we can immediately see the important role played by negotiation.

Matching service users needs with available resources   As part of this central social work activity we may be negotiating internally, lobbying within our own agencies for limited and rationed resources, and the opportunity to apply creative solutions to service users' needs. Externally, negotiations with service providers involve ensuring that the specific needs of service users are addressed.

Planning and implementing care and support   Social workers operate at the interface between the informal world of family, home, social network and community, and the formal world of 'occupations, professions and bureaucracies which comprise the apparatus of the welfare state' (Whittington 1983 p268). Their roles in care planning in this 'intermediate zone' (Christie 1998) involve negotiation between a multiplicity of other agencies, in which they endeavour to ensure the perspective of the service user comes to the fore. In practice this may be achieved through representing this perspective to others or supporting the service user to do this themselves.

Addressing questions of risk and autonomy   When we manage risk to children we are constantly negotiating the delicate balance between supporting and protecting a child and maintaining the cooperation of parents (Broadhurst et al. 2010). When working with adults there is an ongoing negotiation between service users, ourselves and other professionals about the balance between risk and autonomy (Bornat and Blytheway 2010).

A number of key points about the nature of negotiation in social work begin to emerge from this brief overview of its place in practice.

- Social work operates at a pivotal position within networks of care and support which help to sustain 'ordinary people in their natural settings'. As a consequence negotiation in social work can be directed internally towards our own organisations or externally towards other agencies and service providers.
- There are different degrees of informality and formality in negotiation, and the extent to which negotiation is either formal or informal depends upon the practice context. So negotiations with parents about their child within the context of a child protection plan will be very different from talking to a school about how best to ensure that that child's educational needs are met. We may also find ourselves supporting a service user through a formal tribunal of some kind, such as a review of benefits which shapes the structure of the negotiation itself. However, irrespective of the context, many of the approaches we need to adopt and the skills we need to apply will be the same.
- As in any form of advocacy (and our discussion of models of advocacy in Chapter 5 is obviously key here), negotiation will fall within the continuum of empowerment. Within any negotiation we may on the one hand simply be representing the views of a service user, or, on the other, actively supporting the service user to do this themselves.

One final important general point about negotiation is that social work brings its own particular ethos to this process. Social workers will always try to find negotiated solutions to problems and wherever possible not impose them (Jordan 1987, Ford 1988). This is a pragmatic stance, in that such solutions have the greatest likelihood of working, but also a principled one: an approach that is consistent with the principles of inclusivity and empowerment which are such important elements of the social work value base. As social workers we therefore need to employ approaches to negotiation that are consistent with this principled and solution focused orientation.

Strategies for assertive negotiation

What is assertive behaviour?

Being an effective negotiator requires two things. Firstly, we need to be able to communicate effectively in an assertive way. Secondly, effective negotiation requires a familiarity with a range of negotiating strategies. These are not two discrete elements; each feeds into the other. Therefore a good starting point in presenting the account of negotiation we have outlined above is assertiveness. What negotiation demands is clear and direct communication, and this is what the tools of assertiveness can give us.

Two key principles of assertiveness have a close affinity with those of advocacy. At the heart of what we mean by assertive behaviour is the idea that as individuals we have rights, and that we also have a right to assert them (McBride 1998, Back and Back 2005). As an advocate you are standing up for the rights of another person, and, as part of this process, this principle which underlies assertive behaviour is central. Secondly, advocacy requires direct, open and honest communication. This approach to communication is also the hallmark of assertive behaviour and plays a pivotal role in the processes of negotiation which are such an important aspect of advocacy in social work.

Assertiveness is probably most easily understood when we look at how it contrasts with other styles of behaviour. It is only when we look at this contrast between behaviours that we can get a clear picture of what assertiveness really means. So an important distinction to explore at this point is that between *non-assertive* (sometimes referred to as passive), *aggressive* and *assertive* styles of behaviour. I therefore want to explore each of these styles of communication in turn. These distinctions have been explored by a number of writers on assertiveness (Rabin and Zelner 1992, Leebov 2003, Parrot 2006). However, categorising behaviour along these lines is common to them all.

I will start with **non-assertive, or passive behaviour**. Passive behaviour is characterised by standing up for your rights or the rights of others in ways which make it easy for other people to disregard them. This involves a failure to explain honestly and clearly your wants and needs. When we communicate non-assertively we tend to express what we want in indirect, apologetic and self-effacing ways. Those who behave passively do so in order to avoid conflict with others. If we find such conflict anxiety provoking, a non-assertive response relieves anxiety in the short term but in the longer term may leave us feeling exploited or resentful. Other people may respond positively to such passivity, initially feeling sorry for the non-assertive individual. However, in the longer term their respect for the passive individual will diminish.

Aggressive behaviour in contrast involves expressing yourself in ways which may violate the needs and rights of other people. So behaving aggressively involves actively ignoring or dismissing the opinions of other people. Although behaving aggressively may help to get what we want in the short term and make us feel strong and effective we may feel guilty and exploitative in the longer term. Again the net result of this will be the loss of respect from other people.

The underlying principles of assertiveness

Finally, we come to assertiveness. Within negotiation an assertive perspective would have to encompass the following elements:

Clarity about negotiating position   Advocates sit between the service user and the other party involved in the negotiation. Preparation for any negotiation involves a full exploration with the service user of what they want from the process and what sorts of options they might consider. When this happens we begin negotiation clearly understanding where we stand and this enables us to be clear with the other party about what the desired outcomes for the negotiation are and what can and cannot be achieved. Being too passive in negotiation can lead us to understate or be insufficiently explicit about what we want from the process.

Flexibility and openness to compromise   An assertive negotiation is one in which there is space for 'workable compromise' (McBride 1998 p7). The aim of such compromise would be to strive for a win–win situation, identifying circumstances where all parties involved will benefit from the final outcome. It is worth considering the aggressive negotiator here. We can see that in taking an aggressive, bombastic position we fail to give room in the negotiating process for the views of the other party. This is not to say that there will be points at which we have to say no and be very clear about why we are doing this, or circumstances where we do need to reiterate our position repeatedly. However, these firm approaches will only be successful in the context of a framework which allows movement from both parties.

Maintaining open communication and giving feedback   When we are too passive we can fail to give voice effectively to our perspective on a given situation and ignore our own feelings and views about how the other party responds when we are negotiating. So whilst we need to be clear and explicit about what we are saying and what our position is, on the other hand we also need to respond to the other side and attempt to understand their position. There are two elements to this. The first is trying to understand where they stand from the outset of negotiation (one strategy suggested by Back and Back (2005), for doing this is to ask ourselves open questions about the position of the other party in order to gain a better understanding of their perspective). The second is attempting to respond constructively throughout the negotiation. This involves receiving and giving feedback. Challenge is an important part of this work. Aggressive and passive approaches are antithetical to this process. The former involves the maintenance of a dogmatic unmoving stance, the latter a failure to challenge the perspective of the other party (Chambers Clark 2003).

At this point, as we begin to think in more detail about how assertiveness fits into wider strategies for negotiation, I want to introduce a case study (focused on negotiation), which we can draw upon to illustrate our more detailed discussions.

Practice example – Colin

Colin is a 29-year-old black British man who lives on his own in a one bedroom flat rented from a housing association. Colin left school at 16 and worked for around 5 years as an administrator in the civil service. He then abruptly left his job with plans to go to university as a mature student. However, he dropped out of his course and has not worked since then.

It was at this time that he first experienced mental health problems and was diagnosed as suffering from depression. About 5 years ago this diagnosis was changed to one of schizophrenia. Colin was last in hospital about a year ago under section 3 of the Mental Health Act and has managed on his own in the community since then. Colin is very isolated and periodically troubled by voices. He finds it difficult to go out and can neglect himself. He struggles to manage financially on benefits.

He currently receives depot medication by injection from a Community Psychiatric Nurse every week, but feels this makes him lethargic. He would much prefer to take tablets as he has done in the past, but when he raises this issue his psychiatrist is opposed to this plan of action and will not contemplate any changes to his medication. Colin spends quite a lot of time each day in a local café. Now and again, he drops into the local clubhouse drop-in centre (a service user orientated organisation) and has read there about the fact that cognitive psychological help can be of benefit to people who hear voices and would like to try this option as well as medication. However, his psychiatrist, Dr Jenkins, would rather Colin involve himself in social activities at the local day hospital. He thinks this would be more helpful for him and allow psychiatric services to keep an eye on him, and is not keen on him getting one-to-one psychological input. Colin's elderly parents live nearby and are his main source of support. He sees his mother every other day, but their relationship is a difficult one. She feels that he ought to stay on his injection and that he will deteriorate otherwise and begin to neglect himself. Colin's flat is in a poor state of repair with damp in the bedroom, problems with the lock on the front door and graffiti sprayed on the bedroom window. Colin has approached the housing association about these issues and even made a complaint, but nothing has been done. Colin is worried that the landlord wants to get rid of him.

Colin's case presents a number of challenges for a social worker working with him. He clearly wants to try a different approach to treatment, a course of action the psychiatrist treating him feels has some risks attendant upon it. As a social worker you might want to support him in his discussions around medication with his psychiatrist and try to ensure his views are heard (as well as helping sort out the difficulties he has with his flat and his landlord).

We have talked about the sorts of strategies which an assertive approach can bring to negotiation. I also want to look at this point at skills, at how a skilled negotiator manages the process of negotiation from an assertive perspective. There are a range of techniques and verbal and non-verbal approaches which would fall under this category.

Strategies for assertive negotiation – planning and preparation

As has been suggested already, advance preparation is very important in negotiation. Keith Fletcher describes it as 'the vital first key to a successful outcome' (Fletcher 1998 p21). There are three central elements to this part of the negotiation process. Firstly, we need to be clear as to what we want and what our reasons are for wanting it. Secondly, we need to understand the position of those we are negotiating with, to know what they want and to try as far as we can to understand their position. Finally, we need to begin the process of preparing solutions. It may seem to be stating the obvious that clarity about our own position is a prerequisite of successful negotiation. However, achieving this may not always be a completely straightforward task. There are a number of key areas which need to be addressed.

- How flexible are we in terms of outcome? A degree of flexibility will help with the solutions. Can we separate what we want from how we are going to achieve it?
- How specific is what we want? Are there specific timescales within which we are working? Do we have room to try out a particular solution?
- What are our needs and what possible solutions are there? Can you be 'firm about your needs while being flexible over the solutions' (Back and Back 2005 p72)?
- Is there a bottom line, things which are non-negotiable? (We look at this area in more detail later on in this chapter.)

So for Colin there might be scope for negotiating about a medication change at a specific future point, or at day hospital attendance as part of an agreement to change medication, in order that Colin has a little more contact with psychiatric services. An important part of the work that an advocate might undertake in supporting Colin could involve establishing a clearer framework for effective communication between Colin and the mental health team responsible for his care, and separating out the final goals of the negotiation from the process through which they are achieved.

Strategies for assertive negotiation – different levels of assertion

Back and Back (2005) identify different levels of assertion: lower level assertion, where the focus is on finding out about the other party's position whilst at the same time asserting your own, and higher level assertion, where a more forceful and somewhat more confrontational approach is adopted. This is a useful distinction, which we will draw on the case study to illustrate.

In **lower level assertion** we typically indicate an appreciation of the other party's position before we move towards asserting our own perspective. So an example of this approach would be what they term empathetic assertion, where we preface the statement on our own position with an appreciation of the needs and wants of the other party. Adopting this approach, we might preface our discussion of Colin's case with an acknowledgement of the difficulties that Dr Jenkins faces. We might for example want to explain that we know about the pressure on beds the team faces and his fear that if patients relapse in the community this may increase this pressure, before putting forward our own views. Lower level assertion might also include adopting a responsive approach. This is where we check out the perspective of the other party on a particular issue in order to clarify their position. This might involve simply clarifying with Dr Jenkins what his reservations are about the new approach to medication. This serves a number of purposes within the negotiation process. It enables you to find out whether your understanding of the position of the other party is correct and to rectify any misconceptions that exist. It also has the impact of empathetic assertion of overtly demonstrating the fact that you are committed to a shared process at the end of which it may be possible to find solutions. It therefore serves to address both the substance of the negotiation and the relationships between the parties.

In **higher level assertion** we are seeking to be more confrontational and to draw attention either to discrepancies between the position of the other party and their previous behaviour, or to the potential consequences of a particular course of action (what Back and Back call consequence assertion). If for example we know that Dr Jenkins has allowed patients to manage their own medication in the past then we might well want to point out the discrepancies between this and what he is currently proposing for Colin. However, it is important to present this in as positive a framework as possible, perhaps prefaced in this example by a statement acknowledging the shared commitment of all parties to good patient outcomes and seeking a clarification of the reasons for the discrepant decision rather than merely pointing out the fact of its existence.

Consequence assertion involves drawing the attention of the other side to the potential consequences of their proposed course of action. This is the most confrontational form of assertion and is often used as a last resort. It is important, however, that the other party in negotiation is aware of the potential consequences of their action. There are two types of consequence we may be looking at here: the first is some kind of potential sanction or further action like making a complaint or taking the case into a formal process of some kind; the second is drawing attention to potential negative consequences of a particular course of action. This can be presented in a more empathetic way emphasising the common interests of all parties in not having a negative outcome. So in our case we might be pointing out to Dr Jenkins that Colin may become so disenchanted with mental health services should the present treatment arrangements continue that he refuses medication altogether which might be the least desirable consequence for all concerned.

Communication skills for assertive negotiation

Challenging assertively

I want to look now at some examples of how social workers act as advocates. One key communication skill in assertiveness is being able to challenge effectively. In fact, to those unversed in assertiveness, challenging is often regarded as the archetype of assertive behaviour. It is a good place to begin our discussion of communication skills for effective negotiation. Consider the following examples and think about how you would respond assertively in the circumstances described. They are all situations where social workers are advocating on behalf of service users or supporting their advocacy.

Practice examples – challenging assertively

You are a duty social worker working with Jana, a Polish woman who has lived in the UK for the past 5 years with her husband and two small children. In the past 6 months, following the loss of his job, Jana's husband has become increasingly threatening towards her and this has culminated in his assaulting her and her leaving with the children. She has been staying with her sister for a couple of days, but is fearful that her husband will find her there and has approached the local authority for temporary accommodation. When you contact the local authority homeless persons' unit on her behalf a housing officer responds by saying, 'We can't see her today; she'll have to wait in the queue like anybody else: there are plenty of local people looking for accommodation.'

These are some of the possible ways in which you might respond in these circumstances. Which do you think demonstrates assertive behaviour and which are examples of passive and aggressive responses?

- 'Mmm . . . let's move on'
- 'I'm sick of this sort of racism from housing officers'
- 'I don't think that is an appropriate way to respond, and I find your remark offensive. We need to deal with this situation urgently'

You are the manager of a drop-in centre for older people. A group of members of the centre have approached you to ask whether you can help to organise a trip to a 'Pensioner Poverty' rally taking place in central London, for which they will need to use the centre's minibus. You raise this issue at the centre's management committee meeting. When this item comes up on the agenda the chair of the management committee says, 'Before we start discussing this I don't think it is something we can use our resources to back. The centre is supposed to be about providing social contact and friendship for isolated people and the minibus should be being used for seaside trips.'

How should you respond?

- 'You're always so negative about new ideas and developments at the centre. You don't realise how poverty affects the people who come here'
- 'Well if we can't support it I'll go back to the group who want to go. They'll be disappointed'
- 'I think it's perfectly legitimate for members of the centre to be involved in this and we need to have a full discussion of the issues in the meeting. What do other members of the committee think?'

Again, these are some of the possible ways in which you might respond in these circumstances. Which do you think demonstrates assertive behaviour and which are examples of passive and aggressive responses?

(continued)

You are a social worker for Stuart, a young man who has been looked after by the local authority for a number of years. A pathway planning meeting to plan his transition from care has been arranged. Stuart is keen that his friend William should be present at the meeting to support him and to help him present his views to the meeting. You have spoken to the chair of the meeting to agree this in advance. Over the past 2 years Stuart has lived with his foster parent Rachel, who is also at the meeting. When the discussion turns to Stuart's plans for education, Rachel steps in and outlines Stuart's intention to study catering at the local FE college. At this point William interjects; Stuart's uncle, he says, has suggested that Stuart could join him in his small joinery business. Rachel seems quite upset by this suggestion and before William has finished interrupts, saying 'We've already planned what Stuart's going to do and I don't know what he (pointing at William) is doing here. He's never come to any other meetings.'

Discussion point

What do you think you should do in this situation? Think about your own ideas for responses in this situation. How would you apply the key principles of assertiveness? What types of responses might be construed as aggressive? What do you think a passive response might look like?

As we can see from these examples, assertive responses where challenge is called for are characterised by clarity and the opening up of channels of communication so issues can be addressed more effectively.

Verbal and non-verbal skills

In order that these assertive strategies in negotiation are successful it is very important that the assertive negotiator adopts verbal and non-verbal behaviours which support assertion. In relation to verbal behaviour clarity is central. To be clear, statements need to be brief and to the point. This contrasts with non-assertive statements, which can ramble and where the nub of what is being said can be hard to ascertain and hidden within unnecessarily complex discursion. When adopting an assertive approach to verbal behaviour we need to ensure that we distinguish clearly between facts and opinion and that we avoid sarcasm (associated with aggression) or self-deprecation, 'I'm always useless at this' (associated with passivity).

Non-verbally a steadily paced speech pattern and use of consistent volume are important. Facial expressions need to be consistent with our responses to situations and with the message being conveyed. This means the avoidance of 'ghost smiles' where we smile whilst expressing anger or when being criticised, so characteristic of passivity. In assertive communication there needs to be consistency between body language and the message conveyed. 'Where the two do not match we have an incongruous message to unravel' (Koprowska 2010 p12). Equally exaggerated expressions of disbelief, eyebrows raised in amazement for example, which form part of the repertoire of aggressive non-verbal behaviour, are not consistent with assertive negotiation. To be assertive your posture needs to be relaxed and open avoiding either the high crossed arms associated with aggression or the low-crossed arms, hunched shoulders and down-turned head position characteristic of passivity (Back and Back 2005).

It is important as an advocate to be aware of your own preferred communicative style and of your own body language (Fletcher 1998). Even if you are naturally an aggressive or passive communicator, the whole approach to negotiation underlying advocacy demands of the advocate that they communicate assertively. One key theme running through the literature on assertiveness is that the strategies and skills of assertive communication can be adopted by those whose predominant or preferred natural style of communication is different from this (McBride 1998). It is important for social workers to draw on reflective skills when considering these aspects of professional communication, adapting their communication strategies to address the particular demands of the advocacy role (Fook and Gardner 2007). This involves both reflection on action, evaluating the impacts of what you have done after the event and learning from this, and reflection in action, responding within the negotiation to what the other party brings to the situation (Schon 1991). Social workers have a professional responsibility to work to develop this awareness of the self within their working roles (GSCC 2002).

Discussion point

Reflecting on non-verbal communication
It is worth thinking at this point about the extent to which we are naturally passive, aggressive or assertive, and how our non-verbal behaviour can support what we say. One way of doing this is to reflect upon your own natural style. In the case example of Stuart that you looked at, how could you respond assertively in challenging the participants in Stuart's pathway planning meeting? Think now about how your body language and voice might support your assertive behaviour in this example. How easy is it for you to adopt assertive verbal and non-verbal behaviour in a situation like this one? Think about circumstances in your own life when you have had to act assertively and about what aspects of assertiveness come naturally to you and what you have to work on. Finally it is worth thinking about how others perceive you. Do you ever get feedback that 'you put yourself down' too much? Do you sometimes think that people can be 'a bit scared' of you? How might awareness of your own non-verbal communication change others' perspectives of you?

The idea of assertiveness as a sort of panacea which will address all our problems with communication within negotiation comes with some caveats. Negotiations are, for example, not normally conducted within gender free parameters. Gender impacts upon the perception others have of assertive behaviour; 'what is perceived as assertiveness in men can be experienced as aggressive behaviour when expressed by a woman' (Townend 2007 p145). Differences in professional power and other aspects of difference can also impact upon the process of negotiation (Parrott 2006). There are no simple solutions to the issues these aspects of difference may raise for assertive advocacy. There are, however, things we can do to sustain our assertive approach even when in a relatively less powerful position.

Self-belief

Townend (2007) discusses one potential strategy that can be a helpful way of combating some of the impacts of differences in power in negotiation. She argues that 'positive and affirmative self-belief' (Townend 2007 p29) have an important role to play in effective advocacy in circumstances where disparities of power – whether these are the product of differences in gender, ethnicity or professional role – impact upon negotiation. Townend adopts a largely cognitive approach, seeing a lack of self-confidence and what she calls 'self-limiting beliefs and self-recognition' (p28) as having the potential to undermine assertive behaviour. An example of such a belief would be an overarching view within negotiation that the other party will never agree with what is being suggested. Such self-limiting beliefs are not rational, but represent a distorted view of reality, the overarching belief shaping the negotiator's response to the whole process of negotiation. These beliefs are often associated with negative self-talk (Ellis 1997, Clark and Beck 2010), an inner monologue based upon the original distorted self-limiting belief. Examples of this type of negative inner self-talk might be thoughts along the following lines: 'they're not listening to me', 'I'm not presenting this clearly', 'this is not working'.

There are a number of ways of addressing this issue. Firstly, it is important to develop a reflective awareness of these types of restrictive and negative patterns of thinking. Secondly, we need to make use of this awareness to challenge both self-limiting beliefs and associated negative self-talk. Townend suggests that using positive self-affirmation before negotiation can be a helpful approach. This might mean visualising oneself behaving assertively or making self-affirmatory statements, 'I am a skilled and effective negotiator', for example, before we enter into negotiation. Fletcher (1998) gives the following advice in a similar vein. Before any meeting where negotiations are going to take place: 'Remind yourself that you have something to offer which is valuable to the people you are going to meet. There is no reason to assume that they will not think so too' (p77). Also important is being aware of and challenging negative inner self-talk and replacing negative thoughts when they intrude into our consciousness with positive ones.

Service users talking to their doctors: building skills in assertive negotiation

For service users advocating on their own behalf, developing assertiveness skills that can be used in interactions with professionals can play an extremely important part in ensuring their voice is heard and perspective properly understood. One way of doing this is by working together in groups introducing the conceptual framework of assertiveness, and providing participants with the opportunity to share experiences of interaction with professionals, review the approaches they have adopted in the light of their new knowledge about

(continued)

assertiveness, and rehearse and discuss possible future strategies (Bond 1999, Weston and Went 1999). The group context is important here. It allows learning through modelling (Bandura 1977) and a safe environment in which to practise new skills. It can foster a sense of inclusion and confidence amongst groups of service users who are often very isolated (Arroba and Bell 2001, Baird 2005). The benefits of these types of group intervention are not just important for service users themselves, but facilitate effective communication, for as we have seen assertiveness can be very effective in ensuring effective communication.

Frameworks for assertive negotiation

Assertive behaviour and assertiveness skills are only one aspect of assertive advocacy. In order to be an effective assertive advocate we also need a framework around which to shape our negotiation, an important part of moving from a battle of wills to a structured process, in which room to manoeuvre is created for each party. Bateman (2000) uses Fisher and Ury's (1991) framework of principled negotiation as a blueprint for advocacy practice. The central theme of Fisher and Ury's work is the concept of principled negotiation, which shares a substantial amount of common ground with assertiveness. Emphasis is on constructing a framework for negotiation in which the three principles emphasised in assertive communication can come to the fore: clarity of position, flexibility around boundaries (creating space to find solutions) and the maintenance of open communication.

We are all familiar with the 'good cop/bad cop' approach to interrogation we see in police dramas: one attempting to build rapport with the suspect, the other challenging and aggressive. Fisher and Ury's analysis draws an analogous distinction. Their starting point is that without a structured framework there is an inherent tension in any negotiation between 'getting what you want' and 'getting along with people' (Fisher and Ury 1991 pxiv). They argue that traditional negotiation has been perceived as a positional activity, one in which each side in the negotiation adopts a position, and then through a gradual process of conceding elements of each position a compromise is reached. If you want to get along with people you will adopt a soft approach; if you want to get what you want you will adopt a hard approach.

When we start to consider these ideas about negotiation in the context of assertiveness we can immediately see here how the soft approach equates easily with passive non-assertive behaviour and the hard approach with aggressive behaviour. So if you negotiate a 'successful' outcome in which you make the fewest concessions from your starting point by adopting a hard approach, the cost of this may be the potentially damaging impact this has on the other party in the negotiation and the relationship you have with them. On the other hand adopting a soft approach and coming to an amicable resolution may mean making substantial concessions and leave you vulnerable in future negotiations. This may engender feelings of resentment and of being exploited in the soft negotiator. Those adopting a hard negotiating style may feel guilty at their lack of flexibility and victory in a contest of wills in which friendly relationships between the participants in the negotiation are sacrificed.

How does Fisher and Ury's approach offer us a way out of this impasse in conventional negotiation, and steer a way between soft negotiation, where the goal is agreement, and hard negotiation, where the goal is victory?

Assertiveness is often thought of as striking 'a constructive balance between two extremes of being submissive and being aggressive' (Thompson 2009 p38). However, it is probably more helpful to understand assertiveness as offering something different from, rather than an amalgam of, these two extremes of passivity and aggression. This belief that assertive negotiation is different from other approaches rather than a combination of them is the underlying philosophy of Fisher and Ury's work and at the heart of what they call principled negotiation. Theirs is not a style based on compromise where the desire is to partially satisfy everybody's needs by giving something and losing something (Thomas and Kilmann 1974). Principled negotiation is characterised by its focus on problem solving with the participants in any process of negotiation identified as problem solvers rather than opponents. The goal of any negotiation is seen as 'a wise outcome reached efficiently and amicably' (Fisher and Ury 1991 p13).

Fisher and Ury describe their approach to negotiation as a method made up of four elements:

- Separating people from the problem
- Focusing on interests not positions
- Inventing options for mutual gain
- Insisting on using objective criteria

They do not view negotiation as a strictly linear process. In their view, recourse to any element of this framework may be appropriate irrespective of where we find ourselves in the course of any negotiation. However, we can see that separating the people from the problem and focusing on interests and not solutions relate to the process of negotiation, whilst inventing options for mutual gain and insisting on the use of objective criteria have an outcome focus.

What I want to do is to look at a model of negotiation based on this distinction between **process** and **outcome** largely based upon Fisher and Ury's approach, but also using the conceptual framework of assertiveness, and key ideas from solution focused social work. An approach based on these three elements offers a distinctive social work perspective on the process of negotiation within advocacy, allying a capacity to construct a meaningful dialogue with a focus on problem solving and solution finding.

The model has two elements to it: exploring the problem and seeking solutions. Table 7.1 shows the elements of the model.

Exploring the problem

As we have already noted, within negotiation as it is traditionally conceived, there are two types of interest involved: the substance of the negotiation (the primary interest of the hard negotiator) and the relationships between the two sides (the focus of the soft negotiator's concerns). Fisher and Ury argue that an important potential problem

Table 7.1 Model of negotiation: process and outcome

EXPLORING THE PROBLEM		

Preparatory empathy	Understanding our own assumptions
	Understanding motivation of other parties
	Appreciating the emotional meaning and
	    context of the negotiation
		Focus on the processes
		    of negotiation

Separating people from
    the problem
	Separate relationships and substance
	Avoid generalising and challenging
	    preconceptions	

Solution focused approach	Challenging 'impossibility ideas'	

Focusing on interests
    not positions
	Identifying and agreeing shared, mutually
	    identified, common ground	

SEEKING SOLUTIONS		

Holistic systems
    orientation
	Adopting a wide ranging approach to
	    understanding needs and an awareness
	    of systems
		Focus on the outcome
		    of negotiation

Inventing options for
    mutual gain
	Generating a range of different solutions
	    from all the parties in the negotiation	

Solution focused
    approach
	Focusing on strengths, previous successes,
	    resilience and autonomy	

Using objective criteria	Identifying mutually agreed standards Seeking relevant evidence	

in negotiation is the relationship between the parties becoming entangled with what is being negotiated. Fisher and Ury acknowledge that negotiation is shaped by the emotional responses of the parties involved to each other and suggest two key ways in which we might address these aspects of the negotiating process. They call this aspect of principled negotiation **separating the people from the problem**. In order to pursue this end we first need to challenge the underlying assumptions which the parties have about each other. The second strategy we need to adopt is to create an open framework for communication in which emotional and relational issues can be addressed.

The process of challenging assumptions has two elements to it: firstly, you need to think about what assumptions the other party has about you; secondly, you need to consider your own responses to the other party and to interrogate your own fears and any misconceptions you may have about them. It is probably helpful to begin by thinking about the position of the other party in any process of negotiation. Empathy, 'trying to understand, as carefully and sensitively as possible the nature of another person's experience' (Trevithick 2005 p154) is a key element in the social work skills base and a tool in reflective practice, and has an important part to play here.

To understand another's position, we need to try like Atticus Finch in *To Kill a Mocking Bird* to 'climb into his skin and walk around in it' (Lee 1960 p31). Cornouyer (2008) describes two elements of the preparatory process for any social work intervention, preparatory empathy and preparatory self-exploration. Preparatory empathy means putting ourselves in the shoes of another as part of our preparation for intervention, but needs to be combined with a process of also interrogating and confronting our own preconceptions and prejudices. The social worker working as an advocate faces two ways. They represent and work alongside a service user and in doing this they need to understand both that person's perspective and the preconceptions that they bring to the relationship. Rather along these lines, Dominelli (2009) characterises this process as 'developing a deepened understanding of the other person's position while reflecting on the privileged nature of ones own' (p55). However, this is only half the story. The advocate also needs to try to understand the position of the other party.

Returning to our case study it is worth thinking here about the sorts of assumptions we might have about Dr Jenkins and how they may shape our approach to negotiation. What would preparatory empathy look like here? When we put ourselves in Dr Jenkins' shoes we can begin to identify some of his motivation in looking at these issues of medication.

1   He is likely to want the best outcome for those patients for whom he has responsibility.
2   Keeping people out of hospital is likely to be an important motivation for him and influence his approach to treatment. 'His' inpatient beds are a precious resource.
3   He may be unused to patients' views being strongly put forward in ward decision making forums such as ward rounds, and unfamiliar with and possibly a little uneasy about advocacy.
4   He may have a strong sense of professional responsibility to make the right decisions for patients and this may mean at times not going along with everything they suggest.
5   His responsibility is also to engage and sustain contact with patients once they are in the community.
6   He is the leader of a clinical team and needs to sustain a consistent line with patients about taking medication.
7   He may well be receptive to creative and innovative approaches to treatment.

When we look at the obverse of this coin and at our own potential fears and beliefs about Dr Jenkins we can identify a range of potential assumptions we might make.

* He is too focused on risk.
* He works within a very medical model of practice.
* He is likely to equate professional power and responsibility with being firm and therefore will be unlikely to change his mind.

- He has a strong belief that he is right and is resistant to sharing power with patients.
- He doesn't want to lose face in front of his team by being seen to change his mind or to give ground to a patient.

Remember when you think about your own assumptions they will probably comprise general issues relating to all consultant psychiatrists and specific issues relating to Dr Jenkins himself. Social workers acting as advocates need to consider carefully the sorts of assumptions they make going into negotiations alongside a service user. This empathetic appreciation of the position of another and interrogation of our own pre-conceptions, which is such a central element in both reflective and anti-discriminatory practice, needs to incorporate an appreciation of the emotional position of the other party. It is important to consider the impact of these assumptions on the negotiating positions of both parties and their emotional responses to the negotiation. Dr Jenkins is in quite a powerful position in this negotiation, by virtue of his professional status and expertise. This may well mean that he feels a threat from the challenge to this role that a social worker advocating on behalf of the service user may present. This may translate into anger or anxiety or a number of other emotional responses. Equally Colin and his social worker may feel somewhat intimidated and need to be aware of the impact of this response on their own approach to the negotiation. It is through trying to understand this aspect of negotiation that we can start to separate our emotional responses from the core matters being discussed, the people from the problem. Fisher and Ury emphasise the place of what we would understand as assertive communication in this process: managing the emotional content of negotiation whilst separating the person from the problem. A key ingredient is active listening: exploring the position of the other party and making a clear statement of your own position. As part of this they advocate the expression of emotional responses to the situation and the creation of space for the other party to do the same (p30). Questions to find out the thoughts, opinions and wants of the other party are important here (Back and Back 2005) and help to generate 'the satisfaction of being heard and understood' (Fisher and Ury 1991 p35).

How would the principles of separating the person from the problem work in practice? It is important to focus upon the issues at hand and to avoid generalising or making assumptions that what has happened in the past will necessarily happen in the future. Generalising can take two forms. We may be tempted to generalise about psychiatrists; assuming that they are all 'tied to the medical model and want to deliver all medication by injection'. We may also make generalisations about Dr Jenkins' specific approach, thinking 'we know what he's like, he never lets patients manage their own medication'. It is important that we put these preconceptions aside but also that we challenge preconceptions when they are made in relation to our own negotiating position. In the same way that we might make assumptions about Dr Jenkins, he himself may have preconceived ideas about how psychiatric patients should be treated. The potential arguments that he might use here need to be challenged. He might, for example, specifically argue that Colin's previous lack of success managing his own medication in the community suggests he will fail in the future, or more generally that young men in the community always fail if they are not on depot injections. We need to remove the person from the problem here and challenge our own or other people's preconceptions which may damage the negotiating process.

Some useful concepts and techniques, which have their origins in solution focused social work, have a part to play in this aspect of negotiation. Solution focused approaches to social work have their origins in the work of De Shazer (1985) and Berg (1994) and the development of solution focused brief therapy. This is a therapeutic approach which is all about engaging in brief time-limited interventions in order to instigate changes in people's lives. As its name suggests, a key part of the ethos of this approach is the move from understanding the process of change, not as one of overcoming problems, but rather as being about seeking solutions. It is increasingly influential in social work (Tunnell and Edwards 1999, Parton and O'Byrne 2000, Myers 2007). The approach is premised on the idea that people can get stuck with problems, becoming swamped in problem talk and unable to think creatively to find solutions. It presents a number of techniques designed to drive creative thinking about solutions. One such technique is particularly relevant to our discussions of negotiation: exception finding. Exception finding involves identifying circumstances in which there are exceptions to a current problem and hence creating possibilities for change in relation to that problem. 'Talking of exceptions is central to this shift towards solutions' (Parton and O'Byrne 2000 p99). An exception may be a time when things were different, when the problem was lessened and/or the service user felt better about it. Parton and O'Byrne draw our attention to the place of what they call 'impossibility ideas' in preventing us from finding solutions, a way of thinking characterised by the view that a change or a certain course of action is impossible. Exception finding offers us a useful way of challenging this sort of thinking when it comes up in negotiation. As we can see this approach is quite similar to discrepancy based assertion which we discussed earlier, but with a less confrontational orientation. Exception finding is particularly helpful as it does more than merely challenge a fixed set of ideas, but offers us a pathway towards solutions.

If we return to our case study we can begin to see how this might work. One impossibility idea which hangs over our negotiations around Colin's medication is the idea that he cannot manage this aspect of his treatment on his own. Exception finding here offers us an alternative to outright challenge to the psychiatrist's professional perspective. Instead of a positional impasse, we can start to explore exceptions to this fixed rule. We might want to consider initially whether there have been times when Colin has managed his own medication, albeit for a short period of time. It might also be helpful to look at service users in similar positions and whether this has been the case with them. Exception finding is all about small exceptions to what can appear hard and fast rules. Once exceptions are identified they form the first building blocks we can use in constructing a solution. One of the reasons why exception finding is such a helpful tool in these sorts of negotiation is that it does not just direct us towards exceptions, but also enables us to explore what factors contributed towards these. So when we think about occasions when Colin managed his own medication, we can also explore what it was that contributed towards this success. This starts the process of moving towards a solution, from problem based to solution focused talk.

Moving on to look at the second element of Fisher and Ury's typography of negotiation focusing on positions and not interests, solution focused ideas can also help us. As we have already seen, a key concern of solution focused social work is to adopt approaches to practice which help us think differently about problems and creatively find solutions to them. This process, 'in which we create new descriptions about problems in a way that reveals practical solutions', is often described as reframing (Sharry 2001). The identification of shared interests which lies at the heart of Fisher and Ury's framework helps to reframe any negotiation, moving its basis from a positional to a problem solving one. With shared interests established it is then possible to use these to create a common framework within which negotiation can take place. So let us look at our preparatory empathy exercise in relation to Dr Jenkins' position, in order to illustrate what this means. Points 1, 2, 5 and 7 all represent possible positions of potential common interest. Both parties are seeking the best possible outcome here. Neither Colin nor Dr Jenkins (whatever his motivation) wants a return to inpatient treatment. Dr Jenkins knows that he has a responsibility (as does Colin himself with his psychiatrist) to sustain a relationship with a potentially vulnerable patient and it is unlikely that Dr Jenkins would explicitly position himself against creative approaches to treatment. When we start to unpick Colin's situation in this way the differences between the parties in the negotiation begin to lessen and a sense of common purpose emerges. It is possible to start to see here one of the reasons preparatory empathy is so important. It can start to construct the common ground of interests upon which we begin to build our negotiation.

Seeking solutions

We have looked at the two elements of Fisher and Ury's framework that are concerned with exploring the problem and looked at how ideas from solution focused social work can be helpful in this context. The next stage in negotiation is to move towards solutions. Fisher and Ury suggest two approaches to help this part of the process move forward. The first is the generation of a range of options which might be parts of a possible solution to the negotiation. The second is the appeal to objective criteria using which we can evaluate the appropriateness of any proposed solutions.

Generating options is something which needs to be part of the process of negotiation from the beginning and needs to include some discussion of what course of action to take should negotiation break down (an area I will discuss in more detail later). One great professional strength of social work is its capacity to consider service users from a broad holistic perspective within the context of family, social and care systems (Martin 2010). Any social worker working with a service user negotiating with those in positions of authority will need to look at the range of options that are available and also their acceptability as possible outcomes. In Colin's case there are a range of issues relating to his care in respect of which there may be room for compromise. So any solution to Colin's problem with medication might involve negotiation around his day-time activities, the support he receives from his parents and social networks, and improvements to his living conditions. The nature and types of contacts he has with professionals might also be important. It may be that a solution in this scenario, the outcome of which is Colin managing his own medication, may be achievable if changes can be identified in these areas. This may mean more flexible approaches from those involved in his care, supporting him in ways that fit more closely with his needs and way of living, seeing him in the café he frequents for example. This sort of approach, where social workers are on the one hand involved in a wide ranging exploration with service users of how to best to meet their needs, and on the other presenting the outcome of this to those responsible for making decisions on funding care, has quite a lot in common with the sorts of brokerage roles needed as part of personalisation (Bott 2008, Carr 2008, Beresford 2009). Solution-focused approaches can be important here. They are strength orientated and can move the process of solution finding towards an exploration of situations where Colin has in the part demonstrated resilience and exercised choice and autonomy (Myers 2007).

It can be difficult at times to see how the second element of seeking solutions, using objective criteria, might work in respect of social work. If we consider a couple who are divorcing and trying to decide on the value of their mutual assets (which they intend to divide equally) we can see how they might go about this process fairly. They might for example get three estate agents to value their property and decide that they should sell at the average price of the three valuations. This would be quite a common negotiating strategy in these circumstances. With the more complex negotiations entered into by social workers advocating alongside service users, this process of seeking objective criteria is a more complex one. However, there are some general principles which can help us in our search for objective reference points in negotiations.

Firstly, we can apply fair standards to help us negotiate. So, thinking about our example, we have objective market value as the standard for deciding the price of the house. Secondly, we can also apply a fair procedure to the process of negotiation. So the process of obtaining three valuations is an objective procedure for obtaining a fair price. If our separating couple had a shared record collection which they wanted to divide and decided to take turns choosing records until none were left, this again would be an example of seeking fair procedure.

Returning to our case study we can begin to see how these two elements of developing objective criteria might begin to work. In relation to fair standards and fair procedures we can appeal to a number of objective criteria in Colin's case. Firstly, we might think about the sorts of standards that any doctor might apply to any patient she or he was treating. There would be an expectation that medical professionals would provide education and support which would enable the patient to understand the side effects of the medication. Whilst taking the medication there would be good access to advice and assistance about medication and the opportunity to change and adjust the medication to mitigate the worst side effects. From the perspective of medical staff there would be an expectation that anyone taking medication would undertake to do so in a structured and systematic way as instructed. This is the normal contract that doctors have with their patients.

We might also appeal to relevant evidence in our negotiation. Therefore we might consider what makes for a good outcome for those who control their own medication. This might include support from professionals, relevant and meaningful day-time activity, and supportive familial and social networks: all factors likely to make this work. Again there are a set of mutual obligations here. Finally, when we come to think about process we might be able to identify a number of objective criteria, for example government policy on the involvement of service users in their own care planning (Department of Health 2003 for example) or guidance that indicates that multidisci-plinary teams should work collectively with service users accessing their services in formulating treatment plans (Department of Health 1995, Tait and Lester 2005).

What if negotiation does not work? Much of what we have looked at so far assumes that a process of negotiation will come to a successful outcome. However, if despite going through the process of exploring the problem and seeking solutions we are unable to reach an answer, what other options are available? Looking at these types of impasse Fisher and Ury invoke the concept of BATNA, the best alternative to a negotiated agreement. The choice of BATNA depends on the nature of the negotiation. However, Fisher and Ury identify a number of important principles to help shape our thinking in this area. Initially we need to thoroughly explore the options available other than negotiation. This does not mean just looking at a simple bottom line position, but rather looking at a variety of different scenarios which might come into play should negotiation fail. This process should also involve looking at the alternatives available to the other party in the negotiation. Finally, consideration should be given to pursuing the issue through more formal means.

Negotiation and the power of exit

In recent years a clear ongoing trend in UK social policy has been the introduction of choice into the sphere of public services, in an effort to 'make service users sovereign', through 'the extension of choices available to them' (Greener and Powell 2008 p163). The intention of choice models is to enable all of us (and consumers of health and social care in particular) to make active choices about education, health care, housing and social support of one sort and another. This has been achieved through the introduction of markets and quasi-markets into the realm of social goods. In this world of choice we are able to opt for one school as against another or through the personalisation process choose between providers of social care. The provision of choice is often contrasted with voice models of citizen participation (Means and Smith 1994). This is a less market orientated model where changes in the way in which services are managed and delivered are achieved through systems of consultation and the voicing of opinions (Denny 1998). The move towards choice is in part motivated by the belief amongst adherents of this policy that effective service improvement can only be ensured through consumers having the power of exit. The idea of the power of exit derives from the work of Hirschman (1970), who looked at those dissatisfied with the service they were receiving and the options available to them if they wanted an improved service. He argued that two key strategies could be employed. The first of these is exit, where a consumer could move to a new service provider. The

(continued)

second is voice, where through complaint they can attempt to change the service they receive.

It is relatively straightforward to understand how the power of exit might have an impact in relation to standard commercial transactions. I might for example become so dissatisfied with the haircuts I receive from salon A that I withdraw my custom and move to salon B, exercising the power of exit. It is important to remember that voice and exit are not mutually exclusive strategies for those dissatisfied with the services they receive. I might well initially voice my dissatisfaction with salon A before my exit to salon B. However, what exit does provide is a bottom line. If discussion fails to resolve my dissatisfaction, the option to walk away is always available as a last resort. So when we think about our BATNA the power of exit could be important.

However, within the world of social care, despite the rhetoric of successive governments, there are real limitations to the power of exit (Greener 2007). Unless the service user is able to finance alternative care (a rare set of circumstances for those whom social workers work with) then they will not be able to find alternative services to meet their needs. This can put workers in health and social care in quite powerful positions in relation to those they are supporting. If we think about Colin's case we can see the impacts of this lack of an exit option. His choices, other than to remain treated by his current team, are very limited. Although it might appear that he could stop taking his medication, unless it is given to him in a way that he accepts, this is a difficult option for him to pursue, as it may have a damaging impact upon him. This demonstrates the limits of the bottom line and the difficulties of the BATNA model when applied to social work and the type of negotiation we have been describing. It also highlights the centrality of negotiation in ensuring that service users' views are represented and needs met.

Beyond negotiation

As we have seen in our discussion of alternatives to negotiated agreement, that exit, choosing a different service, is often not an option for service users. What choices are available when negotiation fails? The most obvious way to pursue an issue is through some type of formal process of complaint.

Complaints offer a clear and structured process within which disputes about services can be resolved. Within most organisations the process of managing complaints follows a standardised format, beginning with the use of informal methods, where problem solving approaches similar to those we have looked at in relation to negotiation are employed. A continuum of different stages then takes us to a formalised independent review within the organisation itself. As we can see from the following table (Table 7.2), as the process becomes more formal there is greater involvement from those outside the organisation (Williams and Ferris 2010).

The final option for the complainant is to seek to assistance of an external body specifically charged with the role of complaint investigation, an ombudsman for example, or to go through some kind of legal process, for example judicial review.

The power of this structure is that it can effectively give voice to issues raised by service users, often combining independent oversight of the problem with the

Table 7.2 Managing complaints: informal to formal structure

Informal	Informal internal process	Problem solving approaches adopted – limited formal structure – local resolution	Internal subject of complaint and immediate manager	Internal
	Formal internal process	Process with established steps and stages Independent investigation and formal reporting on the complaint	Independent person involved often from within the organisation	
Formal	Formal review process	Review panel	Person external to the organisation itself involved in the process of review within the organisation	External
	External review	Legal enforceable redress Ombudsman judicial review	Case reviewed by an external organisation	

provision of advocacy services (Perry et al. 2008). If we look again at our case study we can see how this might work. Colin has had persistent problems with his flat and the attitude adopted by his landlord to its maintenance and vandalism in the form of graffiti on the windows. Interestingly in this situation we can again see the limitations of the power of exit. Colin is probably not able to find a flat in the private sector: it will be financially very difficult and he will not necessarily be a particularly attractive tenant for a private landlord. His rather frail support networks are also dependent upon his living at his current address. Colin has complained already and the management of his complaint at the informal level has not been entirely successful. It is at this stage that Colin and his social worker may want to look at the housing association's complaints procedure and begin pursuing a more formal process. Gulland's (2009) research into community care complaints found that complainants who did not specifically request independent investigation of their complaints were sometimes denied this by public bodies, even though a system of independent review was a core element in the procedure. This underlines the importance of being familiar with the procedures that relate to the complaint you are making. Colin also retains the option of approaching the Housing Ombudsman; as social landlords, the housing association will have signed up to their services. However, it is unlikely that the ombudsman will consider Colin's complaint until he has exhausted the housing association's complaints procedures.

Key learning points

- Negotiation has a crucial role in social work in general and specifically in advocacy.
- In order to negotiate successfully social workers need to adopt an assertive approach which involves adopting a range of strategies and particular communication skills.
- Adopting a principled and assertive approach to negotiation is consistent with the value base of social work.
- Negotiation has two interlinked aspects: a process and an eventual outcome.
- The process of negotiation involves exploring and sharing the perspectives of the parties involved. Using empathy, exploring each other's preconceptions, and identifying common ground are all key elements of this.
- When seeking outcomes we need to generate as wide a range of possible solutions as we can, focusing on previous successes and trying to identify objective criteria to support the conclusion we come to.
- Beyond negotiation there are a range of more formal mechanisms for resolving differences between parties which can be explored when less formal negotiation is not successful.

Further reading

Back, K. and Back, K. (2005) *Assertiveness at Work: a practical guide to handling awkward situations*, London, McGraw-Hill

Bateman, N. (2000) *Advocacy Skills for Health and Social Care Professionals*, London, Jessica Kingsley

Cournoyer, B. (2008) *The Social Work Skills Workbook*, Belmont CA, Thomas/Brook Cole

Fisher, R. and Ury, W. (1991) *Getting to Yes: negotiating an agreement without giving in*, London Random Century

McBride, P. (1998) *The Assertive Social Worker*, Aldershot, Arena

8   Advocacy Futures

In this final chapter the future of advocacy is explored through a series of interconnected areas. The chapter considers two key themes in the future of advocacy. Firstly, developments in advocacy with marginalised groups in which the role of anti-discriminatory and anti-oppressive practice, are considered. Secondly, it looks at the impacts of recent changes in the delivery of social care on advocacy. We begin with an exploration of advocacy with children and young people and consider the growing theoretical and changing statutory basis for this form of advocacy. It is an area where there is cause for optimism about the future, with independent advocacy increasingly integrated into child care practice. The situation with black and minority ethnic (BME) communities and mental health advocacy, an important way of combating exclusion is less positive. In the international context, however, advocacy can provide a constructive framework for projects centred on creating alliances between the local and the global, particularly around human rights issues.

The fast developing world of adult social care in the UK, within the framework of personalisation, offers opportunities for independent advocacy but also, particularly in the increasingly blurred relationship between brokerage and advocacy, potential changes in the nature of services and how they are delivered. For social work, personalisation may create a greater opportunity to undertake advocacy and may mean social workers operating in a wider range of settings. Finally, the chapter considers evaluation, which may play an increasingly important role as the pace of the changes brought about by personalisation increases.

Advocacy, marginalisation and discrimination

Advocacy is clearly important in relation to marginalisation and discrimination. As Atkinson (1999 p16) points out advocacy 'has a particular resonance for those young people and adults who, for a variety of reasons, are marginalised from society, discriminated against and often excluded from everyday life. In those circumstances advocacy is a lifeline. It is a means of accessing basic human rights.' In this part of the final chapter we are going to explore the role of advocacy with some of the groups who experience the impacts of social exclusion and discrimination most acutely.

Advocacy and anti-discriminatory practice with children and young people

In Chapter 5 we looked at issues around empowerment in advocacy and at how models of the advocacy process can help to encourage empowering practice. In looking at advocacy and young people I want to return again to the theme of empowerment and consider models of practice within this area; my particular focus is going to be Boylan and Dalrymple's account of advocacy as a practice with great potential as a tool for pursuing the goals of anti-oppressive practice (Boylan and Dalrymple 2009).

Boylan and Dalrymple's approach builds on conventional structural accounts of oppression and empowerment (Thompson 2006) to develop a structural model, which analyses empowerment from the perspective of young people and has critically reflective practice at its heart. Underlying this approach is a commitment to advocacy as a potential force for radical change, and an appreciation of the specific oppressive forces impacting upon the most vulnerable children and young people. Boylan and Dalrymple's structural model starts at the level of the individual young person and their interactions with advocacy. At this level advocacy allows 'meaningful dialogue with an adult' in which the young person will 'feel valued and taken seriously' (p142), all of which will enhance their capacity to communicate. This then leads to greater self-awareness, a developing understanding of the 'cultural context of children and young people's lives' (p142), which is enhanced by young people making connections between their own situations and those of others. Finally, the third level refers to collective action by children and young people with adult advocacy support, to actively change the world.

This model has two key features. Firstly, the role of communication and dialogue is extremely important, so a sense of self-worth develops through the dialogue between the advocate and the young person. This then supports the communication between young people, which in turn makes collective action possible. However, it is not just communication *per se* which is important here, but communication which seeks to understand and change. Young people at each stage in the model are communicating with advocates and each other with the goal of understanding their circumstances better and then changing them. This fits with the developmental context of young people's lives, as growing up is characterised by seeking to understand ourselves and the word around us.

So far we have looked at the structural aspects of this model and the important place of purposeful communication within this account of empowerment. However, this account of advocacy as a tool for anti-discriminatory practice also looks at the relationship between advocate and young person. Boylan and Dalrymple argue that, to undertake advocacy in a way which is consistent with anti-discriminatory practice, practitioners need to adopt a reflective and reflexive approach to their interactions with young people.

Before I examine in more detail what Boylan and Dalrymple mean by this, I want to take a step back and think in more general terms about the relationships between advocates and young service users. One interesting thing about the literature on advocacy is that (in contrast to the literature on social work more generally) this relationship is relatively rarely addressed. However, as social workers are aware, to begin to empower service users requires a sensitivity to the nature of these relationships. Person centred practice has often been viewed as a paradigm which helps promote service user choice (Dowling et al. 2006, Koubel and Bungay 2008). Whilst not specifically Rogerian in their focus, these approaches recognise the place of Carl Rogers' work and of person centred counselling as a key element in their underlying philosophy (Elliot and Koubel 2008 p35). Seden (2005) presents a more forceful argument for the use of person centred counselling skills in facilitating service user choice and advocacy. She argues that the application of Rogers' principles of genuineness, acceptance and unconditional positive regard can help support service user self-determination (Rogers 1961): an empathetic relationship built on this framework can enable a service user to explore his or her world and through this exploration come to a point where he or she is able to make positive decisions and choices in their lives. This is in keeping with Ali and Graham's (1996) approach to careers counselling and guidance, where a person centred approach is used to 'give a client a greater sense of control amidst the complexity of life developments' (p12). There is much to be said for an approach to empowering practice which focuses on the relational aspects of empowerment. However, as the following case study illustrates, taking this approach is not entirely unproblematic.

Practice example – Asha

Asha is a 15-year-old black woman. Her parents are both originally from Somalia and are Christians. They came to the UK as refugees 18 years ago. Over the past few months Asha has had some problems at school and on the estate where she lives. These are mainly centred around an ongoing quarrel with a couple of people in her class at the girls' comprehensive school she attends. On the estate, a disagreement at a local youth club led to an altercation between Asha and another girl. Two community police officers who were passing had to calm down everyone involved. At school following another fracas a decision was made to exclude Asha. She was then involved in a fight outside the school gates and the police were called. As a result of this Asha has been asked to sign an Acceptable Behaviour Contract (Home Office 2007). She is currently attending a pupil referral unit and has been referred to a voluntary sector project supporting young women at risk of becoming involved in the criminal justice system.

Asha is angry about being excluded from school. She has always worked hard and feels that the decision is unfair. Asha has been subjected to a campaign of bullying by her classmates. This has taken the form of threatening homophobic texts and emails about Asha and her relationship with another girl in the school. Comments about her have also been posted on social networking sites. Asha has not felt able to raise this issue with her parents, and when she has sought help from teachers they have been quite dismissive of her concerns. One of the other young people at the pupil referral unit tells Asha about a scheme which supports young people who are excluded from school and can help challenge exclusion decisions. Asha makes contact with the project.

It is worth thinking about this referral and about how a person centred approach could help Asha in this context. It offers a number of positives. By creating a safe and secure shared space it would enable Asha to talk about her experience, to begin to understand what it may mean for her and to address some of the psychological impacts of 'cyber bullying' (Mishna et al. 2011). It might also help restore some of her trust in adults and boost her self-esteem. All of this would potentially create a springboard which could enable her with support to advocate on her own behalf. However, what may be lacking is an engagement with the wider context of Asha's life. Of particular importance are likely to be issues around discrimination on a personal level, but also the relationship between these and structural factors, the well-documented relationship between ethnicity and school exclusion for example (Parsons et al. 2004).

If we now return to Boylan and Dalrymple's model of advocacy with children and young people, we will see that this approach has the potential to address the place of the relationship within advocacy, and at the same time, through maintaining a focus on anti-oppressive practice, engage with discrimination. This is achieved through the integration of some of the precepts of critical practice (Fook 2002) into their approach. Essentially this means practitioners recognising the relationship between the specific issues facing particular young people and the broader social and organisational structures which impact upon their lives. This link between the personal and the systemic can leave young people disempowered and inhibit the capacity for both positive decision-making and representing their views to others. In order to achieve this within the relationship between advocate and young person, the advocate needs to have an awareness of the impacts of power. Part of this is to do with matching advocate and service user. The National Standards for the Provision of Children's Advocacy Services (Department of Health 2002) clearly identify the need for advocacy services to embrace diversity and for young people to have a choice in relation to the gender, ethnicity, sexual orientation and disability status of any advocate they might engage with. Research indicates a lack of diversity amongst those acting as advocates (Oliver and Dalrymple 2008) and this is a considerable hindrance to ensuring that services are inclusive. However, advocacy needs to extend the idea of social inclusion beyond the idea of matching advocate and service user in a rather formulaic way. Revisiting our case study illustrates what I mean.

Asha has a choice of advocates who can support her in the school exclusion advocacy project. David is a 30-year-old white gay man who has a lot of experience as an advocate working with young gay men and women. Maya is a black Christian woman from a middle class background, in her late twenties. She is a parent, has a law degree and is volunteering with the project. Summer is a 23-year-old white woman who was excluded from school herself as a child, but went on to train as a social worker and has personal experience of the system of school exclusion.

As we can see it is not entirely clear what a match between advocate and service user would mean here. An awareness of power within advocacy practice therefore needs to be based on more than matching the characteristics of advocate and service user (although this is clearly very important). Advocates need to bring the element of reflexivity to their work. This means being aware of the impacts of who they are on the power balance within a relationship, for example 'to think about how their own gender and ethnicity will affect the interaction between the two' (Boylan and Dalrymple 2009 p141). This critically reflexive position in respect of power within the relationship is the foundation for understanding the impacts of the wider system on the individual and 'challenging the marginalisation and oppression of children and young people' (Boylan and Dalrymple 2009 p141).

Before we leave this area of advocacy, it is worth looking at some of the advocacy and 'advocacy-like' roles that are defined within the legislation governing the care and support of children and young people.

Children and statutory advocacy roles

Legislation governing the care of children and young people has within it a number statutorily identified roles within which advocacy either plays some part or is central. I am going to look at three of these roles: the children's guardian, the independent visitor and the advocate within the complaints procedure.

The role of the children's guardian – best interests and the 1989 Children Act

The role of children's guardian (formerly guardian *ad litem*) within the Children Act 1989 is interesting to consider when thinking about advocacy and best interests. The role combines a perspective which is about enabling a child's voice to be heard, with a primary concern for best interest. Guardians are appointed by the court in child care proceedings (since 2000 under the umbrella of the Children and Family Court Advisory and Support Service, CAFCASS) to advise the court on what they consider to be in the best interests of the child's welfare. They also have the responsibility of appointing a solicitor for the child. The role brings an investigative element to what can be an adversarial court process. In compiling their report the children's guardian has the right to access relevant documents and to interview local authority personnel and others, including the family, evidence from whom they consider would be relevant. They have a responsibility to make the court aware of both the wishes and feelings of the child concerned and what they perceive to be the best interests of that child. This legal role is interesting in that it combines an element of advocacy, from the perspective of 'giving voice', articulating the views and wishes of the child, with an element of best interest advocacy, a professional judgement, grounded in a person centred process of gaining a child's trust and confidence. As a consequence the recommendation of the guardian may not 'always coincide with the views of the child' (Dale-Emberton 2001). This illustrates some of the limitations of the 'best interest' principle which runs through the Children Act as far as advocacy is concerned

Independent visitors – a citizen advocacy role?

The Children Act 1989 (Paragraph 17, schedule 2) places a duty on local authorities to appoint independent visitors in relation to children in their care (although there is evidence that it is a duty that local authorities do not always fulfil successfully (Knight 1998)). Independent visitors are volunteers who befriend and support children and young people

(continued)

who are looked after by the local authority. Visitors are paired with a particular young person and the intention is that they form an ongoing relationship, with the visitor taking an interest in the young person. Independent visitors have a whole range of different roles with young people. Finding out what they like to do, talking about progress at school, becoming involved in sports and hobbies, and social activities (trips to the cinema for example) are just some of the activities in which they can become involved. The independent visitor can also provide help and support when young people are planning for the future, and there is evidence of their advocating for young people in reviews (Knight 1998, DFES 2004). This is an interesting advocacy role and one which has many similarities with citizen advocacy. The focus within independent visiting is on the expressive aspects of the advocacy, on building a relationship. However, through that relationship independent visitors are able to advocate for children.

Advocacy: statutory support with complaints

The Adoption and Children Act 2002 inserted an additional section into the 1989 Children Act which imposed a duty on local authorities in relation to advocacy: to provide access to advocacy services to children and young people wanting to make a formal complaint under the legislation. The driving force behind this move was the negative experience looked after children had had in pursuing complaints, often of a very serious nature, without this additional source of support. The Waterhouse Report, *Lost in Care* (2000), and the Utting Report, *People Like Us* (1997), on the institutional abuse of children were strongly influential. As Corby et al. (2001 p174) point out, 'Most of the inquiries into the abuse of children in residential settings have pointed to the great difficulties children have experienced in making complaints about their treatment.'

The advocacy role in relation to complaints has a number of key features:

- The process should be led by the wishes and views of young people.
- The advocate should be independent of the local authority.
- The advocacy is issue specific with the complaint as its focus.
- The advocate should be able to provide information about the complaints process and the rights and options available to the child or young person.
- The advocate should be attentive to building a relationship, taking the 'time and effort to get to know the young person well' (Department of Health 2002 p3).
- The aim should be to empower young people by 'enabling them to express their views ... or speaking on their behalf' (Department for Education and Skills 2004 p18).

This advocacy role is probably best understood as a version of formal advocacy. The advocate needs to understand the complaints process, and their purpose is primarily to enable the young person to voice their concerns by speaking for themselves or, where necessary, to speak for them. However, it acknowledges the need to address the expressive elements of the advocacy role in building a relationship with the young person. It would fit well with the approach to advocacy grounded in anti-discriminatory practice which we have just been considering.

(continued)

The Children Act, echoing the United Nations Convention on the Rights of the Child, establishes the clear principle that children have a right to participate in decisions made about their care. The development of advocacy services for vulnerable children and young people has been very much shaped by this ethos. We have looked at the specific statutory duty to provide advocacy services in relation to complaints. The guidance in relation to this suggests a broad rather than narrow view of advocacy for this group of young people, envisaging not only a situation where advocacy should be available when a complaint is being made, but that 'children and young people should be able to secure the support of an advocate in putting forward representations for a change to be made in the service they receive or the establishment they live in, without this having to be framed first as a specific complaint' (Department for Education and Skills 2004 p8).

Children's advocacy is important because children are a particularly vulnerable group. As we can see, advocacy in this area therefore makes demands upon the advocate in two ways. The advocate is both supporting child citizenship through representing the child or young person's views and upholding their rights, and is also building a relationship, consistent with the principles of anti-oppressive practice, to enable this to happen. However, advocacy with children and young people is also important as this is an area of social care where there is an acknowledgement that in order to build a 'listening culture' (Department for Education and Skills 2004, National Children's Bureau 2009) in which children's participation is facilitated to the full, advocacy needs to be integrated into service provision. In reality the development of advocacy services has been somewhat piecemeal (Dalrymple 2004). However, the belief in the capacity of advocacy to shape service provision is increasingly influential in policy and practice in relation to children and young people: 'the issue about promoting the child's voice via advocacy is not reducible simply to enhancing some particular role but more a matter of system change.' So in future we may see advocacy services for children and young people 'extended beyond children in need to cover all children's services' (Pithouse and Crowley 2007 p212).

Before we leave the whole area of advocacy marginalisation and discrimination I want to finally look at these issues in relation to mental health and BME communities. We saw in Chapter 3 in our discussions of the IMHA role how advocacy is developing an increasingly prominent presence within the mental health sector. The discrimination experienced within the mental health system by those from BME backgrounds is well attested (Bhui 1998, 2002, Fernando and Keating 2009, Fernando 2010). In a whole range of different areas members of BME communities experience differential outcomes when they experience mental health problems and come in contact with services: examples include higher rates of hospital admission particularly under the Mental Health Act, prescription of more medication, and more involvement by police and courts in admission to hospital. The experience of racism, poverty, poor housing, lack of interpreting services and the trauma of being a refugee all compound this situation (Bhui 2002, Fernando 2003).

The picture that emerges from the research that has been carried out into advocacy support for BME communities, and mental health service users in particular, is one of advocacy which is inadequately resourced, marginalised and struggling to meet widespread demand (Rai-Atkins et al. 2002, Bowes and Sim 2006). Often advocacy is located within community organisations with a wider remit: 'while mainstream service definitions would place advocacy as a distinct service, black projects saw *most* of their work as advocacy' (Rai-Atkins et al. 2002 p32, authors' italics). However, these groups within the BME voluntary sector offer an important and accessible source of support to marginalised people. Their conceptions of the scope of advocacy are often at variance somewhat from that of service providers, with an overall goal of black empowerment, which 'intrinsically and inevitably involves challenging mainstream practice' (Newbigging et al. 2007 p21). Advocacy is often used by professionals as a last resort, when relationships with BME service users are breaking down, rather than proactively, to empower service users from the start of their engagement with mental health services (Rai-Atkins et al. 2002). Both Bowes and Sim (2006) and Rai-Atkins et al. (2002) question the applicability of a eurocentric model of advocacy in a context of cultural diversity, and argue that the understanding of the concept amongst those accessing advocacy services is often different from that of service providers and policy makers. Despite these difficulties, the provision of advocacy which begins to address cultural difference and to meet cultural need is welcomed by service users, who value the fact that advocates are clearly independent of services, have a shared cultural heritage (and language) with service users, and are part of organisations rooted in the BME community (Tam 2004, Newbigging et al. 2007). This begs the question as to how far 'mainstream' services can adequately meet the needs of excluded groups. However, there is a risk that the marginalisation of the BME voluntary sector may reinforce 'the already disadvantaged position of individuals seeking support from services' (Bowes and Sim 2006 p1223). So a mixed picture emerges in relation to mental health advocacy for BME communities. On the one hand it has the potential to make very positive differences in the lives of a particularly excluded group. On the other, 'whether in itself it (advocacy) is capable of delivering social justice – inclusion and access to resources such as services – however remains in doubt' (Bowes and Sim 2006 p1223).

Social work and the global context of advocacy

Within the UK we can have quite a limited view of what social work is about. We are inclined to see it as case based and often practised in a statutory setting. However, the international context of practice is increasingly significant (Healy 2001, Dominelli 2010, Harrison and Melville 2010). Any consideration of the future of advocacy within social work ought to address this. There are two reasons why this is important. Firstly, advocacy and empowerment are common elements in social work across the globe. Internationally the profession shares a common concern with human rights and social justice and a commitment to challenging policies and practices that are unjust. Those who see advocacy as a vital component in social work practice can take heart in its adoption internationally. We share common problems too in the delivery of services and a common interest in advocating against reduced spending on the most vulnerable, managerialism and bureaucracy, and the more negative impacts of social care markets (Dominelli 2010 p130). It is worth remembering that social care in the UK is increasingly influenced by the wider world. The control of residential care in the UK by international venture capital companies is a good example. Secondly, we are 'continually reminded of our interconnectedness with the rest of the world' (Harrison and Melville 2010 p10). These reminders may come in the form of our own awareness of global events and their impacts: wars, economic crises and global warming for example. They may come from closer to home. For all social workers, day-to-day practice is shaped by the experience of working with those whose lives have been shaped by global phenomena. This may take many forms. We may be working with refugees, those physically and psychologically scarred by wars, with people who have been trafficked or families divided between countries. Cultural awareness in practice demands a sensitivity to this global context (Graham 1999).

Within international development the advocacy paradigm has been increasingly used as a framework for connecting grass-roots concerns and activism with campaigns to change policies and institutions on a national level and beyond. VSO's (2009) guidance on participatory advocacy shows how this approach might work in practice. The focus of their method is on empowerment through a continuum of advocacy, from advocacy done for disadvantaged people, through advocacy done *with*, to advocacy *by* (VSO 2009 p11). Underlying this aspect of the model is the idea of capacity building, of using training and the experience of other successful advocacy projects to build skills and confidence in advocacy, which will enable local people to advocate on their own behalf in future. The primary concern of the VSO guidance is on what we would term cause advocacy, and the approach explicitly links advocacy at a local level with advocacy in relation to national issues. It also stresses the importance of participatory research as a way of grounding advocacy efforts in the experience of local people. Ideas which are familiar from cause advocacy are also prominent in this account: the idea of building a coalition of interest and effectively lobbying decision makers for example. What is different in the VSO approach (and other examples of international advocacy) is the sense of a common cause between advocacy in the specific context of one area, or even one country, and global campaigns for rights which transcend national boundaries. So, as well as networking and building coalitions of interest at a national level, links are being made with international and global campaigns for human rights.

Advocacy, HIV and AIDS – the international context

The International Community of Women living with HIV and AIDS (ICW) does work with younger women in Africa which provides a good example of how advocacy can work in this global context (Esplen 2007). In September 2007 the International Project Assistant Services and the ICW collaborated on a joint project designed to develop advocacy in relation to HIV/AIDS in seven African countries. I want to look at the specific example of

(continued)

this work in Namibia as an illustration of how advocacy works in this global context (de Bruyn and Gatsi Mallet 2011). This project shows how local advocacy initiatives can be linked to national advocacy and then into advocacy on an international and global level. The project focused on four key areas: violence towards women, rights to contraception, abortion rights and stigma, and HIV treatment. The project began with information finding and participatory research, and a process of capacity building. Information finding involved the identification of key local issues impacting on the lives of HIV-positive women, and capacity building on beginning to equip those women with the skills and knowledge they would need to become effective advocates. The work undertaken included local initiatives and actions designed to influence national policy, and addressed both case and cause advocacy.

At the local level there were a number of key initiatives. Advocacy support and case advocacy given to individual victims of rape led to a more supportive approach being adopted by the police and health services. The stigmatised treatment of women with HIV/AIDS by medical staff was addressed through the establishment of a pilot project improving the complaints procedure in one clinic and establishing a clearer framework for rights based care. A youth theatre group was supported to use drama as an advocacy tool to raise awareness of issues of domestic violence, abortion and HIV/AIDS. At a national level, campaigns were started using the media, and contact made with politicians and other important opinion makers to change the Namibian abortion legislation and recognise women's reproductive rights (de Bruyn and Gatsi Mallet 2011). This work fitted into a wider international context of other similar projects and advocacy on an international level in Africa and globally through the ICW, in relation to the rights of HIV-positive women (Esplen 2007).

Discussion point

Advocacy in this context presents a particular set of challenges. What do you think the main challenges would be working as an advocate in the global south?

Midgley (2001) argues that the applicability of some aspects of the 'western' model of social work to the developing world can be questioned. It may be that a less individualistic and therapeutic approach to practice than that adopted in the west fits the international context of practice better, particularly in addressing 'problems of poverty, unemployment, hunger, homelessness and ill-health, that disadvantage the global South' (p28). The application of community work principles and an engagement with social activism may be better suited to this context, and link the local and the global more effectively. Dominelli (2010) makes a similar case in her suggestion that 'community social work may provide an interesting way of building on existing theories ... to bring together understandings of the global and the local' (p160). One key element of these types of approaches to practice is advocacy. For Payne and Askeland (2008) these advocacy orientated approaches have much in common with social work and might point towards one way in which social work could be practised internationally.

Advocacy and personalisation

Personalisation is an umbrella term used to describe a number of recent changes in the way social care for adults is delivered in the UK. Personalisation is not an entirely new concept. Its origins can be traced back to the move away from institutional care and the community care legislation of the late 1980s (Department of Health 1989, Department of Health 1990). The disability rights movement has also been influential in its genesis. Care management as it was originally conceived was seen as a system which would allow social workers, in their new role, to respond creatively to the needs of people they were working with using conventional care services, but also funding creative care options and harnessing resources from within the community (Challis and Davies 1985). This was to be achieved through the devolution of budgets to teams or even individual care managers. Disability rights campaigns for people with disabilities to have control over the services provided for them, which led to the 1996 Community Care (Direct Payments) Act, were also influential in the process. The White Paper 'Our Health, Our Care, Our Say' (Department of Health 2006) set out a new vision for the future of adult care where adults were to have much greater control over their care through the two cornerstones of personalisation: self-directed support and personal budgets. One key aspect of self-directed support is the self-assessment process, where service users identify their own needs. The model underpinning the interface between service user and worker is that of 'co-production' a shared process of identifying appropriate support within a broad holistic framework (Needham and Carr 2009). This support might come from within social care or outside (echoing the original philosophy of care management). Personal budgets were clearly identified up-front allocations of money that an individual could use to design and purchase support, from the public, private or voluntary sector. The introduction of the individual budget extended this concept, potentially combining money from several funding sources. This model is grounded in the idea of a diverse social care market where service user purchasing power will shape services and make them more responsive to individual needs.

Advocacy and brokerage

The future for advocacy services within the world of personalised care may be a different one. I want to start by thinking about two roles which are often seen as related to one another: advocacy and brokerage. The process of the provision of care within personalisation is a three-stage one. Firstly, an assessment is made of need and on the basis of this a decision made by the local authority as to a potential service user's eligibility for services or otherwise. This assessment is service user led but supported by a local authority care manager or perhaps a member of staff in a voluntary sector organisation. Secondly, once eligibility for service is decided brokerage comes into play. Brokers work with those who are purchasing a package of care with an individual budget, supporting them through the process and identifying possible service providers. Finally, there are care providers from a range of different statutory, voluntary sector and private organisations.

The role of brokers in social care remains a somewhat unclear one (Carr and Robbins 2009, Scourfield 2010). Emerging from the discussions of this area are two slightly different accounts of how this role might work, which I will describe as the narrow and broad versions of the role. In the narrow version the broker is seen as working to a specific task orientated agenda, identifying care providers and negotiating on price. This is a time limited role which could be undertaken for an hourly rate of pay, in a manner similar to the provision of financial advice by independent financial advisors (Commission for Social Care Inspection 2006 p9). The broad version of brokerage sees it as offering more extended support and a more extensive role. Here the broker is empowering the service user and giving them control over their lives. Brokers are helping people to navigate their way through complex systems of care, drawing on a wide range of resources, including family and friends. In the bigger vision for brokerage it is seen as being concerned with more than 'just accessing specific services' and linked to 'a vision of full citizenship and quality of life to which recipients are entitled' (Carr and Robbins 2009 p14).

Discussion point

Advocacy and brokerage

The following are some of the features of brokerage, probably most applicable to the broad model.

- A clear value base that promotes self-determination
- A fundamental commitment to empowerment
- Identifying and tackling barriers to social exclusion
- Supporting vulnerable people to make decisions about their care
- Providing information about the range of brokerage options available
- Having a knowledge of legislation and policy in relation to health and social care
- Having good communication skills, particularly listening skills
- Mediation and problem solving skills
- Challenging unfair decisions
- Working systematically to collate and interpret material about a resources

Have a look at this list drawn from some of recent accounts of brokerage (Scourfield 2010, Advocacy Resource Exchange 2011, National Brokerage Network 2011). How far do you think that brokerage can be separated from advocacy? How far are they part-and-parcel of the same activity?

Now look at the following statements:

- Brokerage uses 'the language of advocacy' and its key functions 'could very much be seen as activities an advocate would carry out' (Advocacy Resource Exchange 2011 p2).

(continued)

- 'There are similarities with an advocate's role' and 'the two roles cross over' (Advocacy Resource Exchange 2011 p2).
- 'Many advocacy and brokerage tasks are so similar it is clear that both are natural allies in the task of ensuring people who use services gain control over their lives' (Care Services Improvement Partnership 2011 p7).
- 'The broker's work may sometimes include elements of advocacy' but 'brokers provide a skilled technical service that is distinct from the role of advocate' (National Brokerage Network 2011 p1).

Which of the above statements best fits with your view of advocacy and brokerage? What features of brokerage make it similar to advocacy? Can you identify any key differences? Think of the discussions about the defining characteristics of advocacy at the beginning of the book.

So how close are advocacy and brokerage?

- There is common ground in the underlying philosophy of the two approaches and a shared commitment to empowerment.
- As with other roles which relate to care, the job of broker may contain elements of advocacy, 'in situations where people might need help to express and assert their views in relation to their service package' (Key 2006).
- Advocates and brokers both have mediation roles, negotiating and sorting out difficulties between people.
- The provision of information and advice to help people make decisions is an important part of both roles.

Certainly the thrust of the personalisation message is that there needs to be greater overlap between these two roles: a move from 'enabling people to challenge decisions made by others' and 'to argue their case' towards enabling people to 'be in control' and 'to consider how money is spent and support organised' (SCIE 2009 p2).

The rise of brokerage has other implications for advocacy which go beyond any discussion of the similarities and differences between the two roles. Many voluntary sector organisations, which hitherto have provided only advocacy services, have begun now to provide brokerage as an additional complementary activity. In fact this extended role has been actively encouraged: 'Advocates and their organisations may want to consider the full range of tasks needed to enable people to plan and arrange social care support so they can decide where their contribution is best made' (SCIE 2009 p3). This is not an unproblematic thing to do. Brokerage, perhaps slightly differently from advocacy, is a service. The vision of brokerage in the future is of a market place, where different brokerage services will compete with each other (Commission for Social Care Inspection 2006). The quality of these services will depend upon the information available to the broker, and his or her personal qualities and skills. The brokerage role is very much akin to care management, until now the preserve of statutory services (Scourfield 2010). Its incorporation into advocacy projects has the potential to compromise their independence. For some voluntary sector projects in the future, advocacy, brokerage and the provision of services will sit together (possibly as uneasy bedfellows) as part of a portfolio of service provision.

This discussion of brokerage leads us into another aspect of personalisation, its impacts on the nature and the scope of social care markets. The extension and diversification of the marketplace in social care envisioned within personalisation will influence both the nature of independent advocacy and the roles of social workers, particularly as they relate to advocacy.

Independent advocacy and personalisation

Walmsley (2002) rather presciently argues that current trends in advocacy for people with learning difficulties may see us moving towards a situation where advocacy is seen very much as just one element of a range of social care services available to service users. She contends that 'the possibility that self-advocacy becomes one of a range of advocacy services from which consumers might choose appears to undermine its potential as a radical force for change' (Walmsley 2002 p32). This perspective, which Walmsley identifies in *Valuing People* (Department of Health 2001), where advocacy as 'just another service', a commodity, is also potentially present, as part of the wider agenda of personalisation. In this advocacy market place individual budgets could be used to purchase specialist health and social care focused advocacy (SCIE 2009). The idea of having brokerage schemes for advocacy which help direct service users towards the most appropriate and effective advocates (South East Joint Improvement Partnership 2010) might enable new advocacy services to enter the market.

What changes will this market model bring to independent advocacy? Although it is difficult to assess the impacts of personalisation it seems likely that advocacy services will be more dependent on service users using individual budgets to purchase specific advocacy support. This does mean potentially that access to independent advocacy could be restricted to those who hold individual budgets and who therefore meet the local authority criteria for the receipt of a service. The focus of advocacy could be quite narrow, adopting an instrumental task orientated approach and undertaken by paid advocates. This will raise the question of the professional status of these workers. Professionalisation can be a two edged sword. It may perhaps improve practice standards and the status of advocacy, yet can also create distance between advocates and those they are representing (Dalrymple 2004). Advocacy with an expressive focus on long-term relationships between advocate and service user might become more problematic to provide, except by using volunteers. Personalisation may make the scope of advocacy a little narrower. Walmsley points to the role of advocacy in addressing issues of social justice and pushing for social change. However, it is not entirely clear how much space there will be within the reconfigured landscape of adult social care for cause advocacy roles to be pursued.

Despite the possible negative consequences of personalisation on advocacy, it does usher in an era of social care in which the perspective of the service user will be paramount, a system much more in tune with the principles of social inclusion and empowerment which underpin independent advocacy. For independent advocacy it therefore offers the possibility of a pivotal role, albeit one in which the nature of advocacy may need to change somewhat. A theme which runs through this book is the idea that advocacy is a broad concept encompassing a wide range of different activities, tied together by a common value base. Personalisation may require changes in the way in which independent advocacy is undertaken and delivered, but advocacy has always been a flexible activity and able to respond to change. It should have the capacity to embrace personalisation.

Personalisation advocacy and social work

For social work personalisation offers both the positive opportunity to extend practice roles beyond the confines of care management, and the less welcome option of social work being primarily focused on the assessment of service user's eligibility for service and the management of risk (Williams 2009). Where does advocacy fit within this changing professional environment for social workers? In discussions of the changing social work role, advocacy has featured quite a lot. In the local authority circular *Transforming Adult Social Care*, the role of the social worker was seen as 'focused on advocacy and brokerage rather than assessment and gatekeeping' (Department of Health 2009b p4). This idea of advocacy playing a prominent part in the social work professional role is a key theme within discussions of how social work will fit within the new terrain of advocacy (Department of Health 2009b, SCIE 2010, Department of Health/ADASS 2011). There are a number of ways in which this might happen:

- Social workers operate within inter-professional settings where the medical model of care can dominate and can bring a social and holistic approach. Social work advocacy in this context means working within multidisciplinary teams to ensure that their work is consistent with these values.
- Social workers have practical skills in rights orientated practice, a knowledge of the law, and of practical advocacy in relation to a wide range of areas including welfare rights, employment rights and housing.
- There is an advocacy role in safeguarding the most vulnerable at both an individual level and working with communities more widely. One key issue which may arise in personalisation is safeguarding issues arising within care packages purchased through individual budgets (Scourfield 2010).
- Social workers have skills which can be deployed in advocacy and brokerage (Phillips 2010).

What personalisation may herald is a change in the structure of the delivery of social care services. Within the UK social work is understood as being a role that is undertaken within the local authority. This rather parochial understanding of what social work is, in a sense confuses a professional role and a set of skills, with a particular job type and setting. With personalisation, social work roles within local authorities may become less important, with social workers using their skills to operate more in the voluntary and independent sector. Emerging evidence from service users suggests that they value support provided from independent sector organisations (Leece and Leece 2011). This separation of the professional role from a particular job may help in 'developing a much wider concept of the social work role placing it more firmly in line with international understandings' (Lymbery and Postle 2010 p2518).

We have looked at the issues that personalisation presents both to independent advocacy services and for social work. An exercise which is useful as a way of exploring this area is a SWOT analysis of both independent advocacy and social work.

Discussion point

Think about each of the four elements of the SWOT analysis: strengths, weaknesses, opportunities and threats. First of all consider independent advocacy. What are the strengths and weaknesses of independent advocacy in relation to personalisation and what opportunities and threats does it offer/pose? Now do the same exercise in relation to social work, thinking about advocacy roles in particular. Finally compare your two examples of a SWOT analysis. How much common ground is there in your assessment of these two areas and what are the differences?

Evaluating advocacy outcomes

Within a context of personalised services, evaluating the effectiveness of advocacy becomes increasingly significant. If the market is to play its part in the provision of services as envisaged within personalisation, then having a way of distinguishing between the performance of different services may become important. The value for money agenda may become more dominant in the commissioning of services (Davies et al. 2009). The research of Manthorpe et al. provides a snapshot of the evaluation of advocacy projects as it is currently undertaken by those commissioning services within local authorities (Manthorpe et al. 2005). It shows that many local authorities 'do not systematically collect or scrutinise the outcomes of the services they fund' (Manthorpe et al. 2005 p49) and that generally commissioners do not have the necessary tools to evaluate services and are consequently often reliant on contractual arrangements as a mechanism for monitoring services.

The CAPE (Citizen Advocacy Programme Evaluation) and CAIT (Citizen Advocacy Information and Training) evaluation frameworks both apply to citizen advocacy schemes and evaluate schemes against criteria clearly linked to the value base of citizen advocacy and, in the case of CAIT, to the specific principles of local schemes. The CAPE framework was developed by O'Brien and Wolfensberger in the 1970s (Henderson and Pochin 2001), and the influence of the ethos of normalisation can clearly be seen in the approach to evaluation it adopts. It is in part a way of insuring against the danger of citizen advocacy being subsumed into social care and losing its distinctive focus. So the evaluation addresses the question of advocacy schemes operating in a way which is consistent with the underlying principles of citizen advocacy as part of normalisation more generally. The CAIT approach, a development of CAPE, has a similar underlying philosophy, although the voice of the users of advocacy services is more present. However, like CAPE its primary concern is with the principles and process of advocacy. This approach, 'Is what we do consistent with what we say we do?', is a feature of a number of approaches to evaluating advocacy. The Scottish Independent Advocacy Alliance (2010), for example, identifies a range of areas within any advocacy project which could be focal points for evaluation and include service user involvement, management structure, the organisation's accessibility and its adoption of principles consistent with independent advocacy.

The primary problem with these approaches is that they do not have a strong outcome focus. The next approach to evaluation, ANNETTE, that we are going to consider comes much closer to doing this. ANNETTE (Advocacy Network Newcastle evaluation tool) (Henderson and Pochin 2001, Rapaport et al. 2005) was developed by the Newcastle Council for Voluntary Service. The approach records the nature of the work undertaken by advocacy services by dividing advocacy into six different roles – mediator, trouble shooter, special friend, confidant, guide and lifeguard – which gives a more detailed sense of both process and the outcomes for service users, albeit defined by advocates themselves. There is certainly scope for advocates themselves to integrate evaluation into their practice and to use reflective tools to do this, reflective diaries for example (Manthorpe et al. 2005) and supervision. Perhaps the most outcome focused evaluation in this area is the work of the PSSRU in measuring outcomes for advocacy and advice services (Windle et al. 2010). Their work employs a cluster of measures to try to evaluate the empowering impacts of advocacy on service users. They look at increasing service user knowledge, confidence and the capacity to deal with similar problems in the future to gauge the empowering impacts of advocacy. However, this approach adopts an individual focus and the extent to which the broader social goals of advocacy are successfully captured by this type of evaluation is questionable.

Research into advocacy services tend to produce positive feedback from both the commissioners and users of those services (Forbat and Atkinson 2005, Rapaport et al. 2006a), yet the extent to which those service users' voices are heard within evaluations can be limited (Donnison 2009). Certainly for independent advocacy the issue of effectiveness and how to assess it is crucial. It is not only driven by the increasing marketisation of social care, but also by the demands of providing accountable services. This issue of accountability is one not just for organisations, but for individual advocates as well. An awareness of outcome measurement ought to be a cornerstone of good practice in advocacy and personalisation may require it to be.

Key learning points

- The relationship between advocate and young person is a key aspect of practice with this service user group. It is important that advocates adopt critically reflective approaches to this area which are consistent with an anti-discriminatory and anti-oppressive practice, and, most importantly, bring these into the relationships they have with young people.
- In an international context advocacy has the potential to provide a framework for rights based approaches to development and change at a local, national and global level.

- The role of advocacy in personalisation remains somewhat uncertain. New roles such as brokerage may overlap with some aspects of advocacy.
- For independent advocacy the new social care market place may reduce the scope for pursuing causes and campaigning as part of advocacy. It may require a stronger focus on evaluation as more emphasis is placed on the measurement of outcomes. For social workers it may mean taking on a wider range of roles and offer more scope for social workers to be involved in advocacy.

Further reading

Bowes, A. and Sim, D. (2006) Advocacy for Black and Minority Ethnic Communities: Understandings and Expectations, *British Journal of Social Work*, 36(7), October 2006, pp1209–1225

Boylan, J. and Dalrymple, J. (2009) *Understanding Advocacy for Children and Young People*, Maidenhead, Open University Press

Dalrymple, J. (2004) 'Developing the Concept of Professional Advocacy. An examination of the role of child and youth advocates in England and Wales', *Journal of Social Work*, 4(2) pp179–197

Henderson, R. and Pochin, M. (2001) *A Right Result? Advocacy, Justice and Empowerment*, Bristol, Policy Press

Rai-Atkins, A., Jama, A.A., Wright, N., Scott, V., Perring, C., Craig, G. and Katbamna, S. (2002) *Best Practice in Mental Health: Advocacy for African, Caribbean and South Asian Communities*, Bristol, Policy Press

SCIE (2010) *Personalisation briefing; implications for advocacy workers*, London, SCIE

Scourfield, J. (2010) Going for Brokerage: A Task of 'Independent Support' of Social Work? *British Journal of Social Work*, (40) 858–877

VSO (2009) *Participatory Advocacy: a tool kit for VSO staff volunteers and partners*, London, VSO

Conclusion

One purpose of anyone writing a book about advocacy is to be an advocate for advocacy and I hope I have achieved this. In a world of increasing complexity where sources of power and authority are remote and often diffuse, the role of advocate is an important one wherever it is practised, as one part of a professional role or as a role in its own right.

A number of key themes emerge from this exploration of advocacy. There is much going on within the world of advocacy which is very positive; the development and consolidation of statutory advocacy roles has been extremely important. However, independent advocacy as it is currently constituted faces a range of challenges. Not least amongst these is the insecurity of the funding which the sector receives, which puts it at risk when spending is cut. Some parts of the sector, funding for BME groups for example, may be particularly vulnerable. Personalisation may have a substantial impact on advocacy. The nature of advocacy may change from 'enabling people to be in control rather than supporting people to argue their case' (SCIE 2009). How far brokerage roles are consistent with the underlying principles of advocacy and how organisations will adapt to them remains to be seen.

For statutory social work an awareness of how conflicts of interest can limit advocacy roles is an important issue. The role of advocacy within protection and the maintenance of an open and supportive perspective to independent advocates are developing areas. I started this book by presenting the case for social work to be understood in a broad sense rather than confined to the limited bureaucratic roles with which it is sometimes currently associated. It seems possible now that this breadth will be thrust upon us with personalisation ushering in an era when social work will not be confined to and synonymous with what takes place within a local authority. This decoupling of social work from the local state may provide opportunities for a greater diversity of practice, one part of which may be a stronger focus on advocacy. We shall see.

I want to end on a personal note. In Chapter 1 I asked readers to think about their own personal journeys towards and into social work and about how advocacy fitted into their own personal models of practice. I was fortunate to start my working life working (as what was called a community worker) in a service user run project in which much of my work involved advocating on behalf of individuals, equipping them with the skills they needed to be successful advocates on their own behalf, and supporting collective campaigns about issues which had an impact on those using our services. I had some trepidation coming into social work, about whether it would afford opportunities to advocate on behalf of service users and to work within empowering frameworks. However, becoming a social worker was not a disappointment. I met many colleagues who shared my enthusiasm for empowerment and advocacy (from whom I learnt a lot) and many opportunities for advocacy.

References

Action for Advocacy (2002) *The Advocacy Charter*, London, Action for Advocacy

Action for Advocacy (2006) *The Advocacy Charter*, London, Action for Advocacy

Action for Advocacy (2009) *Human Rights: A tool kit for advocates*, London, Action for Advocacy

Adams, R. (2008) *Empowerment, Participation and Social Work* (4th edn), Basingstoke/New York, Palgrave Macmillan

Advocacy Resource Exchange (2011) *Where does advocacy fit in with Brokerage for self-directed support and personal budgets?*, Southampton, Advocacy Resource Exchange

Aldridge, J. and Becker, S. (1993) *Children Who Care: Inside the World of Young Carers*, Loughborough, Department of Social Sciences, Loughborough University

Ali, L. and Graham, B. (1996) *The Counselling Approach to Careers Guidance*, London, Routledge

Allan, K., Stappleton, K. and Maclean, F. (2005) *Dementia and Deafness: an exploratory study*, Edinburgh, Deaf Action

Arnstein, S. (1969) A Ladder of Citizen Participation, *Journal of the American Institute of Planners*, 35(4) pp216–222

Arroba, T. and Bell, I. (2001) *Staying Sane: managing the stress of caring*, London, Age Concern

ASIST (2007) *Non-instructed Advocacy: the Watching Brief*, Stoke, Staffordshire, ASIST

Aspis, H. (1997) Self-advocacy for people with learning difficulties: does it have a future? *Disability and Society*, 12, pp647–654

Atkinson, D. (1999) *Advocacy: A review*, Brighton, Pavillion/Joseph Rowntree

Audi, R. (1995) The ethics of advocacy, *Legal Theory* (1), pp251–281

Back, K. and Back, K. (2005) *Assertiveness at Work: a practical guide to handling awkward situations*, London, McGraw-Hill

Baird, J. (2005) Reflections on the effects of group work with older people with impaired vision, *International Congress Series*, 1282, pp360–364

Baldwin, C. and Capstick, A. (eds) (2007) *Tom Kirkwood on Dementia*, Maidenhead, Open University Press

Baldwin, M. (2000) *Care Management and Community Care: social work discretion and the construction of policy*, Aldershot, Ashgate

Bandman, E. and Bandman, B. (2002) *Nursing Ethics through the Life Span*, Upper Saddle River NJ, Prentice Hall

Bandura, A. (1977) *Social learning Theory*, Englewood Cliffs/London, Prentice Hall

Banks, S. (2009) *Ethics in Professional Life: virtues for health and social care*, Basingstoke, Palgrave Macmillan

Bateman, N. (2000) *Advocacy Skills for Health and Social Care Professionals*, London, Jessica Kingsley

Becker, S., Aldridge J. and Dearden, C. (1998) *Young Carers and their Families*, Oxford, Blackwell Science

Beckett, C. and Maynard, A. (2005) *Values and Ethics in Social Work*, London, Sage

Beresford, P. (2001) Service users, social policy and the future of welfare, *Critical Social Policy*, 21(4), pp494–512

Beresford, P. (2009) Personalisation, brokerage and service users: time to take stock, *Journal of Care Services Management*, 4(1), pp24–31

Beresford, P. and Croft, S. (1993) *Citizen Involvement: a Practical Guide for Change*, Basingstoke, Macmillan

Beresford, P. and Postle, K. (2007) Capacity Building and the Re-conception of Political Participation: A Role for Social Care Workers? *British Journal of Social Work*, 37, pp143–158

Berg, I.K. (1994) *Family-Based Services: A Solution Based Approach*, New York, Norton

Berridge, D. and Brodie, I. (1996) Residential child care in England and Wales: The inquiries and after, in Hill, M. and Aldgate, J. (eds) *Child Welfare Services: developments in law policy and practice*, London, Jessica Kingsley

Bersani, H. (1998) From social clubs to social movement: land-marks in the development of the international self-advocacy movement, in Ward, L. (ed.) *Innovations in Advocacy and Empowerment for People with Intellectual Disabilities*, Chorley, Lissieux Hall

Bhui, K. (1998) London's ethnic minorities and the provision of mental health services, in Johnson, S. et al. (eds) *London's Mental Health: the report for the King's Fund London Commission*, London, King's Fund Publishing

Bhui, K. (ed.) (2002) *Racism and Mental Health: prejudice and suffering*, London/Philadelphia, Jessica Kingsley Publishers

Biddle, W.W. (1969) *Encouraging Community Development*, New York, Holt, Rinehart and Winston

Blytheway, B. and Johnson, J. (1998) The social construction of 'carers', in Symonds, A. and Kelly, A. (eds) (1998) *The Social Construction of Community Care*, Basingstoke, Macmillan

Bobo, K., Kendall, J. and Max, S. (1996) *Organising for Social Change*, Santa Anna CA, Seven Locks Press

Bond, H. (1999) Hear Their Voice, *Community Care*, 9.9.99, pp30–31

Bornat, J. and Blytheway, B. (2010) Perceptions and Presentations of Living with Everyday Risk in Later Life, *British Journal of Social Work (2010)*, 40(4), pp1118–1134

Bott, (2008) *Peer Support and Personalisation*, London, Centre for Independent Living

Bowes, A. and Sim, D. (2006) Advocacy for black and minority ethnic communities: understandings and expectations, *British Journal of Social Work*, 36(7), October 2006, pp1209–1225

Boylan, J. and Dalrymple, J. (2009) *Understanding Advocacy for Children and Young People*, Maidenhead, Open University Press

Bradshaw, J. (1972) A taxonomy of social need, *New Society* (March), pp640–643

Bramer, A. (2009) *Social Work Law* (3rd edn), Harlow, Longman

Brandon, D. (1995a) *Advocacy Power to People with Disabilities*, Birmingham, BASW

Brandon, D. (1995b) Peer Support and Advocacy: international comparisons and developments, in Jack, R. (ed.) *Empowerment and Community Care*, Chapman Hall, cited in Brandon, D. and Brandon, T. (2001) *Advocacy in Social Work*, Birmingham, Venture Press

Brandon, D. and Brandon, T. (2001) *Advocacy in Social Work*, Birmingham, Venture Press

Braye, S. (2000) Participation and Involvement in Social Care, in Kemshall, H. and Littlechild, R. (eds) *User Involvement and Participation in Social Care*, London, Jessica Kingsley

Braye, S. and Preston-Shoot, M. (1995) *Empowering Practice in Social Care*, Buckingham, Open University Press

Brechin, A. and Swann, J. (1989) Creating a 'working alliance' with people with learning difficulties, in Brechin, A. and Walmsley, J. (eds) *Making Connections: Reflections on the Lives and Experiences of People with Learning Difficulties*, London, Hodder and Stoughton in association with the Open University

Briskman, L. (2008) *Recasting Social Work Human Rights and Political Activism*, Eileen Younghusband Memorial Lecture, International Federation of Schools of Social Work Conference, Durban

Broadhurst Hall, K., Wastell, C., White D. and Pithouse S. (2010) Risk, instrumentalism and the humane project in social work: identifying the *informal* logics of risk management in children's statutory services, *British Journal of Social Work (2010)*, 40(4), pp1046–1064

Brody, S. (2010) Did more people with learning disabilities vote in the general election? *Community Care*, 7 May 2010

Brooker, D. (2007) Introducing SOFI: a new tool for inspection of care homes, *Journal of Dementia Care*, 15(4), July/August, pp22–23

Brown, R. and Barber, P. (2008) *The Social Worker's Guide to the Mental Capacity Act 2005*, Exeter, Learning Matters

Brown, R., Barber, P. and Martin, D. (2009) *The Mental Capacity Act: a Guide to Practice*, Exeter, Learning Matters

Brueggeman, W. (2002) *The Practice of Macro Social Work* (2nd edn), Belmont CA, Brooks/Cole

Buchanan, Ian and Walmsley, Jan (2006) Self-advocacy in historical perspective, *British Journal of Learning Disabilities*, 34(3), pp133–138

Butcher, H. (2007) Power and empowerment: the foundations of critical community practice, in Butcher, H., Banks, S. and Robertson, J. (eds) *Critical Community Practice*, Bristol, Policy Press

Cantley, C., Steven K. and Smith, M. (2003) *Hear what I say: Developing dementia advocacy services*, Newcastle upon Tyne, Dementia North

Caplan, G. (1965) *Principles of Preventative Psychiatry*, London, Tavistock

Capstick, A. (2003) The theoretical origins of dementia care mapping, in Innes, A. (ed.) *Dementia Care Mapping: Applications across cultures*, Baltimore, Health Professions Press

Care Service Improvement Partnership (2011) *Self Directed Support: The Role of Support Brokerage within Individual Budgets*, Care Service Improvement Partnership available at http://www.nationalbrokeragenetwork.org.uk/documents/downloads/csip.pdf (accessed 30 June 2011)

Carlyle, Thomas (1888) *On Heroes, Hero-Worship and the Heroic in History*, New York, Fredrick A. Stokes & Brother

Carr, S. (2004) *Has Service User Participation Made a Difference to Social Care Services?*, London, Social Care Institute for Excellence

Carr, S. (2008) *SCIE Report 20: Personalisation: A rough guide*, London, Social Care Institute for Excellence

Carr, S. and Robbins, D. (2009) *The Implementation of Individual Budget Schemes in Adult Social Care*, London, Social Care Institute for Excellence.

Challis, D. and Davies, B. (1985) Long term care for the elderly in the community: the community care scheme, *British Journal of Social Work* (15), pp363–379

Chambers Clark, C. (2003) *Holistic Assertiveness Skills for Nurses*, New York, Springer Publishing

Charity Commission (2008) *The Prevention or Relief of Poverty for the Public Benefit*, Liverpool, Charity Commission

Christie, A. (1998) Is Social Work a 'Non-Traditional' Occupation for Men? *British Journal of Social Work*, 28(4), pp491–510

Chronnel, C. (2011) *A Guide to Grants for Individuals in Need, 2011/12*, London, Directory of Social Change

Clark, C. (2000) *Social Work Ethics Politics, Principles and Practice*, Basingstoke, Macmillan

Clark, D. and Beck, A. (2010) *The cognitive treatment of anxiety disorders: Science and practice*, New York, Guilford Press

Commission for Social Care Inspection (2006a) *See me not just the dementia: Understanding people's experience of being in a care home*, London, Commission for Social Care Inspection

Commission for Social Care Inspection (2006b) *Support Brokerage: A Discussion Paper*, London, Commission for Social Care Inspection

Cook, T. (2007) *The History of the Carers Movement*, London, Carers UK

Corby, B., Doig, A. and Roberts, V. (2001) *Public Inquiries into Abuse of Children in Residential Care*, London, Jessica Kingsley

Corrigan, P. and Leonard, P. (1978) *Social Work Under Capitalism*, London, Macmillan

Coulshed, V. and Orme, J. (2006) *Social work practice : An introduction* (4th edn), Basingstoke, Palgrave Macmillan

Cournoyer, B. (2008) *The Social Work Skills Workbook*, Belmont CA, Thomas/Brook Cole

Cox, M. (1998) Whistleblowing and training for accountability, in Hunt, G. (ed.) *Whistleblowing in the Social Services*, London, Arnold

Croft, S. and Beresford, P. (1993) *Getting Involved: A Practical Manual*, Joseph Rowntree Foundation, London

Currer, C. (2007) *Loss and Social Work*, Exeter, Learning Matters

Daily Mail (2007) Thousands are claiming incapacity benefit for stress in sick note Britain, *Daily Mail*, 31 January 2007

Daily Mail (2009) Just one in six incapacity benefit claimants is genuine as tough new test reveals two million could be cheating, *Daily Mail*, 20 October 2009

Dale-Emberton, A. (2001) Working with Children: a Guardian Ad Litem's Experience, in Lull, C. and Roche, J. (eds) *The Law and Social Work: Contemporary issues for practice*, Basingstoke, Palgrave Macmillan/Open University Press

Dalley, G. (1986) *Ideologies of Caring: Rethinking community and collectivism*, London, Macmillan/Centre for Policy on Ageing

Dalrymple, J. (2004) Developing the Concept of Professional Advocacy: An examination of the role of child and youth advocates in England and Wales, *Journal of Social Work*, 4(2), pp179–197

Dalrymple, J. and Burke, B. (2006) *Anti-oppressive practice: Social care and the law* (2nd edn), Maidenhead, Open University Press

Davies, M. (1994) *The Essential Social Worker: An Introduction to professional practice in the 1990s*, Aldershot, Arena

Davies, L. and Duckett, N. (2008) *Proactive Child Protection and Social Work*, Exeter, Learning Matters

Davies, L., Townsley, R., Ward, L. and Marriot, A. (2009) *A framework for research on costs and benefits of independent advocacy*, London, Report for the Office of Disability Issues, Office for Disability Issues

Day, P.R. (1981) *Social Work and Social Control*, London, Tavistock

Dearden, C. and Becker, S. (2003) *Young Carers and Education*, Loughborough, The Centre for Child and Family Research, Loughborough University

Dearden, C. and Becker, S. (2004) *Young Carers: the 2004 Report,* London, Carers UK

De Bruyn, M. and Gatsi Mallet, J. (2011) *Expanding reproductive rights knowledge and advocacy with HIV-positive women and their allies in Namibia: An action-orientated initiative: Summary report.* Chapel Hill NC, Ipas

Dementia Advocacy Network (2011a) *Dementia Advocacy Good Practice Guidelines*, London, Dementia Advocacy Network/Advocacy Plus

Dementia Advocacy Network (2011b) *Four Approaches to Non-Instructed Advocacy*, London, Advocacy Plus/Dementia Advocacy Network

Denny, D. (1998) *Social Policy and Social Work*, Oxford, Oxford University Press

Department for Education and Skills (2004) *Get it Sorted: Providing Effective Advocacy Services for Children and Young People Making a Complaint under the Children Act 1989*, London, Department for Education and Skills

Department of Health (1989) *Caring for people in the next decade and beyond*, London, HMSO

Department of Health (1990) *Caring for people: Policy Guidance*, London, HMSO

Department of Health (1995) *Building Bridges: A guide to arrangements for interagency working for the care and protection of severely mentally ill people*, London, Department of Health

Department of Health (2000) *No Secrets: Guidance on developing and implementing multi-agency policies and procedures to protect vulnerable adults from abuse*, London, Department of Health

Department of Health (2001) *Valuing People: A New Strategy for Learning Disability for the 21st Century*, London, The Stationery Office

Department of Health (2002) *National Standards for the Provision of Children's Advocacy Services*, London, Department of Health

Department of Health, (2003) *Building on the Best: Choice, Responsiveness and Equity in the NHS*, London, Stationery Office

Department of Health (2006) *Our Health, Our Care, Our Say: A New Direction For Community Services*, London, Department of Health

Department of Health (2008) *Transforming Social Care*, (LAC (DH) (2008) 1), London, Department of Health

Department of Health (2009a) *Making decisions: the independent mental capacity advocate service*, London, Department of Health/Office of the Public Guardian

Department of Health (2009b) *Transforming Adult Social Care*, (LAC (DH) (2009) 1), London, Department of Health

Department of Health (2010a) *Adult protection, care reviews and Independent Mental Capacity Advocates (IMCA): Guidance on interpreting the regulations extending the IMCA role*, London, Department of Health

Department of Health (2010b) *The Third Year of the Independent Mental Capacity Advocacy (IMCA) Service 2009/2010*, London, Department of Health

Department of Health/Association of Directors of Adult Social Services (2011) *The Future of Social Work in Adult Social Services in England*, London, Department of Health

De Shazer, S. (1985) *Keys to Solutions in Brief Therapy*, New York, Norton

Doel, M. and Best, L. (2008) *Experiencing Social Work Learning from Service Users*, London, Sage

Doel, M. and Marsh, P. (1992) *Task Centred Social Work*, Aldershot, Ashgate

Dominelli, L. (2002a) Anti-oppressive Practice in Context, in Adams, R., Dominelli, L. and Payne, M. *Social Work: Themes, Issues and Critical Debates* (2nd edn), Basingstoke, Palgrave

Dominelli, L. (2002b) *Anti-Oppressive Social Work Theory and Practice*, Basingstoke, Palgrave Macmillan

Dominelli, L. (2009) Anti-oppressive practice: the challenges of the twenty-first century, in Adams, R., Dominelli, L. and Payne, M. (eds) *Social Work, Themes, Issues and Critical Debates* (3rd edn), Basingstoke, Palgrave Macmillan

Dominelli, L. (2010) *Social Work in a Globalizing World*, Cambridge, Polity

Donnison, D. (2009) *Speaking to Power: Advocacy for health and social care*, Bristol, Policy Press

Dowling, S., Manthorpe, J. and Cowley, S. (2006) *Person-Centred Planning in Social Care: A Scoping Review*, York, Joseph Rowntree Foundation

Dybwab, G. (1996) Setting the Stage Historically, in Dybwab, G. and Bersani, H. (eds) *New Voices: Self-Advocacy by People with Learning Disabilities*, Cambridge MA, Brookline Books

Elliot, P. and Koubel, G. (2009) What is Person Centred Care?, in Koubel, G. and Bungay, H. (2009) *The Challenge of Person Centred Care: An Interprofessional Perspective*, Basingstoke, Palgrave Macmillan

Ellis, A. (1997) *Stress Counselling: A rational emotive behaviour approach*, London, Cassell

Emerson, E. (1992) What is normalisation?, in Brown, H. and Smith, H., *Normalisation: a reader for the nineties*, London/New York, Tavistock/Routledge

Equality and Human Rights Commission (2009) *From safety net to springboard: A new approach to care and support for all based on equality and human rights*, London, Equality and Human Rights Commission

Esplen, E. (2007) *Women and Girls Living with HIV/AIDS: Overview and Annotated Bibliography*, Brigthon, Bridge/Institute of Development Studies

Evans, T. and Harris, J. (2004) Street Level Bureaucracy, Social Work and the (Exaggerated) Death of Discretion, *British Journal of Social Work*, 34(6), pp871–897

Ferguson, I. and Woodward, R. (2009) *Radical Social Work in Practice: Making a difference*, Bristol, Policy Press

Fernando, S. (2003) *Cultural Diversity, Mental Health and Psychiatry: The Struggle Against Racism*, Hove, Routledge

Fernando, S. (2010) *Mental health, Race and Culture* (3rd edn) Basingstoke/ New York, Palgrave Macmillan

Fernando, S. and Keating, F. (eds) (2009) *Mental Health in a Multi-ethnic Society: A multidisciplinary handbook* (2nd edn), London/New York, Routledge

Finch, J. and Groves, D. (1980) Community Care and the Family: A case for equal opportunities, *Journal of Social Policy*, 9, p4

Fisher, R. and Ury, W. (1991) *Getting to Yes: Negotiating an agreement without giving in*, London, Random Century

Fitzgerald, F.S. (1926) *The Great Gatsby*, London, Penguin

Fletcher, K. (1998) *Negotiation for Health and Social Care Professionals*, London, Jessica Kingsley

Fook, J. (2002) *Social Work Critical Theory and Practice*, London, Sage

Fook, J. and Gardner, F. (2007) *Practising Critical Reflection: A resource handbook*, Maidenhead, Open University Press

Forbat, L. and Atkinson, D. (2005) Advocacy in Practice: The Troubled Position of Advocates in Adult Services, *British Journal of Social Work* (35), pp321–335

Ford, J. (1988) *Negotiation (Counselling, Advocacy): A Response to Bill Jordan, British Journal of Social Work*, 18(1), pp57–62

Ford, P. and Postle, K. (2000) Task-centred practice and care management, in Stepney, Paul and Ford, Deirdre (eds) *Social Work Models, Methods and Theories: A Framework for Practice*, Lyme Regis, Russell House, pp52–64

Freddolino, P., Moxley D. and Hyduk, C. (2004) A differential model of advocacy in social work practice, *Families in Society*, 85(1), pp119–128

Freire, P. (1972) *Pedagogy of the Oppressed*, Harmondsworth, Penguin

Gates, B. (1994) *Advocacy: a Nurse's Guide*, Harrow, Scutari Press

Goldberg Wood, G. and Tully, C. (2006) *The Structural Approach to Direct Practice in Social Work*, New York, Columbia University Press

Gorman, H. (2009) Frailty and Dignity in Old Age, in Adams, R. Dominelli, L. and Payne, M. (eds) *Practising Social Work in a Complex World* (2nd edn) Basingstoke/New York, Palgrave/Macmillan

Graham, M. (1999) The African Centred World View: Developing a paradigm for social work, *British Journal of Social Work*, 29(2), pp251–267

Greener, I. (2007) Choice or Voice, *Social Policy and Society*, 7(2), pp197–200

Greener, I. and Powell M. (2008) The Evolution of Choice Policies in UK Housing, Education and Health Policy, *Journal of Social Policy*, 38, pp163–181

Gregory, S., Caldwell, G., Ronit, A. and Harding, T. (2005) *Video for Change: A Guide for Advocacy and Action*, London, Pluto

GSCC (2002) *Codes of Practice for Social Work*, London, GSCC

GSCC (2009) *Social Work Connection*, 6, September 2009, London, GSCC

Gulland, J. (2009) Independence in complaints procedures: Lessons from community care, *Journal of Social Welfare and Family Law*, 31(11), pp59–72

Hanay, C., Banks, W.C., and Zimbardo, P.G. (1973) Interpersonal dynamics in a simulated prison, *International Journal of Criminology and Penology*, 1, pp69–97

Hardman, D. (2009) *Judgement and Decision Making: Psychological Perspectives*, Chichester, BPS/Blackwell

Harnett, R. (2004) *Models of peer advocacy developed by selected projects funded by the Princess of Wales Memorial Fund*, London, National Children's Bureau

Harrison, G. and Melville, R. (2010) *Rethinking Social Work in a Global World,* Basingstoke/ New York, Palgrave Macmillan

Healy, K. and Mulholland, J. (2007) *Writing Skills for Social Workers*, London, Sage

Healy, L.M. (2001) *International Social Work: Professional action in an interdependent world*, Oxford, Oxford University Press

Henderson, C., Flood, C., Leese, M., Thornicroft, G., Sutherby, K. and Szmukler, G. (2004) Effect of joint crisis plans on use of compulsory treatment in psychiatry: single blind randomised controlled trial, *British Medical Journal*, 329(7458), pp136–138

Henderson, C., Swanson, J., Szmukler, G., Thornicroft, G. and Zinkler, M. (2008) A typology of advance statements in mental health care, *Psychiatric Services*, 59, pp63–71

Henderson, P. and Thomas, D. (2002) *Skills in Neighbourhood Work* (3rd edition), London, Routledge

Henderson, R. (2007) *Non-instructed Advocacy in Focus*, London, Action for Advocacy

Henderson, R. and Pochin, M. (2001) *A Right Result? Advocacy, Justice and Empowerment*, Bristol, Policy Press

Hervey, N. and Ramsay, R. (2004) Carers as partners in care, *The Royal College of Psychiatrists: Advances in Psychiatric Treatment*, (10), pp81–84

Hill, M., Davis, J., Prout, A. and Tisdall, K. (2004) Moving the Participation Agenda Forward, *Children & Society*, 18, pp77–96

Hirschman, A. (1970) *Exit, Voice and Loyalty: Responses to Decline in Firms, Organizations, and States*, Cambridge MA, Harvard University Press

Hodgson, D. (1995) Advocating self-advocacy: partnership to promote the rights of young people with learning disabilities, in Dalrymple, J. and Hough, J. (eds) (1995) *Having a Voice: An exploration of Children's Rights and Advocacy*, Birmingham, Venture Press

Home Office (2007) *Acceptable Behaviour Contracts and Agreements*, London, Home Office

Howell, A. (2003) A Minority Experience, in Cree, V. (ed.) *Becoming a Social Worker*, London, Routledge

Hugman, R. (2005) *New Approaches in Ethics for Caring Professions*, Basingstoke, Palgrave Macmillan

Hunt, G. (ed.) (1998) *Whistle blowing in the Social Services*, London, Arnold

Hunter, M. (2009) A Blow for Social Care, *Community Care* 28.5.09

Hurstfield, J. Prashar, U. and Schofield, K. (2007) *The Costs and Benefits of Independent Living*, London, HMSO

Ife, J. (2008) *Human Rights and Social Work: Towards rights-based practice*, Cambridge/ New York, Cambridge University Press

International Federation of Social Workers (2000) *IFSW Definition of Social Work*, Montreal, IFSW [Online] Available from http://www.fsw.org/p38000208-html (Accessed 12.10.11)

Johnson, S. and Chronnel, C. (2009) *A Guide to Grants for Individuals in Need*, London, Directory of Social Change

Jones, C. (1983) *State Social Work and the Working Class*, Basingstoke, Macmillan

Jones, C (2002) *Social Work and Society* in Adams, R., Dominelli, L., and Payne, M., *Social Work: Themes, Issues and Critical Debates* (2nd edn). Basingstoke, Palgrave Macmillan

Jordan, B. (1987) Counselling, Advocacy and Negotiation, *British Journal of Social Work*, 17(2), pp135–146

Joyce, T. (2007) *Best interests: Guidance on determining the best interests of adults who lack the capacity to make a decision (or decisions) by themselves*, Leicester, British Psychological Association

Keating, F. (1997) *Developing an integrated approach to oppression*, London, Central Council for Education and Training in Social Work (CCETSW)

Key, P. (2006) 11 Questions and Answers about Brokerage, in *Control Briefing Paper 1*

Killick, J. and Allan, K. (2001) *Communication and the Care of People with Dementia*, Buckingham, Open University Press

Kirkwood, A. (1993) *The Leicestershire Inquiry 1992* Leicester, Leicestershire County Council

Kitwood, T. (1993) Person and Process in Dementia, *International Journal of Geriatric Psychiatry*, 8(7), pp541–545

Kitwood, T. (1996) A dialectical framework for dementia, in Woods, R.T. (ed.) *Handbook of the Clinical Psychology of Ageing*, London, John Wiley and Sons

Kitwood, T. (1997) *Dementia Reconsidered: The Person Comes First* Buckingham, Open University Press

Knight, A. (1998) *Valued or forgotten? Disabled children and independent visitors*, London, National Children's Bureau, Joseph Rowntree Foundation

Kondrat, D. (2010) The strengths perspective, in Teater, B. (2010) *An Introduction to Applying Social Work Theories and Methods*, Maidenhead, Open University Press

Koprowska, J. (2010) *Communication and Interpersonal Skills in Social Work*, Exeter, Learning Matters

Koubel, G. and Bungay, G. (eds) (2008) *The Challenge of Person-Centred Care: An Interprofessional Perspective*, Basingstoke, Palgrave Macmillan

Lansley, A. (2010) The principles of social care reform, The 5th International Carers Conference, Leeds, 9 July

Laraña, E., Johnston, H. and Gusfield, R. (eds) (1994) *New Social Movements: From ideology to identity*, Philadelphia: Temple University Press

Lawton, A. (2007) *Supporting Self-Advocacy*, London, Social Care Institute for Excellence

Ledwith, M. (2005) *Community Development a Critical Approach*, Bristol, Policy Press

Lee, H. (1960) *To Kill a Mockingbird*, London, Mandarin

Leebov, W. (2003) *Assertiveness Skills for Professionals in Health Care*, Lincoln NE, Authors Choice

Leece, J. and Leece, D. (2011) Personalisation: Principles of the role of social work in a world of brokers and budgets, *British Journal of Social Work*, 41(2), pp204–223

Levy, A. and Kahan, B. (1991) *The Pindown Experience and the Protection of Children*, Staffordshire, Staffordshire County Council

Lymbery, M. and Postle, K. (2010) Social work in the context of adult social care in England and the resultant implications for social work education, *British Journal of Social Work*, 40(8), pp2502–2522

Lyons, K. (2003) Historical Portraits: Dame Eileen Younghusband, *Social Work and Society*, (1)

MacDonald, A. and Bailey, S. (2008) *Why Family Carers Matter: A Local Study of the Work of Suffolk Family Carers*, Norwich, University of East Anglia

Maden, A. (2007) *Treating Violence: A guide to risk management in mental health*, Oxford, Oxford University Press

Maglajlic, R., Brandon, D. and Given, D. (2000) Making direct payments a choice: a report on the research findings, *Disability and Society*, 15(1), pp99–113

Manthorpe, J. and Bradley, G. (2002) Managing Finances, in Adams, R., Dominelli, L. and Payne, M. (eds) *Critical Practice in Social Work*, Basingstoke, Palgrave Macmillan

Manthorpe, J. and Bradley, G. (2009) Managing Finances, in Adams, R., Dominelli, L. and Payne, M. (eds) *Practising Social Work in a Complex World*, Basingstoke, Palgrave Macmillan

Manthorpe, J., Rapaport, J. Hussein, S., Moriaty, J. and Collins, J. (2005) *Advocacy and People with Learning Disabilities: Local Authority Perceptions of the Scope of its Activity, Extent and Effectiveness*, London, King's College

Mantle, G. and Backwith, D., (2010) Poverty and Social Work, *British Journal of Social Work*, (40), pp2380–2397

Marsh, P. and Doel, M. (2005) *The Task Centred Book*, Abingdon, Routledge

Marshall, M. and Tibbs, M. (2006) *Social Work and People with Dementia*, Bristol, Policy Press

Martin, R. (2010) *Social Work Assessment*, Exeter, Learning Matters

Maughan, C. and Webb, J. (2005) *Lawyering Skills and the Legal Process*, Cambridge, Cambridge University Press

Mayo, M. (1994) Community Work, in Hanvey, C. and Philpot, T. (eds) *Practising Social Work,* London, Routledge

Mayo, M. (2002) Community Work, in Adams, R., Dominelli, L. and Payne, M. (eds) *Social Work Themes, Issues and Critical Debates*, Basingstoke, Palgrave Macmillan

McBeath, G. and Webb, S. (2002) Virtue Ethics and Social Work: Being lucky, realistic and not doing one's duty, *British Journal of Social Work*, 32(8), pp1015–1036

McBride, P. (1998) *The Assertive Social Worker*, Aldershot, Arena

Means, R. and Smith, R. (1994) *Community Care: Policy and Practice*, Basingstoke, Macmillan

Mental Health Alliance (2007) *The Mental Health Act 2007: The final report*, London, Mental Health Alliance

Mercer, K. (2008) Non-directed advocacy, in CROA, Further down the rights track, Belper, CROA, cited in Boylan, J. and Dalrymple, J. (2009) *Understanding Advocacy for Children and Young People*, Maidenhead, Open University Press

Midgley, J. (2001) Issues in International Social Work: Resolving Critical Debates in the Profession, *Journal of Social Work*, 1(1), pp21–35

Milgram, S. (1963) Behavioural Study of Obedience, *The Journal of Abnormal and Social Psychology*, 67(4), pp371–378

Mill, J.S. (1972) *Utilitarianism*, London, Dent

Miller, W.R. and Rollnick, S. (2002) *Motivational interviewing: Preparing people for change* (2nd edn), New York/London, Guilford Press

Milner, J. and O'Byrne, P. (2002) *Assessment in Social Work* (2nd edn), Basingstoke, Palgrave Macmillan

Milner, J. and O'Byrne, P (2009) *Assessment in social work* (3rd edn) Basingstoke, Palgrave Macmillan

MIND (2010) *The MIND Guide to Advocacy*, London, MIND

MIND Information Unit (2010), *Crisis Services*, London, MIND

Mishna, F., Cook, C., Saini, M., Meng-Jia, W. and MacFadden, R. (2011) Interventions to Prevent and Reduce Cyber Abuse of Youth: A Systematic Review, *Research on Social Work Practice*, 21(1), pp5–14

Morgan, S. (2000) *Clinical Risk Management: A clinical tool and practitioner manual*, London, Sainsbury Centre for Mental Health

Mullally, R. (1993) *Structural Social Work: Ideology, Theory and Practice*, Toronto ON, McClelland Stewart

Myers, S. (2007) *Solution Focused Approaches*, Lyme Regis, Russell House

National Brokerage Network (2011) *Ten Broker Statements*, Fulbourn, Cambridge, National Brokerage Network

National Children's Bureau (2009) *Listening as a Way of Life*, London, National Children's Bureau

National Council for the Single Woman and her Dependants (1977) *The Impacts of Caring*, London, National Council for the Single Woman and her Dependants

Needham, C. and Carr, S. (2009) *Co-production: An emerging evidence base for adult social care transformation*, London, Social Care Institute for Excellence

Newbigging, K., McKeown, M., Hunkins-Hutchinson, A. and French, B. (2007) *Mtetezi: developing mental health advocacy with African and Caribbean young men*, London, Social Care Institute for Excellence

Nursing and Midwifery Council (2008) *The Code: Standards of conduct, performance and ethics for nurses and midwives*, London, NMC

Oak, E. (2009) *Social Work and Social Perspectives*, Basingstoke/New York, Palgrave Macmillan

O'Connor, I., Hughes, M., Turney, D., Wilson, S. and Sutterlund, D. (2007) *Social Work and Social Care Practice*, Basingstoke, Macmillan

Okitikpi, T. (ed.) (2011) *Social Control and the Use of Power in Social Work with Children and Families*, Lyme Regis, Russell House

Okitikpi, T. and Aymer, C. (2010) *Key Concepts in Anti-Discriminatory Social Work*, London, Sage

Oliver, C. and Dalrymple, J. (eds) (2008) *Developing Advocacy for Children and Young People: Developing Issues in Research, Policy and Practice*, London, Jessica Kingsley

Oliver, M. (2009) *Understanding disability: From theory to practice* (2nd edn), New York, Palgrave Macmillan

Oxford University Press (1992) *Concise Dictionary of National Biography*, Oxford, Oxford University Press

Parker, J. and Bradley, G. (2010) *Social work practice: Assessment, planning, intervention and review* (3rd edn) Exeter, Learning Matters

Parrot, L. (2010) *Values and Ethics in Social Work Practice*, Exeter, Learning Matters

Parrott, A. (2006) *Assertiveness, Negotiating and Influencing Skills*, Buckinghamshire, Institute for Clinical Research

Parsons, G., Godfrey, R., Annan, G., Cornwall, J., Dussart, M., Hepburn, S. and Howlett, K. (2004) *Minority Ethnic Exclusion and the Race Relations (Amendment) Act 2000*, London, DFES/HMSO

Parton, N. and O'Byrne, P. (2000) *Constructive Social Work*, Basingstoke, Palgrave Macmillan

Payne, M. (1991) *Modern Social Work Theory*, Basingstoke, Palgrave Macmillan

Payne, M. (1995) *Social Work and Community Care*, Basingstoke: Macmillan

Payne, M. (1997) *Modern Social work Theory* (2nd edn), Basingstoke, Palgrave Macmillan

Payne, M. (2000) *Anti-bureaucratic Social Work*, Birmingham, Venture Press

Payne, M. (2005a) *Modern Social Work Theory* (3rd edn), Basingstoke, Palgrave Macmillan

Payne, M. (2005b) *The Origins of Social Work, Continuity and Change*, Basingstoke, Palgrave Macmillan

Payne, M. (2006) *What is Professional Social Work?* (2nd edn) Bristol, Policy Press

Payne, M. and Askeland, G.A. (2008) *Globalization and International Social Work: Postmodern change and challenge*, Aldershot/Burlington VT, Ashgate

Pease, B. and Fook, J. (eds) (1999) *Transforming Social Work Practice: Postmodern critical perspectives*, London, Routledge

Perry, O., Pithouse, A., Anglim, C. and Batchelor, C. (2008) 'The Tip of the Ice Berg': Children's Complaints and Advocacy in Wales: An Insider View from Complaints Officers, *British Journal of Social Work (2008)*, 38(1), pp5–19

Phillips, J. Ray, M. and Marshall, M. (2005) *Social Work with Older People* (4th edn), Basingstoke, Palgrave Macmillan

Phillips, T. (2010) Personalisation, support brokerage and social work: what are we teaching social work students? *Journal of Social Work Practice*, 24(3), pp335–349

Pilgrim, D. (1995) Explaining abuse and inadequate care, in Hunt, G. (ed.) *Whistleblowing in the Health Service: accountability, law and professional practice*, London, Edward Arnold

Pithouse, A. and Crowley, A. (2007) Adults Rule? Children, Advocacy and Complaints to Social Services, *Children and Society*, 21, pp201–213

Pizzey, E. (1974) *Scream Quietly or the Neighbours Will Hear*, Harmondsworth, Penguin

Pochin, M. (2002) Thoughts from a UK Citizen Advocacy Scheme, in Gray, B. and Jackson, R., *Advocacy and Learning Disability*, London, Jessica Kingsley

Preston-Shoot, M. (2000) What if? Using the Law to uphold practice standards, *Practice*, 12(4), pp49–63

Rabin, C. and Zelner, D. (1992) The Role of Assertiveness in Clarifying Roles and Strengthening Job Satisfaction of Social Workers in Multidisciplinary Mental Health Settings, *British Journal Social Work*, 22(1), pp17–32

Rai-Atkins, A., Jama, A.A., Wright, N., Scott, V., Perring, C., Craig, G. and Katbamna, S. (2002) *Best Practice in Mental Health: Advocacy for African, Caribbean and South Asian Communities*, Bristol, Policy Press

Rapaport, J., Manthrope, J., Hussein, S., Moriaty, J. and Collins, J. (2005) Advocacy with people with learning disabilities in the UK: How can local funders find value for money? *Journal of Intellectual Disabilities*, 9(4), pp299–319

Rapaport, J., Manthrope, J., Hussein, S., Moriaty, J. and Collins, J. (2006a) Old issues in new directions: Perceptions of advocacy, its extent and effectiveness from a qualitative study of stakeholder views. *Journal of Intellectual Disabilities*, 10(2), pp191–210

Rapaport, J., Bellringer, S., Pinfold, V. and Huxley, P. (2006b) Carers and confidentiality in mental health care: considering the role of the carer's assessment: a study of service users', carers' and practitioners' views, *Health & Social Care in the Community*, 14(4), pp357–365

Redley, M., Clare, I., Luke, L., Holland, A. and Keeley, H. (2006) *The Evaluation of the Pilot Independent Mental Capacity Advocacy Service*, Cambridge, Learning Disability Research Group

Redley, M., Clare, I., Luke, L. and Holland, A. (2010) Mental Capacity Act (England and Wales) 2005: The Emergent Independent Mental Capacity Advocate (IMCA) Service, *British Journal of Social Work*, (40), pp1812–1828

Redley, M., Clare, I., Dunn, M., Platten, M. and Holland, A. (2011) Introducing the Mental Capacity Advocate (IMCA) and the Reform of the Adult Safeguarding Procedures, *British Journal of Social Work*, Advance Access, January 26

Reichert, E. (2003) *Social Work and Human Rights: A foundation for policy and practice*, New York, Columbia University Press

Reid W.J. (1978) *The Task Centred System*, New York, Columbia University Press

Reid, W.J. and Epstein, I. (1972) *Task Centred Case Work*, New York, Columbia University Press

Reid, W.J. and Shyne, A.W. (1969) *Brief and Extended Case Work*, New York, Columbia University Press

Rethink (2003) *Who Cares? The experience of mental health carers accessing services and information*, Kingston upon Thames, Rethink

Reynolds, L. and Smith, J. (2009) *Taking the Strain: The private rented sector and the recession*, London, Shelter/Money Advice Trust

Rhoades, C. (1995) Self Advocacy: Readings on Self Advocacy with groups of people with developmental difficulties, cited in Brandon, D. (1995a) (ed.) *Advocacy Power to People with Disabilities*, Birmingham, BASW

Ritchie, J., Dick, D. and Lingham, R. (1994) *The Report of the Inquiry into the Care and Treatment of Christopher Clunis*, London, HMSO

Roberts, A.R. (ed.) (2005) *Crisis Intervention Handbook: Assessment, treatment, and research* (3rd edn) Oxford/New York, Oxford University Press

Rogers, C.R. (1961) *On Becoming a Person: A therapist's view of psychotherapy*, Boston, Houghton Mifflin

Rojek, C., Peacock, G. and Collins, S. (1989) *Social Work and Received Ideas*, London, Routledge

Romme, M. and Escher, S. (2000) *A guide for mental health professionals working with voice hearers*, London, MIND

Rose, S. and Black, B. (1985) *Advocacy and Empowerment: Mental health care in the community*, London/New York, Routledge

Rosenhan, D.L. (1973) On being sane in insane places, *Science*, 179(4070), pp250–258

Ruch, G., Turney, D. and Ward, A. (eds) (2010) *Relationship Based Social Work: Getting to the heart of practice*, London, Jessica Kingsley

Russell-Day, Peter (1981) *Social Work and Social Control*, London, Tavistock

Sale, A. (2009) Charitable Causes, *Community Care*, 1 July

Saleebey, D. (2009) *The Strengths Perspective in Social Work Practice* (5th edn) Boston, Allyn and Bacon

Schneider, R. and Lester, L. (2001) *Social Work Advocacy: A New Framework for Action*, Belmont CA, Brooks Cole

Schon, D. (1991) *The Reflective Practitioner: How Professionals Think in Action*, Aldershot, Arena

SCIE (2009) *Personalisation Briefing: Implications for advocacy workers*, London, SCIE

SCIE (2010) *Personalisation Briefing: Implications for social workers in adult services*, London, SCIE

Scottish Independent Advocacy Alliance (2010) *Independent Advocacy: An Evaluation Framework*, Edinburgh, Scottish Independent Advocacy Alliance

Scourfield, J. (2010) Going for Brokerage: A Task of 'Independent Support' or Social Work? *British Journal of Social Work*, (40), pp858–877

Seden, J. (2005) *Counselling Skills in Social Work Practice*, Maidenhead, Open University Press

Sharry, J. (2001) *Solution Focused Group Work*, Thousand Oaks CA, Sage

Sheldon, B. and MacDonald, G. (2009) *A Text Book of Social Work*, Abingdon, Routledge

Sheppard, M. (2006) *Social Work and Social Exclusion*, Aldershot, Ashgate

Simons, K. (1992) *Sticking Up for Yourself: Self-advocacy and people with learning difficulties*, York, Joseph Rowntree Foundation

Smart, C. (2000) Reconsidering the Recent History of Child Sexual Abuse, 1910–1960, *Journal of Social Policy*, 29(1), pp55–71

Smith, R. (2008) *Social Work and Power*, Basingstoke, Palgrave Macmillan

Social Work Reform Board (2010) *Building a Safe Confident Future: One year on*, London, Crown Copyright

Solomon, B. (1976) *Black Empowerment*, New York, Columbia University

South East Joint Improvement Partnership (JIP) (2010) *'Signposts': Towards Universal Information and Advice*, London, JIP

Southgate, J. (1990) Towards a Dictionary of Advocacy based Self Analysis, *Journal for the Institute of Self Analysis*, 4(1) (December), cited in Brandon, D. (1995a) *Advocacy Power to People with Disabilities*, Birmingham, BASW

Spencer, B. (2009) The Poor-Man's Lawyer Service: a precursor to legal aid, *Legal Action* (May), pp6–7

Stationery Office (2007) *The Mental Capacity Act 2007: Code of Practice*, Norwich, Stationery Office

Stepney, P. and Popple, K. (2008) *Social Work and the Community: A critical context for practice*, Basingstoke, Palgrave Macmillan

Stevenson, O. and Parsloe, P. (1993) *Community Care and Empowerment*, York, Joseph Rowntree

Sutherby, K., Szmukler, G.I., Halpern, A., Alexander, M., Thornicroft, G., Johnson, C. and Wright, S. (1999) A study of 'crisis cards' in a community psychiatric service, *Acta Psychiatrica Scandinavica*, 100(1), pp56–61

Szasz, T.S. (1961) *The Myth of Mental Illness: Foundations of a theory of personal conduct*, New York, Hoeber-Harper

Szivos, S., (1992) The limits to integration? in Brown, H. and Smith, H. *Normalisation: A reader for the nineties*, London/New York, Tavistock/Routledge

Tait, L. and Lester, H. (2005) Encouraging Service User Involvement in Mental Health Services, *Advances in Psychiatric Treatment*, 11, pp168–175

Tam, D. (2004) Culturally Responsive Advocacy Intervention with Abused Chinese-Canadian Women, *British Journal of Social Work*, 34, pp269–77

Taylor, A. (1998) Hostages to Fortune: The abuse of children in care, in Hunt, G. (ed.) *Whistleblowing in the Social Services*, London, Arnold

Teater, B. (2010) *An Introduction to Applying Social Work Theories and Methods*, Maidenhead, Open University Press

Thomas, K.W. and Kilmann, R.H. (1974) *Conflict Mode, Instrument*, California, Xicom

Thomas, P.F. and Bracken, P. (1999) The Value of Advocacy: Putting ethics into practice, *Psychiatric Bulletin*, (23), pp327–329

Thompson, N. (2002) Social Work with Adults, in Adams, R., Dominelli, L. and Payne, M. *Social Work: Themes, Issues and Critical Debates* (2nd edn), Basingstoke, Palgrave

Thompson, N. (2006) *Anti-discriminatory Practice* (4th edition), Basingstoke, Macmillan

Thompson, N. (2009) *People Skills,* Basingstoke, Palgrave Macmillan

Topss (2002) *The National Occupational Standards for Social Work,* Leeds, Topss

Townend, A. (2007) *Assertiveness and Diversity,* Basingstoke, Palgrave Macmillan

Townsend, P. (1996) *A Poor Future: Can We Counteract Growing Poverty in Britain and Across the World?,* London, Lemos and Crane

Trevillion, S. (1999) *Networking and community partnership* (2nd edn), Aldershot, Ashgate/ Arena

Trevithick, P. (2005) *Social Work Skills: A practice handbook,* Maidenhead, Open University Press

Turnell, A. and Edwards, S. (1999) *Signs of Safety: A Solution and Safety Oriented Approach to Child Protection Casework,* London, Norton

Tyne, A. (1992) Normalisation from theory to practice, in Brown, H. and Smith, H. *Normalisation: A reader for the nineties,* London/New York, Tavistock/Routledge

UN Centre for Human Rights (1994) *Human Rights and Social Work,* Geneva, UN Centre for Human Rights

Utting, D. (1997) *People Like Us: The report of the safeguards for children living away from home,* London, Stationery Office

VSO (2009) *Participatory Advocacy: A tool kit for VSO staff volunteers and partners,* London, VSO

Wade, C. and Tavris, C. (2000) *Psychology,* Upper Saddle River NJ/London: Prentice-Hall International

Walker, A. and Walker, L. (1991) Disability and financial need: the failure of the social security system, in Dalley, G. (ed.) *Disability and Social Policy,* London, Institute for Policy Studies

Walmsley, J. (2002) Principles and Types of Advocacy, in Gray, B. and Jackson, R. *Advocacy and Learning Disability,* London, Jessica Kingsley

Waterhouse, R. (2000) *Lost in Care: Report of the Tribunal of Inquiry into the abuse of Children in Care in the former county council areas of Gwynedd and Clwyd since 1974,* London, The Stationery Office

Waterston, T. (2009) Teaching and Learning about Advocacy, *Archives of Disease in Childhood: Education and Practice Edition,* 94(1), pp24–28

Weinstein, J. (2008) *Working with Loss, Death and Bereavement: A guide for social workers,* London, Sage

Wells, S. (2006) *Developments in Dementia Advocacy: Exploring the role of advocates in supporting people with dementia,* London, Westminster Advocacy Service for Senior Residents

Weston, C. and Went, F. (1999) Description and evaluation of an assertiveness group for people with learning disabilities, *British Journal of Learning Disabilities,* 27(3), pp110–115

White, I. and Hart, K. (1995) *Report of the Inquiry into the Management of Child Care in the London Borough of Islington,* London, London Borough of Islington

Whittaker, A. (1995) The Fight for Self-Advocacy, in Mittler, P. and Sinason, V. (eds) *Changing Policy and Practice for People with Learning Disabilities*, London, Cassell

Whittaker, A., Gardner, S. and Kershaw, J. (1991) *Service Evaluation by People with Learning Difficulties*, London, Kings Fund.

Whittington, C. (1983) Social Work in the Welfare Network: Negotiating Daily Practice, *British Journal of Social Work*, 13, pp265–286

Wilcox, D. (1994) *A Guide to Effective Participation*, York, Joseph Rowntree Foundation

Williams, C. (2009) Personalisation: is the social work role being eroded? *Community Care* (1 April)

Williams, C. and Ferris, K. (2010) *Complaints Panels in Social Care*, Lyme Regis, Russell House

Williams, C., Harris, J., Hind, T. and Uppal, S. (2009) *Transforming Adult Social Care: Access to Information Advice and Advocacy*, London, IDEA

Williams, J. (2001) 1998 Human Rights Act: Social Work's New Benchmark, *British Journal of Social Work*, 31, pp831–844

Williams, P. (2006) *Social Work with People with Learning Difficulties*, Exeter, Learning Matters

Williams, P. (2009) *Social Work with People with Learning Difficulties* (2nd edn), Exeter, Learning Matters

Wilson, E. (1980) Feminism and Social Work, in Brake, M. and Bailey, R. (eds) *Radical Social Work and Practice*, London, Edward Arnold

Windle, K., Netten, A., Caiels, J., Masrani, R., Welch, E. and Forder, J. (2010) *Measuring the Outcomes of Information and Advice Services: Final report,* Kent, PSSRU.

Wolfensberger, W. (1977) *PASSING: Program analysis of service systems implementation goals*, Canada, National Institute on Mental Retardation

Younghusband, E. (1947) *Report on the Employment and Training of Social Workers*, London, Carnegie United Kingdom Trust

Younghusband, E. (1968) *Community work and social change: The report of a study group on training set up by the Calouste Gulbenkian Foundation*, Harlow, Longman

Younghusband, E. (1971) *Social Work and Social Change*, London, Allen & Unwin

Index